First published in the United Kingdom
by International Masters Publishers Ltd

First published in the USA
by International Masters Publishers Inc
(under licence from IMP AB)

ISBN 1 930560 34 6

Printed and bound in the United Kingdom
by Cox & Wyman Limited
Cardiff Road
Reading
Berkshire RG1 8EX
United Kingdom

Picture Credits:
Corbis: Beltmann 290 (br), 293 (bl), 295 (cl), 299 (tl),
Hulton Getty Picture Collection 288 (tr), 291 (b), 298 (bl),
301 (tr), 302 (tl); **Hulton Getty Picture Collection:**
289 (tr), 294 (cl), 295 (bl), 298 (tr), 299 (br), 300
(tr & bl), 302 (cr & bl); **Peter Newark Pictures:** 288 (cl),
289 (cr), 296 (cr), 298 (cl), 299 (bl), 301 (bl);
Popperfoto: 288 (br), 290 (t & cr), 289 (t), 292 (tl),
294 (b); **Richard Opie:** 289 (cl & bl), 292 (cr), 295 (tr),
296 (tr & bl), 297 (br); **Topham Picturepoint:** 290 (bl),
293 (t), 295 (cr), 297 (tl, cr & cl), 298 (br), 301 (cr).

Wings of Hope

Shirley Worrall

~ *Notes from Lilian* ~

'Curiosity killed the cat,' my mother used to tell me. I was a child who always asked questions. I was also a bit of a dreamer, always begging to be told stories about far-away places and people I'd never met. Sometimes, my mother would tell me real-life stories, the ones that even my vivid imagination couldn't have created – the ones about the Penrose family – my family.

My mother had a tiny miniature painting handed down through my father's family that she knew was a picture of a Penrose who had lived one hundred years before. Stories about other Penroses had also survived and enthralled me on many a rainy day indoors by the fire with my mother. I loved to hear about these colourful characters, and I promised myself that one day I would learn more about the Penroses and tell my own children their stories. Indeed, it's become a bit of a personal passion over the last few years to build up a record of my family tree and to research all the characters and times in history that have shaped the Penrose saga. It has involved many hours of delving into records and writing letters to distant places, but it has been the most incredible journey. I feel I've met many of these ancestors and know them now as if they were friends.

As I was growing up in an ordinary home in an ordinary town before the war, I never imagined how my life might weave into the lives of those who came before me. I was more anxious to spread my wings and learn about the world outside. It so happened that the years of my youth coincided with a truly dramatic moment in history that shaped my life and changed the world forever. Unknown to me, my own story was becoming part of the Penrose family saga, in the same way that all those fascinating ancestors' lives had done, whose stories my mother told me. Looking back, and knowing now what I know of my family tree, I can see that I too was becoming part of the bigger picture – a part of the past, present and future of the Penroses.

My own story is not unlike those of many of my generation who lived through the war – a story of courage in the face of adversity as the world fought off a brutal enemy – but it is also the story of a loss of innocence, of enduring spirit and above all, love.

Lilian Penrose

~ *Chapter One* ~

DECEMBER 1939

Lilian was so excited she could hardly breathe. She had kept the letter safely hidden inside her diary since the day before, when it arrived. But she had to keep taking it out and reading it. If she didn't tell someone soon, she felt sure she would burst... Not Maud though.

Her sister came into the bedroom and Lilian quickly hid the letter.

Lilian had grown used to having the bedroom to herself, and it was far too small a room for two, but she wouldn't have minded sharing it with anyone but Maud.

Maud and her husband, Joe, had been renting a house of their own but as soon as Joe joined up – and he had been eager to volunteer on the day Prime Minister Chamberlain declared war – Maud came home, bringing their two children with her. Having the children in the house was lovely, but sharing a bedroom with Maud was awful. Everything had to be just so. If Lilian put something down, Maud immediately moved it. She would pick up Lilian's shoes with a heavy sigh and put them under the bed. The time Lilian had wasted looking for her shoes was legendary.

Soon, though, it wouldn't be a problem. Maud would

have the room all to herself. Lilian felt that familiar thrill of excitement at the thought.

'You're looking pleased with yourself,' Maud commented suspiciously.

'And why not?' Lilian retorted. 'I'm going to Grace's party tonight. It should be fun.'

Maud sat down on the bed.

'You don't even like Grace,' she pointed out dryly.

That was true enough. Lilian Penrose and Grace Cotterill had attended the same school, and they only lived two streets apart. Two streets were enough in Sunderland, though. Those two streets convinced Grace she was better than any of them, a view her parents encouraged wholeheartedly. Only Grace's parents could throw what was sure to be a lavish party for their precious daughter when the country was at war.

'She's alright,' Lilian replied with a shrug. 'Besides, all my friends will be there. Joan and Margaret are going, and so is Joyce. Kathleen and Eileen are going. Barbara, Ivy, Violet –' And Roy, she added silently. 'Just because you didn't get an invitation…'

No one in their right mind would invite Maud to a party, Lilian thought crossly. She was guaranteed to put a damper on anything. She had always been the same, ever since Lilian could remember.

At twenty-four, six years older than Lilian, Maud felt obliged to show Lilian the error of her ways, and it drove Lilian mad. Since Maud had married Joe, and especially now she was the perfect mother of their two children, things were even worse.

Lilian's mood softened immediately as she thought of her nephew and niece. Credit where it was due,

Maud was a wonderful mother. John at just five years old and three-and-a-half year old Rose were the most adorable children Lilian had ever known. She loved them dearly. She wanted to see a lot more of life and have some fun before she thought of settling down and having children of her own but, when she did have children, she hoped they would be exactly like John and Rose.

'Have you heard from Joe?' she asked Maud.

'I had a letter yesterday,' Maud nodded, but said no more.

'And?' Lilian prompted. 'Is he having a good time?'

'No, he's not having a good time. For heaven's sake, Lil. He's up in Scotland, miles away from me and his children, he doesn't know where he'll be sent next – how can he have a good time?'

Lilian bit back the retort that sprang to her lips. Joe was a lovely man. He was far more capable of having a good time than Maud was. He was always ready with a joke or a witty retort which is why everyone, especially his children, loved him so much.

'It's funny, isn't it?' she said instead. 'He joins up in Newcastle then ends up with the Argyll and Sutherland Highlanders. They'll have him wearing a kilt and playing the bagpipes yet,' she added with a giggle.

'A lot of Geordies have ended up there,' Maud replied. 'And do you know, according to Joe, the Scots call everyone from this part of the world Geordies – not just them from Newcastle.'

'Do they?' That wouldn't go down well! 'But fancy him joining a Scottish regiment.'

'Oh, Joe's happy enough about that. It's a great

regiment by all accounts. And he's already wearing a kilt.'

'He is? You're joking!'

'No. It's part of the uniform.'

Lilian laughed at the thought of Joe baring his knees in a kilt, but it was a waste of time trying to have a smile about anything with Maud. She took life far too seriously.

Giving up on Maud, Lilian took down her outfit from where it was hanging on the back of the door. She would have loved something new to wear to the party but that was out of the question so, once again, she had to resort to her faithful blue dress. It fitted well and everyone said it suited her, but she would have loved to wear something a little more grown-up and a little more stylish. Heaven alone knew what glamorous creation Grace would be wearing – something new, sophisticated and expensive, Lilian suspected.

'Oh, that looks pretty,' Maud said suddenly. 'Is that the length of ribbon Aunt Elsie gave you for your birthday?'

'Yes.' Lilian wasn't so sure about the ribbon now. She'd sewn a length around the neckline and two lengths down the bodice in an attempt to give her old dress an added sparkle, but 'pretty' wasn't the effect she had been after. She had been aiming for 'glamorous', but she supposed there was only so much that could be done with a plain blue dress and a length of ribbon. 'Does it look all right, Maud? Really?'

'It looks lovely, Lil, it really does. No one would believe it was the same dress. You've always been clever with a needle, haven't you?' she added. 'Think of that dress you made for Rose. It's still her favourite – and mine. I can do the basics, but you're really good. You have an eye for it.'

Praise from Maud was so rare that Lilian felt herself blush. Maud certainly wouldn't say such things if she didn't mean them. In a sudden, rare rush of affection for her sister, Lilian reached for her diary.

'Guess what, Maud. God, I'm so excited I'll explode if I don't tell someone soon. You must promise not to tell Mam and Dad though. Not yet. I'll break it to them tomorrow, after the party.'

'Now what have you done?' Maud was wary.

'Here.' Lilian handed her the letter.

'Oh, my – Lilian! Are you mad? You can't –'

'It's too late now,' Lilian said, taking the letter back. 'I'm joining the Women's Auxiliary Air Force and that's that. If they'll have me, of course,' she added, chewing on her bottom lip. 'Oh, I'm sure they will. I'm bright enough. I'm willing to learn, eager to please –'

'Totally irresponsible and far too young!' Maud finished for her. 'Dad will go wild, and quite right too. He'll kill you, Lil.'

The thought of telling her father had filled Lilian with dread ever since the letter asking her to report to the recruiting office had arrived. Clive Penrose was a loving father, but they didn't come much stricter. He had always been able to quell any nonsense from his daughters with one stern glance. He certainly wouldn't take kindly to his youngest daughter gallivanting around the country where he couldn't keep an eye on her. Of course, for Lilian, that was one of the main attractions. She would be able to go where she pleased, with whom she pleased. She wouldn't have to report her every movement to her parents. She wouldn't have to go home just when her friends were starting to enjoy themselves. And she wouldn't have to share a room with Maud. Oh, it would be wonderful!

She still had to break the news to her father though.

Their mother wouldn't take the news well either, Lilian knew that. Dorothy Penrose wasn't such a problem however. Lilian could usually get round her.

'Dad will forbid it,' Maud said simply. 'And don't think you'll get any support from me. I've never heard such a stupid idea. You know nothing about that sort of life. You know nothing about anything!'

'But they train you.'

'To do what? What do you imagine you'll be doing for heaven's sake?'

'I don't know,' Lilian admitted. The Women's Auxiliary Air Force – oh, it sounded grand. She had no idea what the WAAF girls did it was true. She had simply seen the recruitment notice in the newspaper, decided the girls would be having a lot more fun and freedom than she was, and made up her mind to volunteer. 'But I'm not an idiot.'

'No,' Maud retorted. 'You're not an idiot, you're just insane.'

'That's not what you said when Joe volunteered. It's no different, just because I'm a girl. I can do my bit for the country too, you know.'

'God help us,' Maud said with a heavy sigh.

'It will be –'

'It won't be anything,' Maud cut her off, 'because Dad will forbid it.'

Lilian knew there was an awful ring of truth to those

words, but she refused to accept it. She was joining the WAAF and no one, not even her father, was going to stop her. Never in her life had she felt so strongly about anything. She would go to the recruitment office no matter what. If her father forbade it, then she would defy him. The thought made her shiver, but she would do it if she had to.

'But you're doing so well at Singleton's,' Maud said earnestly. 'Old man Singleton thinks very highly of you.'

Mr Singleton senior was a lovely man and Lilian knew he was pleased with her work, but she didn't want to be stuck in that dreary solicitor's office for the rest of her working days.

'It's so boring,' she replied with a groan. 'The work's boring and the people are even more boring. No one has a laugh. It's all taken so seriously.'

'Not half as seriously as Dad will take this WAAF nonsense,' Maud countered grimly.

Lilian knew her sister was right about that. But she refused to think about it now. Tonight she would enjoy her party and tomorrow she would worry about her father...

∽∾

As Lilian had guessed, Grace's party dress made all the other girls look dowdy.

'A birthday present,' Grace boasted, twirling around so that the full red skirt flew out. 'I chose the pattern, and Mrs Gregson made it for me.'

'It's very nice,' Lilian said as graciously as she could.

In truth, it was gorgeous. The bodice was tight, the neckline far lower than anything Lilian would have been allowed to wear, and the skirt danced provocatively around Grace's slim legs. She looked at least twenty, Lilian thought gloomily. Even her shoes looked new. Lilian had polished her own shoes to within an inch of their lives, but it had been a long, long time since they had looked new.

'Come and get something to eat,' Grace said.

A long table was groaning beneath the weight of enough food to keep the whole street going for a week. Everyone in the country was worrying about the possibility of food shortages – everyone except the Cotterills it seemed.

'We've been busy all week preparing it,' Grace added.

It showed, too.

'Thanks,' Lilian murmured, her eyes scanning the room for her friends as she helped herself to a sandwich.

'Your dress looks pretty,' Grace remarked. 'You'd never guess the ribbon hadn't always been there. Did you do it yourself?'

'Yes,' Lilian replied through clenched teeth. She wished she hadn't bothered. Twice now it had been described as 'pretty', whereas no one would describe Grace's dress as 'pretty'.

Lilian spotted Joan and Margaret and quickly made her escape. While she was crossing the room to them, she caught sight of her reflection in the mirror hanging above the fireplace. It did nothing to improve her mood. She had nice cheekbones, her nose wasn't too big or too small, and her eyes were an attractive shade of green, but her hair, long and auburn, had a will of its own and curled wherever it felt the need to. She was passably attractive, she supposed, but she wasn't a beauty like Grace, and never would be. She was one of those girls that people didn't give a second glance to.

She had been hoping that, this evening, Roy would give her a second glance. But there was fat chance of that happening with the blonde-haired, blue-eyed, stylishly dressed Grace in the same room.

'What do you think of all that food?' Joan asked in a whisper when she joined them. 'It's all for show, of course. Me mam said they were going overboard for this.'

Joan's mother worked in the butcher's shop and had an uncanny knack of knowing what every family in the neighbourhood was putting on their plates each evening.

'Perhaps they'll live on the leftovers for the next month,' Lilian replied with a laugh.

'Leftovers?' Margaret grinned. 'What leftovers? I'm starving!'

'Bread and dripping more like,' Joan muttered. 'Serves 'em right too. Show-offs!' She suddenly nudged Lilian. 'Don't look now but Roy Walker's giving you the eye.'

Lilian immediately spun round and found herself making eye contact with Roy. It was true; he was looking straight at her. She blushed, her skin feeling as if it was on fire, and quickly turned back to her friends.

'He's looking at us, not me,' she said, flustered.

'Rubbish,' Joan scoffed. 'He's had his eye on you for

weeks now. What do you think of him?'

'He's OK.' Lilian tried to sound disinterested, but it was difficult. She'd known him for years, although she hadn't really noticed him until he walked her home from a shopping trip last Christmas. Since then, she had only seen him half a dozen times, but she had thought of him frequently. He was eighteen, the same age as Lilian, and worked at the same factory as her father. 'He's not very tall, is he?'

Joan and Margaret spluttered with laughter.

'Tall enough!' they said in unison, making Lilian laugh.

'It's just that you're a beanpole,' Margaret added.

And that was another thing. Unlike Maud, Lilian had inherited their father's height. She was five feet nine inches tall and if there was one thing she hated it was the thought of having a boyfriend she had to look down on. Roy was possibly an inch taller, she supposed.

'He's coming over,' Joan hissed.

'Oh, no!' The heat in Lilian's face had died down a little but now her whole body was burning. 'What's he doing?' she whispered.

But Roy was already at her shoulder.

He flirted with the three of them but made it plain he had eyes only for Lilian. She couldn't believe it. For preference he could have been a bit taller, but there was no denying that he was a very handsome young man. His hair was dark, swept back from a face dominated by piercing blue eyes that always looked as if he was laughing at a private joke.

If only she could look like her screen favourite Lana Turner, Lilian thought desperately. She would give anything to be Roy's girl. Anything!

Not that she could be anyone's girl if – no when – she joined the WAAF, she supposed. Would Roy wait for her?

The front room had been cleared and Grace's mother was soon sitting at the highly polished baby grand piano.

'What a snob,' Joan muttered. 'She can't play it. She just likes everyone to know they've got one.'

'It was my mother's,' Margaret mimicked in a brilliant imitation of Mrs Cotterill's posh accent.

They fell about laughing, but everyone joined in to sing 'Happy Birthday' to Grace.

Mrs Cotterill's playing certainly left a lot to be desired but no one could fault her for effort and a few couples began to dance.

'Lilian?' Roy put out his hand.

Lilian might not look like a Hollywood star, but she knew she could dance well. She had spent hours with Joan, practising in the cramped confines of her bedroom. Because she was taller, Lilian usually took the lead, and it was wonderful to dance with Roy. He was a good dancer too.

'When are you going to join up?' she asked him.

'Who says I'm going to?' he replied. 'I expect it will all be over soon.'

'That's not what Dad says,' Lilian retorted. 'He reckons it'll last a year or more.' She was desperate to tell him her news, but knew she couldn't. She had to tell her parents first. 'Everyone else is joining up,' she added, taken aback somehow that he wasn't rushing off to do his bit for king and country.

'Which means there's less competition when it

comes to dancing with the prettiest girls,' he responded immediately.

Lilian didn't know what to say to that. All she knew was that when she was dancing with Roy, she could almost believe she was Lana Turner.

'Do you think it's going to be as bad as everyone says?' she asked him. 'The way everyone talks, you'd think Hitler was on his way to Sunderland right now.'

'The north-east coast is certain to suffer the most, I suppose.'

That's what everyone said.

'But seriously, don't you want to join up?' she asked curiously. 'Joe couldn't wait to go. I'd be the same – if I was a man.'

'I'm in no rush,' he answered with a shrug.

Lilian searched his handsome face for any sign that he might be teasing her. He was quite serious though. She was surprised, but more than that, she was bitterly disappointed.

'When you're twenty, you'll have to join up,' she reminded him. 'You'll have no choice.'

'But I'm not twenty,' he replied, grinning. 'And it'll all be over when I am.'

'My dad reckons they'll lower the conscription age to nineteen.'

'Lilian Penrose!' He laughed at her. 'Will you stop talking about the war? I've got far more important things on my mind. How can I even think about the war when I'm with you? So – are you going to let me walk you home?'

'Well – I suppose so. I was going to walk with Joan and Margaret, but I suppose you can.'

It was what she had dreamed of, the perfect end to

a perfect evening. She brushed aside her doubts about him. He would sign up soon, she knew it.

Grace quickly claimed a dance with him and Lilian returned to Joan and Margaret.

'He's walking me home,' she whispered, her voice tight with excitement.

'Make sure you keep him at a distance,' Margaret said with a giggle. 'You know what he's like.'

'No. What's that supposed to mean? What is he like?'

'Well, he's got a bit of a reputation as a ladies' man,' Margaret said.

'Has he?' Lilian hadn't heard anything. She wondered briefly if Margaret was jealous, but she knew Margaret better than that and quickly dismissed the unkind thought. 'Who says so?'

'He was courting Emily Pearson,' Joan said.

'I know.' Lilian frowned. 'So what?'

'She dumped him when she discovered he'd been two-timing her,' Joan explained. 'She found out he was seeing that Beverley. And you know what she's like. Mind you, it's no wonder. Her dad's never sober and her brothers are just as bad.'

Lilian felt some of the pleasure of the evening seep away from her.

'He's only walking me home,' she pointed out. 'It's not as if we're courting or anything...'

~⚬~

When it was time to leave, Joan and Margaret went on ahead and Lilian walked with Roy. She felt on edge and couldn't think of anything to say to him. It would have been good to talk about their hopes for the future, but Roy didn't seem to have any and, as much as she wanted to, she couldn't really tell him of her own plans.

'You're quiet,' he said.

'So are you.'

'But I'm the strong, silent type,' he quipped.

She laughed at that and felt a bit better.

It wasn't his fault that nothing felt as special as she'd hoped. Shivering in the cold, and groping their way through the darkness was hardly romantic. Lilian had found the blackout quite exciting at first, but that was before she'd bruised every part of her body colliding with things.

Roy held her hand, which was nice, but it didn't feel right somehow and she was pleased when they reached the house.

'Thanks for walking with me,' she said, pulling her hand from his.

'Hey, don't I even get a goodnight kiss?'

Lilian blushed, not knowing how to respond to that. She was so long thinking about it that it was too late to make any response. His hand went to the back of her head and his lips came down on hers. His kiss took her completely by surprise. She had expected to receive a brief peck on the cheek, not a full assault on her mouth. He pressed his body close to hers, too close, and she had to struggle to get away.

'You've had your kiss,' she said, trying to keep her voice light. 'Good night, Roy. Thanks again for walking home with me.'

She hurried down the back path away from him, wiping at her mouth with her hand as she did so. For weeks she had dreamed of his kiss. Her very first kiss and she had so wanted it to be from Roy. In her dreams his kiss had been full of tenderness, but there had been no tenderness in that kiss. His mouth had bruised hers and she hadn't enjoyed it at all.

She wished now that she'd walked home with Joan and Margaret. They would have talked about the party; it would have been far more fun.

She opened the door quietly, so as not to wake anyone, but she needn't have bothered. Her father was standing by the stove, her mother was sitting in her chair on one side of it and Maud was sitting on the other. Three pairs of eyes turned on her.

'What's wrong?' she asked, her face flooding with guilty colour. Surely they hadn't seen Roy kissing her. 'What's happened?'

'Go to bed!' Her father nodded at his wife and Maud. How Lilian wished the order had included her. He must have seen Roy kissing her. She was for it now.

The two women left the room without a word, leaving Lilian shaking just inside the door. She swallowed painfully and waited. She didn't have long to wait.

'I hope you're proud of yourself, young lady.' His voice was menacingly quiet. 'You've deceived me, you've deceived your mother –'

'I haven't deceived anyone,' Lilian cried, confused.

'Oh, you haven't? So you haven't written to these WAAF women behind our backs?'

Maud!

Anger at Maud made her feel a little more brave. Just wait till she got her hands on that tattle-tale sister of hers. How could Maud do such a thing?

'I was going to tell you both tomorrow,' she said.

'Now isn't that handy.'

'I was! If you'd asked that sneak of a sister, she would have told you that. I told her I was going to tell you tomorrow.'

'Don't call your sister a sneak!' His voice changed to a roar. 'She has your best interests at heart, as we all do. It wouldn't cross your mind to mention it to us, would it? Oh, no. You go on in your own sweet way without a thought of anyone else, without a thought of your mam worrying herself into an early grave.'

'I saw it in the paper,' Lilian said, trying without much success to keep her voice from shaking, 'and I thought I'd find out more about it. There was no point mentioning it to anyone until I knew what it was about.'

'And now you know all about it?' he said. 'Well, that's a relief. Then do share your great knowledge.'

Lilian felt herself sag with relief. When her father's anger was replaced by sarcasm, she knew the worst was over. He was strict, he could terrify the life out of her with one look and had raised his hand to her on more than one occasion, but she had never had the slightest doubt that he loved her as much as she loved him.

'I didn't mean to deceive anyone, Dad,' she said earnestly. 'There just seemed no point telling anyone about it until I knew it was for me. I want to do something for the war effort and –'

'The best thing you can do for the war effort is behave yourself and help your mam and your sister,' he barked out.

'But how can I help? Mam doesn't need me, and

Maud could raise sixteen kids on her own if she had to.' Her mind raced. 'I want to do something positive, Dad. Lots of girls are joining the WAAF and I want to too.' And then she hit on it. 'All my friends think of nothing else but going out with boys and stuff like that. I'm not interested in any of that. I want to do something useful with my life.'

That last bit was a gem and she pushed on.

'You were proud of Joe when he joined up, we all were. Obviously women can't go off and fight, but there are lots of useful things we can do. I thought you'd be proud of me, Dad.'

'Ha!'

'You said yourself that everyone has to pull their weight now. Look at you – who'd have thought you'd be shop-floor manager of a munitions factory? You're proud of that, surely? I know I am. You're doing your bit, Joe's doing his and I want to do mine. And at least you'll know I'm behaving myself,' she went on earnestly. 'They're really strict with you and it's very hard work.'

'Doing what?' he asked knowingly.

'Lots of things.' Lilian didn't have a clue. 'I've got an appointment at the recruiting office, and I thought Mam could come with me. That way, she'll know what I'll be doing. That's if they take me, of course.'

There was a long silence.

'Lilian Penrose,' her father said at last, 'you'll be the death of me.'

'So I can go?'

'Your mother will go with you!'

'Of course. I wouldn't want to go without her.'

'It's the deceit though, Lilian. I will not tolerate that.'

He sighed loudly. 'Now, off to bed with you.'

'Yes, Dad.'

Lilian escaped while the going was good, part excited, part relieved, and part furious with Maud...

∞∞∞

Clive Penrose climbed into bed beside his wife and wondered, not for the first time in his life, what would happen to his youngest daughter. She worried them to death with her madcap schemes and always, without fail, managed to twist him round her finger. Being master in his own house was the devil's own job with Lilian around.

'Well?' Dorothy asked.

'What do you think?' he replied. 'Who do you think won that one? Me or Lilian?'

Chuckling, Dorothy rolled onto her side and slipped her arm through his.

'Lilian has always been good at getting her own way,' she said. 'She's a little horror, and the Lord alone knows what sort of mess she'll make of her life, but she's inherited her dad's spirit and I'm not sure –'

'Her dad's spirit?' he repeated in astonishment. 'She's inherited her spirit from her mother. I knew she was trouble the moment I laid eyes on her.'

Dorothy laughed.

'I suppose so. And yes, in Lilian's shoes, I'd want to do something similar.'

'And she's inherited her mother's looks,' Clive went on. 'Every time I look in her eyes, I see you gazing straight back at me. It's always been the same, and it's always been my downfall.'

'I don't know whose looks she's inherited,' Dorothy said, her brow creasing into a worried frown. 'She can't see it yet, thank the Lord, and until she wakes up one morning, looks in the mirror and sees some film star staring back at her, she'll always think she's a Plain Jane, but she's turning into a real beauty.'

Clive knew it. He had noticed how she'd turned men's heads on the occasions she'd met him outside the factory. She was just like her mother. He could remember now how quickly Dorothy had turned his own head. Dorothy had been beautiful – she still was in his eyes – but it had been so much more than that. It had been the way her eyes had constantly sparkled with life and laughter, the way she met life head-on. The first time he laid eyes on her she had been chatting excitedly about her meeting with Sylvia Pankhurst, the suffragette leader and daughter of the infamous Emily Pankhurst who had spent much of her time on hunger strike or in jail. Clive had had little patience with the exploits of the suffragettes, but he hadn't said as much to Dorothy. Not then…

'I wouldn't want to be in Maud's shoes now.' Dorothy stifled a laugh.

'Me neither.'

They were both laughing as Clive wrapped his arms tightly around his wife.

'Perhaps this WAAF business won't be so bad,' he said thoughtfully. 'They must have some responsible people in charge, mustn't they? And they can hardly run the outfit without plenty of discipline.'

'I suppose you're right.'

'And it might keep her mind off the lads for a while,' Clive pointed out.

'Yes, it might. But will there be any other girls like our Lilian there?' Dorothy asked worriedly. 'I get the impression it's more for – well, not people like us.'

'The landed gentry's daughters?' he asked, and she nodded.

'I don't know, pet,' he said.

Not for the first time, they both fell asleep worrying about their youngest daughter.

∽∾∽

~ *Chapter Two* ~

JANUARY 1940

Lilian couldn't sleep. It was her last night at home, the last night she would have to share a room with Maud. She rolled over onto her back and pulled the blankets up to her chin. What would tomorrow bring?

'I wish you'd stop fidgeting, Lil,' Maud complained.

'Sorry.' She refused to waste her last night at home arguing with Maud.

'You'll be worn out tomorrow if you don't sleep. Mind you, you'll be worn out even if you do.' Maud yawned loudly. 'Now go to sleep.'

Lilian knew she had a tiring day ahead of her tomorrow, but she was far too excited to sleep. She was a little nervous, too. Going to the recruiting office with her mother had been an eye-opener.

'You should have seen her strutting –'

'Seen who?' Maud demanded with an impatient sigh.

'Mam. D'you know, I bet she wishes she was joining the WAAF.'

'You could be right,' Maud replied, her voice softening momentarily. 'Just make sure you don't follow in her footsteps and get yourself arrested.'

Lilian sat bolt upright. 'Arrested?'

'Yes.' Maud clearly wished she hadn't said anything. 'Go to sleep, Lil!'

'In a minute. What do you mean, Maud? Mam was

never arrested, was she?'

'A long time ago.'

'When she lived in London?'

'Yes. Now go to sleep.'

Lilian couldn't sleep now!

'What on earth did she do?'

'Nothing. It was in her suffragette days – half a dozen of them were arrested. They spent a night in jail.'

'How exciting!'

'A night in a cell with criminals? It certainly was not exciting! Now – for heaven's sake, Lil, let's get some sleep. You've got an early start in the morning.'

'Do you think,' Lilian asked after a few minutes, 'that Mam has regrets? Do you think she finds life a bit dull – you know, marrying Dad, having us, living here?'

'No, I don't! She got involved with those suffragettes when she was young – about your age – and went off to London with them. She soon saw sense and came back north. Now not another word. Sleep!'

Realizing that her hands were going numb with cold, Lilian slid back under the blankets. But she still couldn't sleep. Fancy their mother getting arrested. Lilian could hardly believe it. And despite what Maud said, Lilian would bet anything that their mother found life a bit dull these days. As much as Lilian loved their father, it had to be said that he wasn't the most exciting of men, although, she reasoned, there must have been something about him that had attracted their mother in the first place. But then, Dad had always been a bit of a dark horse. She had often talked to him about his family, but there were still so many things she didn't know... so many unexplained mysteries. Lilian made a mental note to herself to find out all about the Penroses one day. But not just yet…

With this thought in mind, she finally fell into a restless sleep…

∼∽∾

Dorothy Penrose stood on the platform at Sunderland station in the biting cold feeling strangely detached from everything. Part of her was worried to death about her youngest daughter, and yet a small part of her was envious. Lilian had her whole life ahead of her and this adventure was just the beginning. She guessed her daughter was experiencing mixed emotions – excitement and trepidation.

Maud didn't appear to be envious of her sister, quite the reverse. She was happy keeping an eye on John and Rose, holding their hands tight as they walked along the platform. Maud's children were her life, just as Dorothy's were, but it seemed to Dorothy that Maud had never wanted to see anything of life before settling down with a family. It wouldn't have done for Dorothy. It wouldn't do for Lilian, either.

'You've got that rail warrant?' Dorothy asked her.

'Yes, Mam!' Lilian laughed despairingly. 'I've got everything I need. Don't worry.'

Don't worry? When would they do anything but worry when it came to Lilian? Once again, Dorothy realized how her own parents must have worried about her. She'd led them a merry dance one way and another.

'And you'll write as soon as you get there?'

'Yes, Mam. I'll write – before I even report to

wherever it is I'm supposed to report to.'

Clive, busy at work by now, had given Dorothy a long list of things she must tell Lilian. There seemed little point though. Lilian would make her own mistakes, just as Dorothy herself had had to at the same age.

Oh – she would miss Lilian. She would miss her fun and sparkle, her lively mind and that wicked sense of humour.

'Here it is!' John shouted excitedly, tugging on Dorothy's coat.

'So it is, sweetheart.' A shudder ran through Dorothy as she hugged her grandson to her and gazed through a sudden shimmer of tears at the approaching train. 'You're sure you've got everything, Lilian?'

'Yes, Mam.' Lilian hugged little Rose, then ruffled John's dark curls. 'You be good for your mam.'

'You be good, too,' Dorothy told Lilian sternly, blinking back the moisture in her eyes.

'I shall, Mam.' Lilian hugged her, almost crushing the breath from her body. 'Don't worry. WAAF here I come!'

Lilian turned and gave Maud a quick hug.

'Er – excuse me –'

Dorothy turned to the woman who had spoken. She was about her own age, Dorothy supposed, and with her was a nervous-looking girl of around Lilian's age.

'I was just wondering,' the woman said shyly. 'Did I hear you mention the WAAF? My daughter, Sarah, is a new recruit, and I thought perhaps your daughter – this young lady is your daughter?'

'Yes. Yes, this is Lilian, my daughter, and yes, she's joining the WAAF too. Oh, they'll be wonderful company for each other.' Dorothy suddenly wondered if she'd misunderstood. 'Is Sarah joining the WAAF then?' It seemed so unlikely, she thought, smiling at the anxious-looking girl.

'Yes.' From the expression on the woman's face, Dorothy suspected she was no happier about losing her daughter to the WAAF than she was.

'Come on – we won't be going anywhere if we don't get a move on,' Lilian urged the other girl.

As she watched them step onto the train, Lilian striding on confidently with her suitcase and Sarah hesitating shyly and waving at her mother while clutching an identical suitcase, Dorothy didn't know whether to laugh or cry. She was pleased Lilian would have some company though. Between them, the two girls ought to get there safely. Doubtless Lilian would chatter for the duration, and doubtless poor Sarah would wonder what sort of life she was joining. Sarah certainly didn't look like a recruit.

Lilian was soon leaning out of the window.

'Tell Dad he won't recognise me the next time he sees me,' she shouted out. 'And I'll expect him to salute me,' she added cheekily.

'He'll salute you with the back of his hand if you don't behave yourself, my girl,' Dorothy called back sternly, but Lilian simply threw back her head and laughed.

''Bye, Mam. 'Bye, Maud. Take care. Take care of your little sister for me, John. And Rose, don't let him pull your hair. 'Bye!'

The train began pulling out of the station and Dorothy strode along beside it.

'Come straight home if you don't like it, pet,' she shouted. 'Don't let your pride get in the way. Everyone will understand.'

'And have Maud say "I told you so"? Ha! Not on your life. 'Bye, Mam!'

''Bye, love,' Dorothy shouted, but she doubted if Lilian would have heard her.

She stood at the end of the platform, waving until long after the train was out of sight. It was just as bad as waving the menfolk off, she decided. There was the same horrible knot in the stomach that fear of the unknown brings with it. Unlike Joe, who could be sent heaven knew where after he'd finished his training in Scotland, Lilian wasn't going off to fight but, until this war was over, there was no knowing what dangers lay ahead – for any of them.

❧

'Freedom here we come!' Lilian said, throwing herself down in the seat opposite Sarah.

Despite the number of people boarding the train, it had looked as if they might have the carriage to themselves, but then a young family joined them; harassed-looking parents and their three young charges, two boys and a girl.

Lilian smiled at the youngest of the boys and had to chuckle when he stuck out his tongue at her.

Sarah wasn't going to be the liveliest of companions, she decided. The girl had barely spoken a word so far. She was a plain-looking thing and her spectacles gave her a startled expression. Without the glasses, and with something done to her fair hair to stop it looking as if she'd just had a shock, she could be quite pretty. Her chubby face had an enviable rosy complexion.

'Let's introduce ourselves properly,' Lilian suggested.

'I'm Lilian Penrose and I'm eighteen years old. On the platform, you saw my mam – a born worrier – my elder sister, Maud – a born meddler – and Maud's children, John and Rose.'

'Sarah Harris,' the other girl replied with a shy smile. 'I'm twenty and that was my mam. Another born worrier, but quieter than your mam.'

'Most are quieter than Mam,' Lilian responded with a grin. 'And are you really twenty?'

'Yes. The people at the recruiting office didn't believe me either.'

Lilian wasn't surprised. Sarah didn't look eighteen, never mind twenty.

'Are you excited?' she asked her.

'I was,' Sarah replied slowly, 'but now, well I'm a bit scared to be honest. I would have changed my mind but my dad said he was proud of me and, after that, I didn't have the heart to say anything.'

'I'm sure there's nothing to be scared of.'

But Lilian could understand Sarah's feelings. If she were completely honest with herself, she was a bit scared too. She'd never been away from home before, except to her aunt and uncle's farm in Norfolk for holidays, and that was different because her parents had been there. Having a strict father who insisted on knowing and approving her every movement didn't seem quite so terrible when she was sitting on a train which was putting distance between her and everything that was familiar. Even sharing a bedroom with Maud didn't sound too bad.

'My fella –' Sarah blushed. 'Well, he's not really my boyfriend but I like him a lot. He joined up and I was so proud of him that I decided I wanted to do something too. But now…' Her voice trailed away.

'There was a boy I liked too,' Lilian confided, thinking of Roy, 'but he's in no hurry to join up. I can't understand it. Mind you, now that they're calling up nineteen-year-olds, he soon won't have any say in the matter.'

She had only seen Roy once since the night of the party. He'd been walking into the shop as she had been walking out so they hadn't been able to say much. Lilian had asked him if he wanted her to write to him and he'd said she could if she liked. Thinking about it now, he hadn't seemed particularly bothered one way or the other.

'If I was a man,' she told Sarah dreamily, 'I'd want to fly. Can you imagine that?'

'I don't want to. I can think of nothing worse. What keeps those planes up in the sky?'

'I don't know!' Lilian spluttered with laughter. 'Something keeps them up there, that's all that matters.'

'Horrible noisy things,' Sarah said with a shudder.

They were noisy, and they didn't look particularly safe. They had to be safe though, otherwise people wouldn't go in them Lilian assumed. She thought it would be grand to fly over the country and know that down below you, people were looking up and, more often than not, waving at you.

'At least we're not locked in,' Sarah said, looking round the carriage. 'One girl who lives near us joined the WAAF and on her way to her depot, the train was full of soldiers. Anyway, they locked the girls away so they couldn't mix.'

'Spoilsports!' Lilian was eager for more gossip. 'This friend of yours, does she like it in the WAAF? What's she doing? Where is she?'

'I don't know. She's not a friend. Me mam heard her mam telling someone in the butcher's.'

'I don't know much about the WAAF,' Lilian admitted. 'Do you?'

'Only what they told us at the recruiting office,' Sarah replied. 'And I've heard that they're getting so many volunteers they're running out of accommodation. We'll probably end up sleeping in tents. Still, it's too late to worry now. We'll soon find out for ourselves...'

On arrival at Bridgnorth railway station they had half an hour to wait. Another train pulled in and soon there were around twenty recruits waiting for the promised station bus to collect them and take them to RAF Bridgnorth. The other girls waited in groups of twos and threes and Lilian was glad of Sarah's company. They said little, they were too busy stamping their feet and trying to bring some feeling back to their toes, but it was good to know someone was there.

Eventually the bus arrived and, amid a lot of nervous laughter, they all climbed aboard and grabbed seats. Lilian managed to sit next to Sarah.

'They seem all right,' she murmured, gesturing at a group of four girls who were sitting in front of them.

'Yes.'

And again, they lapsed into a thoughtful, tentative silence.

The bus bumped its way up the hill so slowly that Lilian wondered if they would ever get there. Straining her neck to see where they were going, she saw they were following a shiny green sports car being driven by a young girl. A shiver of excitement ran through Lilian when she spotted the guardroom in the distance, and she was surprised when the car drove straight up to the gate.

The service policeman on the gate gave the girl a smart salute and Lilian wondered who she could be. Then, to Lilian's complete amazement, the girl handed over what looked like a pink recruiting summons. But surely not.

As the driver opened the bus door they all heard the policeman's shocked, 'A recruit? In that bloody thing?'

Everyone on the bus erupted into gales of laughter and a lot of the tension was broken.

'Get that bloody car out of sight,' the girl was told, 'and then sort yourself out with that lot.' The policeman gestured to the girls on the bus.

The bus was allowed through the gate and when Lilian got off and looked around her, she was highly amused to see the girl who had been driving the car walking towards them carrying two – two! – suitcases.

The next few hours passed in a blur and Lilian struggled to keep close to Sarah as they signed this and collected that. In the reception area she noticed a poster that read: Homesickness is like seasickness – it soon wears off. She noticed little else, however. By the end of the day, her head was spinning.

The supper was good, but by that stage Lilian felt sure she could have eaten anything, and then they were sent to their huts. Lilian was relieved to discover that Sarah was in the same hut as her and they quickly made for a couple of beds next to each other.

Lilian found that her companion on the other side was the girl who had caused such merriment in her car. She gave the girl a shy smile but was quite lost for words. Without doubt, she was very different to the others

Lilian had come across so far. She looked friendly enough, though. She had blonde hair, the colour of ripe corn, lovely clear skin with peach coloured dashes of colour, bright, sparkling eyes and a confident smile.

Just as Lilian was about to speak, the other girl beat her to it.

'I'm Prudence Fitzwilliam,' she said in a very posh voice, putting out her hand.

Fascinated and bemused, Lilian shook the hand. 'Lilian – Lilian Penrose. And this is Sarah Harris. We travelled from Sunderland together. Oh, and I love your car.'

'Don't remind me!' Prudence rolled her eyes to the heavens. 'That little episode has earned me a few enemies already.' She looked around her. 'I don't know how they expect us to sleep in here. It's freezing!'

'It is cold,' Lilian agreed. 'But then I've been cold all day.'

'Trust us to come here now. I heard the Thames froze over. Ugh! Mark my words, January 1940 will go down in history as the coldest winter ever.' Prudence sat on the unmade bed and groaned. 'We'll never sleep,' she announced in a matter-of-fact way.

While they were busy trying to sort out their blankets, Lilian had to ask. 'What made you volunteer, Prudence?'

'It was my father's idea. He's with Air Ministry and he thinks the WAAF will make something of me.' She gave the bed a scowl. 'The Lord alone knows what it will make of me. Oh, and by the way, my friends call me Prue.'

Lilian was pleased to be thought of as a friend.

'Daddy says the WAAF is a real dog's breakfast at the

moment,' Prue went on with a giggle. 'It's getting better, I gather, but there's still very little accommodation or clothing or anything.'

It was ironic, Lilian thought. Prue's father had wanted his daughter to volunteer, and her own father had been against the whole idea. Or had he? she wondered. He'd given in quite easily, far more easily than Lilian had expected. Perhaps, deep down, he was proud of her.

'Who cares, though?' Prue said with a laugh. 'It should be a lark.'

There was no chance to chat further with Prue or Sarah. Chaos reigned in the hut as everyone frantically tried to sort themselves out.

It was certainly an eye-opener for Lilian. She hadn't known quite what to expect, but she certainly hadn't expected this. One thing was certain, if her father could see her now, he would march her straight back to Sunderland in record time. He would think his youngest daughter had been let loose in a real den of iniquity. Bad enough to have to wash and undress in front of strangers, but having to avert your eyes from a near-naked girl who didn't seem to give the matter a second thought was something else.

Lilian welcomed lights-out. She was weary to her bones and thought she would be asleep within seconds. But she wasn't; the sound of girls sobbing beneath their blankets kept her awake long into the night.

∽✑∾

Maud couldn't sleep either. During the day, with the young ones to keep her busy, she managed to feel quite optimistic about life. As soon as she climbed into bed, however, the worries descended. Joe was a good letter writer, but it was hard not knowing where he would be sent when he'd finished training. She worried, too, about how the threatened food shortages would affect the children. And one of her biggest worries was keeping the children safe in an industrial north-east coast town that everyone felt certain was high on Hitler's list of priorities. Sunderland would be a prime target, she knew it. The whole length of the River Wear consisted of shipyards, engineering works, Wearmouth Colliery, the goods station –

With so much to worry about, she wished Lilian was in the room with her. Lilian was wild and reckless, but it had to be said that her ever-optimistic attitude to life rubbed off on those around her. It made a refreshing change to get into bed without climbing over heaven knew what clutter, but the house was surprisingly quiet without her.

Perhaps Lilian was safer where she was, Maud thought wryly as she remembered her meeting with Roy Walker.

Maud had been walking back from the shop, with two shopping bags in one hand, and Rose's hand in the other, when Roy caught up with her.

'Let me,' he said, taking the bags from her.

'Thanks.' She wasn't keen on Roy but she was grateful to let go of her shopping and flex her sore fingers.

'Did your Lilian get away all right?' he asked.

'Yes. We saw her off this morning.'

'Why is it that all the pretty ones have to go off and join the WAAF or take up nursing?' he complained.

'I've no idea, Roy. The same reason that all the decent men join up, I suppose,' she replied sweetly, unable to resist having a dig at him.

Sarcasm was wasted on Roy; he simply laughed.

'You'll be gone yourself soon,' she added. 'When are you nineteen?'

'July.' The prospect of conscription clearly didn't please him.

'I'll miss Lilian,' he said, changing the subject. 'All I had was one kiss. Never mind, I suppose there are plenty more fish in sea.'

'Plenty!' Maud retorted, shocked. Lilian had let him kiss her? Whatever had the stupid girl been thinking of? Roy was a good-looking chap, there was no disputing that, but his reputation went before him.

They had reached the house so she grabbed her bags from him and marched down the alley. She was annoyed with Lilian, and she was even more annoyed with Roy. People like him belittled everything that all the men like Joe were doing. As much as she longed for Joe to be back with them, she took comfort from the fact that he was where he should be, doing what had to be done, and she was proud of him...

She pulled the blankets tight around her neck and tried to push her worries from her mind. If she could have had Joe with her, just for a night, she felt sure she would be stronger. As it was, all alone with the silence, she found it impossible to ignore a sense of dread. Just what would become of them all?

∼ *Chapter Three* ∼

FEBRUARY 1940

Lilian woke early to the sound of sobbing coming from the next bed.

'Sarah?' she whispered in amazement. 'Sarah, what's wrong?'

But the sobbing increased. Lilian grabbed a blanket, wrapped it tight around herself, and groped her way through the darkness to the side of Sarah's bed.

'What on earth's the matter?'

'I want to go home,' Sarah sobbed. 'I can't bear it, Lil. I really can't. I can't cope with the cold, the endless square-bashing – my feet will never recover. I can't stand the food. I can't stand being just a number to be sent here, there and everywhere.'

Sarah wouldn't be the first girl to give up and go home, and Lilian sympathised to a degree. She longed for her mother's cooking, a good night's sleep in a comfortable bed – just a good night's sleep would do. Life was hard for them all. They did their best and yet they always ended up in trouble for something or other. They couldn't give up though, not now they'd come this far.

'You'll make it,' she said softly. 'We've almost finished our basic training now. Life will be much better soon.'

'It won't,' Sarah wailed. 'It will be more of the same – you know it will. Endless square-bashing. Washing up for hundreds. Oh, Lilian, I hate it.'

'I know. We all hate it.'

'No.' Sarah dried her face on her blanket. 'You and Prue complain about it, but you manage to see the funny side of it. You're quite happy to be away from home, taking orders from everyone. You two are happy; I'm not. I hate every second of it. I'm going home, Lilian.'

Lilian could feel her toes going numb but she ignored her discomfort. She hated the thought of Sarah giving up. For one thing, she felt sure Sarah would live to regret it. She would go home feeling like a failure. And for purely selfish reasons, she wanted her to stay. Sarah was the first friend she'd made. The train journey they had made together provided a link with home somehow.

In all honesty, Lilian couldn't say she was homesick. And, yes, Sarah was right. She might complain about the life, but she was happy. It was hard work – no one knew what they were supposed to be doing, and they spent half their time wandering around in an exhausted daze saluting everything that moved – but Lilian thrived on the laughter and the fun they shared. She missed her mother, of course. She would love to go home at the end of the day and sit in front of the stove to tell her all about her new life. She wrote long letters, usually while she was struggling to stay awake before lights-out, and her mother wrote equally long letters in return, but it wasn't the same.

'Why don't you just stay until the end? Finish your training, and then see how you feel,' Lilian suggested. 'If you still hate it, and if you don't like the thought of your first posting, then you can go home.'

'I can't bear it. I have to go home now.' She was calmer now. 'Sorry, but I can't stay. I'll miss you, and Prue, of course, but I can't stay.'

In the end, Lilian stumbled her way round her bed and woke Prue, never a wise, or an easy thing to do.

'She's just tired, Lil,' she mumbled, rolling away from Lilian. 'We're all tired.'

'No, it's worse than that. You'll have to talk to her, Prue. Make her see sense.'

Prue reluctantly left the relative warmth of her bed and tried to persuade Sarah to stay. It did no good, though. Before they knew it, it was time for washing, dressing, daily inspection, and all the other horrors of the day.

By the end of the day, Sarah was on her way back to Sunderland.

≈≈≈

Two weeks of initial training seemed to have made a world of difference to Lilian. When she finally made it back to Sunderland on a three-day leave, she felt at least a foot taller than when she'd left. There was so much news to catch up on and so many tales to tell her family – and all in the space of three days. She had been hoping for at least a week's leave, but they'd only been given three days. Lilian hardly knew where to start.

'So what exactly are you going to do in Blackpool?' Maud wanted to know. 'I thought you'd done your training.'

Lilian couldn't claim to have suffered from homesickness, but it was bliss to sit around the stove, surrounded by her family and all that was familiar.

Everyone accepted the thick blackout curtains now; in fact, they gave the kitchen a warm feel.

'We have,' Lilian answered Maud. 'And passed our exams. How we managed that I don't know.' She laughed happily. 'We're doing trade training now: they're going to teach us how to drive. Well, when I say teach us, I mean teach me. Oh, you can't imagine how pleased I am that Prue's coming to Blackpool too. But, of course, she can already drive. We did have a laugh about her car. The chap on the gate treated her like royalty until he knew she was a volunteer. He said "A recruit? In that bloody thing?" and I swear –'

'Lilian! I will not have language like that in this house,' her father barked out.

'But Dad, I was only telling you what he said.'

'If folk are using language like that, I don't want to know, thank you very much. He should have had more sense. In front of ladies, too!'

Lilian chuckled to herself. If her father only knew it, that was nothing to the language that had been bandied around the hut. Some of the women had been worse than the men. In fact Elsie, who before volunteering for the WAAF had made her living from prostitution on Liverpool docks, had introduced Lilian and the rest of them to a whole new vocabulary. Elsie was guaranteed to make any man blush.

'A lot of people thought Prue was a snob from that day on,' she told them, 'but nothing could be further from the truth. Her dad – she calls him Daddy – works for the Air Ministry and they've got pots of money, but she's a great laugh. You'll never believe what she did. We kept getting bits of clothing, all coming in dribs and drabs. Anyway, Prue took one look at it, decided she didn't like it, and simply parcelled it up and sent it to her mother for the church jumble sale. Prue thought they were giving it to us; she didn't realize it was WAAF property.'

'Daft 'aporth,' her father said, but even he was laughing.

Her mother rose to her feet. 'Let's have another cup of tea – before that's on ration. And that's another thing, our Lilian, did I tell you about Emily Patterson?'

'No.'

'She got hit by a car and had her leg broken. I tell you, this blackout will cause more injuries than the Germans will.'

'Had she been drinking?' Emily's drinking habits were well known.

'I wouldn't know.' Her mother handed Lilian a cup of tea. 'And I can't see that it matters. Drunk or sober, she's always managed to cross the road. I tell you, it's this dratted blackout.'

Lilian sipped her tea, unable to remember when a drink had tasted so good. And the luxury of drinking from a proper cup instead of those horrid tin mugs.

Very little had changed at home, although Lilian couldn't help noticing that Maud was quieter than usual. She looked pale and tired, too.

'What's the news from Joe?' she asked her sister.

'I had a letter,' Maud said, 'and I reckon he's being sent abroad any day now. I can't say for sure because of course he can't say anything. I don't think he knows himself. Before he left though, we joked about things he could say that would let me know where he was going. He was going to mention that he'd seen some fictitious uncle and the uncle's name would be connected to wherever he was. In his last letter, he said he might go and see Uncle Abraham.'

'Abraham? Abraham sounds nothing like abroad,' Lilian retorted on a burst of laughter.

'So what is it like, clever clogs?' Maud demanded.

'Well, I don't know.' Lilian couldn't come up with anything, and she could see Maud wasn't in the mood for jokes. 'But Joe's all right?'

'I suppose so.' Maud nodded.

Lilian let it drop. It was clearly preying on Maud's mind, but if she didn't want to talk about it, that was her choice.

Her father looked tired too, Lilian thought, but that was probably due to the long hours he was working at the factory.

It was late when Lilian finally stopped chattering and climbed into bed. She couldn't help smiling to herself when she remembered how she had longed for the first night when she wouldn't have to share a room with Maud. Having shared an icy hut with such a varied assortment of strangers, it was bliss to settle down in her own comfortable bed with only Maud in the room. And the bed was unbelievably comfortable. It was warm and soft, and the blankets didn't scratch. Maud didn't snore either – Lilian had soon reached the conclusion that being able to snore loudly throughout the night was obligatory for WAAF girls.

She wondered briefly what Blackpool had in store for them. One thing was certain, good or bad, at least they wouldn't be stuck in a freezing, makeshift hut. They were to be billeted in private accommodation.

She would miss the friends she'd made though. They had promised to keep in touch and she hoped they did. It was ironic to think of the tears that had been shed on that first night at the depot. Even more had been shed on the last day when friends realized they were being sent to different parts of the country. She and Prue had hardly been able to believe their good fortune when they discovered that not only were they both being sent to Blackpool to train as drivers, they were to be billeted in the same building.

'I've heard of Blackpool,' Prue had said, 'but I know nothing of the place.'

Lilian had laughed at that. Blackpool would be a different world for her well-to-do friend.

'According to a girl at the depot,' Prue had gone on, 'a rather loud girl with bleached hair – don't know her name – Blackpool is the best place in the country to find good-looking men. Mind you, I expect they'll have all joined up by now.'

'Never mind the men,' Lilian had retorted with a laugh. 'I've got to learn how to drive. Me! I'll never do it.'

'Of course you will, Lil. I haven't managed to hit anything yet.'

Nevertheless it sounded interesting to Lilian. She didn't know, very little had been said, but she supposed they would eventually be driving the top brass here, there and everywhere. And they were sure to go to all the best places.

Her mind was busy but the unaccustomed comfort soon claimed her and she fell into a deep sleep.

∽∾∽

'The WAAF doesn't seem to have changed our Lilian,' Dorothy murmured as she snuggled up close to Clive for warmth in their bed.

'Nope. She's still as daft as a brush.' But Clive was smiling and Dorothy knew how pleased he was to have her home again, if only for a brief time.

'This Prue sounds a right character,' Dorothy went on. 'Fancy Lilian hitting it off with her.'

'That's Lilian for you.' Clive slipped his arm around her and pulled her close. 'She's always expected folk to take her as they find her. And if this lass's dad is with the Air Ministry, she should know the meaning of discipline.'

Dorothy didn't comment on that. In her experience, that sort of girl was the worst sort imaginable. They tended to rebel. In her days with the suffragette movement, Dorothy had mixed with girls from all walks of life. Most had been passionate about the cause but some, and it seemed to Dorothy that they were nearly always girls from the upper class, simply wanted excitement, or to rebel against their parents. She was glad Lilian had made friends, though, and it was a comfort to know she would be going to Blackpool with someone she knew.

'And fancy her learning to drive,' she murmured, smiling. 'Whatever next?'

'It's a whole new world,' Clive said with a sigh. 'The world, or the world as we know it, is changing, and I doubt if it will ever be the same again. Every family has at least one man away, and life at home's getting more and more difficult – what with the rationing and the blackout.'

'Don't talk to me about the blackout. No matter how carefully I close them, those curtains always seem to let out a small chink of light. We've painted the edges of the windows black, and still the air raid warden finds cause for complaint,' said Dorothy wearily.

'And the government's wasting money on posters,' Clive went on scathingly, 'telling us that walls have ears of all things…'

Dorothy's mind drifted back to her daughters. Lilian took everything in her stride, but Maud was a born worrier. It wasn't surprising, Dorothy supposed, that she was worrying now. She had a lot to worry about. She didn't know where her husband was going to be sent, or when she'd see him again, and then there was the ever-present threat of air raids. It was a terrible time to be a young mother.

'I wish it would all end, Clive,' she whispered fervently into the dark room.

'Aye, and that thought's being echoed all over the country. I fear it will get a lot worse yet though, pet.'

Dorothy shivered at his words and tightened her grip on his arm.

∽∾

Lilian's first impression of Blackpool was not a good one. A strong wind was blowing in from the sea, bringing heavy rain with it that made everything look grey and gloomy. As she got off the train, she thought she had never seen such a depressing place in her life. Only the posters springing up everywhere, reminding them that 'walls have ears' and that they must 'keep it dark', cheered up the place.

Then she saw Prue dashing along the platform, dragging her kit bag behind her, and in an instant everything looked better.

'What a day!' Prue greeted her. 'I've been here for what seems like hours and of all the people I've asked, no one knows where our billet is.'

'Hello to you too,' Lilian replied with a laugh. 'And yes, I enjoyed my leave. Thank you so much for asking.'

Prue spluttered with laughter. 'Sorry, but I'm wet, cold and thoroughly fed up with life.'

'Let's ask that guard,' Lilian suggested. 'He's sure to know where we need to go.'

Lilian strode over to him and two minutes later, she not only had directions to their billet, but had also learnt of a café on the way where they were assured of a good hot cup of tea and a sandwich.

They set off in the rain and, sure enough, there was the café. It was small, clean, welcoming and, most important of all, warm and dry. It was also empty. A young woman smiled a welcome and Lilian suspected she was glad of something to relieve the boredom.

While she went into a back room to make their tea, Lilian and Prue took off their coats and hung them on pegs to drip.

By the time the tea was brought to the table, they were feeling far more human. Lilian sat with her hands warming around her cup.

'So tell me about your leave,' she said.

'Oh, it was wonderful. It was sheer heaven to crawl into my own bed. And guess what, Molly even brought me breakfast in bed.'

'You call your mam Molly?' Lilian was horrified. She could imagine her own mother's reaction if she suddenly started calling her Dorothy. Not only that, her father would threaten her with his belt for showing such disrespect.

'No, idiot! Molly's our housekeeper. And a friend for life now. I think I ate the whole bacon ration.'

A housekeeper? Lilian supposed she should have guessed. She knew Prue came from a completely different background, of course, but because she couldn't relate to it, she often forgot. She wondered briefly what Prue would make of her own family, and what her family would make of Prue. Prue might have her eyes opened, she supposed, but she felt sure her family would take to Prue. She might have been born with a silver spoon in her mouth but she had no airs and graces. She certainly didn't consider herself better than everyone else just because her family had money. All the same, it bothered Lilian now and again that they were so very different.

'What about you?' Prue broke into her thoughts. 'Did you do anything exciting?'

'Not really. It was good to see everyone and I swear John and Rose have each grown six inches – Oh, I did do something exciting. I visited Sarah. You'll never guess where she's working.'

'Then I won't even bother trying. Where?'

'The same factory as my dad. Lots of the girls have jobs there now by all accounts. It makes sense I suppose, with all the men being away. Anyway, she loves it. She's as happy as Larry. She sends her love, of course, but I don't think she's in the least bit envious of us.'

Prue looked out at the steadily falling rain and pulled a face. 'I'm not surprised!'

And on that less than optimistic note, they left the warmth of the café and walked on to their billet.

Their destination was easy to spot; a tall, imposing

building standing in a row of equally imposing buildings. It looked clean and well-cared for, and Lilian felt her spirits lift. This was the life; no more freezing huts to endure. They would sleep in warm, comfortable beds in a warm, comfortable house. No matter what was thrown at them during the day, at least they would come home to comfort.

Prue rapped sharply on the door and they waited – and waited.

'They are expecting us, aren't they?'

'Sure to be.' But Lilian was a lot less confident than she sounded.

Their patience was finally rewarded when the door was opened a full six inches.

'Yes?'

Prue introduced them in a way that said they didn't intend to stand in the rain all the day. The door was opened fully so that they could see their landlady. She was a large, unsmiling woman in her mid-fifties, wearing a grubby brown skirt and cardigan, and a pair of slippers that were so worn, it was impossible to say what colour they had once been.

'You'd better come in then,' she said. 'And wipe your feet!'

Lilian exchanged a bemused look with Prue as they stepped inside and dutifully wiped their shoes on a threadbare mat that probably made their shoes dirtier than they'd been to start with.

'It's Mrs Marston, is it?' Prue asked in what Lilian thought of as her Miss High-And-Mighty voice.

'Aye, it is. You're at the top,' she said, clearly not inclined to make small talk, 'and once I've shown you the room, I don't expect to have to come up these stairs again.'

Lilian could see why Mrs Marston was so reluctant; she was overweight and far from fit. She puffed her way very slowly up the two flights of stairs.

So much for comfort, Lilian thought grimly, as they ascended. The smell of damp got stronger at every step and it felt no warmer inside than it did out. The stairs were bare and her mother would have had forty fits if she could have seen the thick layers of dust clinging to the banister.

They arrived at their room. With Mrs Marston's ample bulk in it, there was no space left for Lilian and Prue. No one said a word. Lilian wrinkled her nostrils at the smell of damp and stared in dismay at the four beds that had been crammed into the small, dreary room.

'I'll expect you to leave it as you find it,' Mrs Marston said. 'The other two –' she nodded at two of the beds '– will be back this evening. WAAF girls like you.'

Four of them in this tiny room? Lilian couldn't believe it. They would surely suffocate.

Mrs Marston rattled off a long list of rules and regulations and then left them.

'And I'll have no men in the house,' she called out from the bottom of the stairs. 'I know what you WAAF girls are like!'

Lilian and Prue stared at each other with identical expressions of outraged indignation on their faces.

'Fat chance!' Prue spluttered to Lilian. 'There's no room for us, let alone a man as well!'

They heard a downstairs door slam shut, sank onto the nearest bed and burst into hysterical laughter.

'This isn't funny, Lil,' Prue said, wiping tears of mirth from her eyes.

'I know!' But Lilian was still bent double.

'It's a pity we can't parcel up the confounded woman and post her off to Hitler.' Prue looked around the room. 'Daddy wouldn't keep the spaniels in conditions like this,' she muttered scathingly. She climbed across the two beds to the window. 'And look at this – there's a gale blowing through this –'

A scurrying sound stopped her in mid-sentence.

'What was that?' she asked anxiously.

'I don't know. It couldn't be – no, it couldn't be. I mean, not a rat.'

'For heaven's sake, Lil!'

All was silent and they relaxed a little.

They took off their wet coats and hung them on the back of the door. Like it or not – and they didn't – this room would be their home for a while. It wasn't a comforting thought.

'What a let down after our leave,' Prue said with a sigh. 'I had such a lovely time too.'

'Yes, well. Don't expect to eat the whole bacon ration here,' Lilian said with a wry smile.

'Or any bacon at all,' Prue muttered. 'Blasted woman. Honestly, here we are doing our bit for king and country; there's Charlie off to heaven knows where with the army –' For once, words failed Prue.

Lilian had heard a lot about Charlie, otherwise known as Captain Charles Wainwright, and felt she would dearly like to meet him. He was Prue's neighbour and they'd grown up together, but Lilian couldn't help thinking there was more to it than that. Prue insisted they were 'just friends', but he cropped up in conversation on a very regular basis.

'Have you heard from him?' she asked.

'Better than that,' Prue replied, smiling. 'He was at home on a forty-eight hour pass.'

Lilian waited to hear more but nothing was forthcoming. Prue spoke of him fondly, and she mentioned him often, but she didn't give much away.

'What does he look like?' Lilian asked curiously.

Prue reached across for her kit bag, delved inside and brought out a tiny photograph. Lilian was amazed; she had no idea Prue carried a photograph of him with her. Charles Wainwright, or Charlie as she thought of him, wasn't particularly handsome but he had a relaxed smile and looked to be an easygoing sort of man. He was wearing uniform in the photograph.

'He looks very kind,' Lilian said.

'Yes. Yes, he is. He's two years older than me and he's always had the job of getting me out of scrapes. I've never heard him say a bad word about anyone. He's a lovely man.'

'How does he feel about you?' Lilian ventured.

'He claims he's going to marry me,' Prue answered with a burst of laughter. The laughter died and she smiled the fond smile that was always reserved for Charlie. 'And he probably will.' She returned the photograph to her kit bag. 'And what about you, Lilian Penrose? Who are you going to marry?'

'If no one better comes along,' Lilian responded immediately, 'I expect I'll settle for Clark Gable.'

It was fine to joke, but she wished she carried a nice young man's photograph around with her. Perhaps she was too fussy. She had half-imagined herself in love with Roy, but at times she found herself wondering if that had been based on anything other than his good looks. She seemed to find fault with all the men she came across. They were too short, too quiet or too talkative.

The door to their room burst open and in came Mary and Eve, the two girls they were to share this small room with. It was odd, Lilian thought as they introduced themselves, how totally unlikely friendships developed in the WAAF. Eve was as shy as Mary was outgoing. Eve smiled a lot but said very little whereas Mary didn't stop talking. She could even out-talk Prue, Lilian thought with amusement, and that took some doing.

'Have you met Harvey yet?' Mary asked.

'Harvey?' Lilian and Prue spoke in unison.

'Our resident mouse,' Eve explained. 'We see him most days.'

'Oh, no,' Prue wailed. 'I'll never sleep if I think a mouse is on the loose.'

'I just hope Harvey turns out to be a Harriet,' Mary said with a raucous laugh. 'I trust you've been warned about having men in the room?'

'We certainly have!' Once again, Prue bristled with indignation. 'She said "I know what you WAAF girls are like". The cheek of it!'

'Two men spent the night here on Tuesday night,' Mary confided, lowering her voice. 'They returned to their own billet to find all their belongings out on the pavement. Apparently, the landlady had other more lucrative plans for their room and just threw their stuff out. It poured with rain all night and they had nowhere else to go so they came here.'

'How did you get them past Mrs Marston?' Lilian asked in amazement.

'They climbed up the drainpipe and came in through the window. Mind you, when the powers that be found out they'd been thrown out of their billet, there was a huge flap on.'

'I'm not surprised,' Prue said, her eyes dancing with laughter.

If she had to share such a small room with three other girls, Lilian decided as she tried to get comfortable in her bed that night, she couldn't have asked for better roommates. Mary and Eve had almost finished their training as drivers and had been able to answer the hundreds of questions she put to them. When Lilian finally fell asleep, it was with a fairly confident feeling that she might, just might, cope with Blackpool.

⚬⚭⚬

Maud had thought this moment would never come. Ever since Joe had phoned the newsagent yesterday to leave a message saying he was coming home, she had been on tenterhooks. She threw open the door, letting light spill onto the pavement with no thought of the blackout, and hurled herself into Joe's arms. He felt warm and smelt wonderfully familiar. Neither spoke as he held her tight. Maud could feel his body trembling, and she could taste her own salty tears on her lips. When he lifted her face to kiss her, Joe tasted them too.

'And I thought you'd be pleased to see me,' he teased.

'I am,' she sobbed. 'So very pleased, Joe. I can't bear it without you. I honestly can't bear it.' She had promised herself that, for Joe's sake, she would put on a brave face, but the tears poured down her cheeks and she was powerless to stop them. 'Sorry, love.'

'Hey, come on, pet,' he whispered, kissing away her tears. 'I'm here now. I'm home, sweetheart.'

She nodded, and brushed at her tears. He was home,

but this wasn't their home, it was her parents' home, and he was only with her for forty-eight hours. When that was up, he would be on a ship...

'Let's get this door shut,' Joe said, dragging his kit bag through the door.

Once inside, with the night safely locked out, Maud took a good look at him. Lines of weariness circled his eyes, she noticed. He looked older, too, and she regretted her outburst. He was having a tough enough time without having to worry about her as well.

'John and Rose are in bed.' Selfishly, Maud had wanted Joe to herself for a few hours. She would have to share him with her parents, but hopefully they would go to bed soon. 'They wanted to wait up but –'

'How are they?' His expression was wistful.

'They're grand. Just grand, love.' She felt even more guilty about her outburst now. At least she had the children, which was more than Joe had. 'You'll see for yourself in the morning. Come and see Mam and Dad.'

Maud saw that her parents both had tears in their eyes as they greeted their son-in-law. While her mother flitted about making tea and finding food, her father questioned Joe about his new life. All Maud could do was gaze at her husband and wish with all her heart that this war would end and let them get on with their lives again. It seemed no time at all since she had walked up the aisle on Joe's arm looking forward to a bright future full of hope. She certainly hadn't imagined the country would be at war.

But it was so good to be able to look at him. Joe wasn't particularly handsome, she supposed. His hair was a nondescript brown and it curled untidily in all directions. His eyes were a very ordinary blue-grey colour and he was stocky rather than well-built. But to Maud he was everything. He was kind, thoughtful and generous. He loved her in a way that made her feel special. He was a born optimist and could see a good side to anyone. Oh, she loved him so much...

She couldn't sleep that night. It seemed criminal to squander their precious time together by sleeping. To be held in his arms was all she asked.

'I had a letter from Lilian,' he said, softly stroking her hair. 'She's enjoying the war if no one else is.'

'That's Lilian,' Maud said with a wry smile. 'You'll never believe this,' she added, 'but I really miss her. She's totally irresponsible and drives me crazy, but she used to make me laugh. I miss that.'

'She's a good kid,' Joe murmured. 'Her letter made me smile, too. I showed it to some of my mates. We had a good laugh.'

'Joe?'

'Mmmm?'

'Talking of Lilian – well, talking of Norfolk –'

'Yes?' he prompted.

'Aunt Violet wondered if I'd like to take the children and stay with them on the farm for a while. What do you think?'

'Really? Why, I think it's a great idea, love. How do you feel about it?'

Maud didn't really know. She wanted the children to be safe, that was her main priority, and she felt sure they would thrive in Norfolk. On the other hand, she wanted to be with her parents, and she wanted the children to be with them.

'I don't know,' she confessed. 'I just don't know.' She moved closer to him. 'How long are we going to have to live like this, Joe?'

'If I knew that, pet, I'd be a clever bloke. Now it looks like Winston Churchill will be Prime Minister, perhaps things will start to happen.' He was thoughtful for a moment. 'I'd feel a lot better if I knew you and the kids were in Norfolk though,' he said eventually. 'I know there are RAF stations there but it's still bound to be safer than Sunderland. Which is going to take a real hammering.' He pulled her close as she shuddered. 'I know, love,' he whispered. 'I know exactly how you feel. But we have to face facts.'

'We'll see,' she whispered. 'Let's talk about it tomorrow. Just hold me, Joe...'

She didn't sleep well, but it was heaven to wake up and feel the strength of Joe's arms around her. He slept well, hardly moving during the night, and she was pleased. He didn't say too much about his life, but she could tell he needed the sleep.

The children demanded all his attention and more the following day. Rose insisted on clinging to him the whole time – not that Joe minded – and John reeled off question after question, not waiting for the answer before he fired off the next question.

As a treat, they took the children out to tea. Rose looked very grown up, in spite of the cake crumbs that clung to her chubby face, and John looked painfully like his father. They were good kids, Maud thought. They were well-mannered and polite and it was heart-warming to take them to the tea rooms and feel proud of them. It was even better to feel like a real family again.

'Where are you being sent?' Maud asked Joe, as she poured them another cup of tea.

'We haven't been told,' he answered slowly, looking at the children briefly before turning his gaze back to her, 'and there are so many rumours going round that you might just as well stick a pin in the map. Yesterday, the clever money was on Jericho. Tomorrow – who knows?'

Maud simply nodded. She could think of nothing worse than his being sent to some foreign place to fight. She could hardly bear the thought of it, yet there was nothing she could say. All they could do was hope and pray. That, and try to keep each other cheerful.

They walked home in a row; Maud held Rose's hand, Joe held John's, and the two children held hands in the middle. Anyone looking at them would have thought they were the perfect family without a care in the world. If it hadn't been for the fact that Joe's forty-eight hour pass was rapidly running out, they would have been...

The following evening, it was all over.

Maud left the children with their grandparents and went to the station with Joe. The platforms were packed with soldiers waiting for trains, and wives or girlfriends waiting with them. There were a lot of tears being shed but Maud wanted Joe to remember her with a smile on her face.

They hardly spoke a word until his train pulled into the station.

'This is it, love,' Joe said, his voice hoarse with emotion.

'Oh, Joe.' Maud clung to him. 'You take good care of yourself for me.'

'I will, pet,' he promised.

Maud could feel her heart hammering painfully fast. In a second, he would be gone and the Lord alone knew when she would see him again. Her mouth was dry and she was finding it almost impossible to swallow.

'I'd better go, love,' he said, shouting over the noise.

Maud held his face in his hands, and gazed at him intently as if she could imprint his features in her mind.

'I love you so much, Joe. Don't forget how much. I'll write every day.'

'And so will I. I love you too, Maud. Take care of the children for me.' He held her close. 'Just pray that I'm home soon – eh?'

'I will.' She buried her face in the scratchy collar of his jacket and sniffed loudly.

And then he was gone.

Maud stood on the platform, searching for his face among the milling soldiers, but she couldn't see him.

She stood there long after the train had left the station. Her heart was racing with a sudden wild panic. For a moment, just for a brief moment, she had thought she would never see him again. The thought had flashed through her mind from nowhere, but it had terrified her.

Pull yourself together, she told herself shakily. There was nothing to panic about. Joe would be home again soon.

Tears streamed steadily down her cheeks as she walked slowly home...

∽⌒∽

∽ *Chapter Four* ∽

APRIL 1940

Three letters arrived that morning, and Dorothy recognised the handwriting on each one. The neat, slightly forward-sloping script on the bulky envelope belonged to Lilian, the slightly disjointed writing on the envelope addressed to Maud was Joe's, and the barely legible, spidery writing belonged to Violet, Dorothy's sister.

Maud had taken the children to the shops so Dorothy put Joe's letter on the table where she would see it as soon as she came home. Dorothy only hoped he'd written a cheerful letter because poor Maud was looking more worried every day. Joe usually did write a good letter, so Dorothy had no real worries on that score. Maud usually read them – or the less personal parts – out loud to the family.

Dorothy took a knife from the drawer, slit the flaps on both her envelopes and sat by the stove to read them. She started on Lilian's first. Inside the thick envelope were pictures of Blackpool Tower for John and Rose.

Dorothy loved Lilian's letters. She wrote in a disjointed fashion, making it easy for Dorothy to imagine her daughter sitting opposite her and talking nineteen to the dozen. This letter was four pages long, half of it written in parenthesis as Lilian went off at a tangent. It consisted mostly of amusing anecdotes but was enough to reassure Dorothy that her daughter was happy and enjoying life. Lilian had almost completed her training as a driver but there was very little about that in her letter. All she said was 'The trucks are huge but I haven't managed to crash one yet.'

Smiling to herself, Dorothy returned the letter to its envelope and read Violet's note. This one was completely different. Violet had always taken life very seriously. She was warm and generous though, and the two of them had always got along well. As children they had been as close as two peas in a pod and now, despite the miles separating them, they were still the best of friends.

'I know you're worrying about Maud,' Violet wrote, 'and I can imagine how Maud is worrying about the children, so I wondered if she'd thought any more about coming to stay with us until this terrible war is over.'

Dorothy couldn't answer that. Maud had thought about it, she knew that, but she didn't think her daughter had made a decision. Something was holding her back.

Violet had married her farmer, Jack, and lived happily on his farm in Norfolk for the last twenty years. Dorothy still had fond memories of the holidays she and Clive had spent with them when Maud and Lilian were young. It was the ideal place for children. The fresh country air had always put a glow in the girls' cheeks.

The rest of the letter was quickly read – news from the farm mostly, and worries about how those in the towns were suffering.

Dorothy sat back in her chair and wondered what

Maud would do. She would hate to see her daughter go to Norfolk – she loved having her grandchildren in the house – but all in all it was for the best. It was true the farm was near an RAF station, but it still had to be safer than Sunderland which was bound to be a prime target. The children would be safe and they would be able to play on the farm, and they would drink fresh milk and have fresh butter on their bread.

It saddened her to think how families were being torn apart by this war. Joe should have been at home with his wife and children, Lilian could soon be posted to the other end of the country, and Maud might decide to take the children to Norfolk. At times, Dorothy was grateful they hadn't been blessed with sons. She didn't know how mothers coped with knowing their boys were away fighting. She prayed for those mothers and their sons every day. She prayed for them all every day…

∽∾∾

Lilian could hardly believe her eyes! She'd been awaiting news of her first real posting with mixed feelings. Having amazed herself by passing her exams and qualifying as a driver, part of her couldn't wait to get out there and start work on a proper RAF station. The other part of her had dreaded the thought of leaving Prue behind. She couldn't believe it when she saw they were both being sent to Norfolk.

'I think it's a conspiracy,' Prue said, laughing happily. 'If I didn't know better, I'd think Daddy was involved. And just think, no more Mrs Marston. We'll never have to set eyes on the confounded woman again.'

Lilian looked around their small room and had to agree that it was wonderful to see their kit bags lying on the beds ready to move on.

She threw herself down on the lumpy bed.

'Are you serious?' she asked thoughtfully. 'About your dad, I mean? Do you really think he could be behind it?' Lilian was amazed that anyone could have such power.

'No.' Prue shook her head. 'At least, I wouldn't think so. But I do know he'll be delighted. I've told him all about you and –'

'Told him what?' Lilian sat up.

'Oh, everything. Mummy can be a bit of a snob,' she confided, 'and Daddy has always insisted on me mixing with –' She stopped mid-sentence.

'Ah,' Lilian said softly.

'Don't look like that, Lil!' Laughing, Prue leaned across the beds and gave Lilian a quick hug.

'I do have a titled relative, you know,' Lilian said, feeling uncomfortable with Prue for the very first time. 'On my dad's side. Not that we have anything to do with him – some sort of family dispute, I think. And it's not as if there's any family money or anything. But he is a baronet. Honestly! He is! Can you imagine that? Me, of all people, related to a baronet!'

'Will you stop it!' Prue cried. 'I don't care a fig how many rich relatives you have.'

'But it is pretty amazing. I mean – a real baronet.'

'It is, but I still don't care. I was merely saying that Daddy would call you the salt of the earth. He's delighted to know that my best friend, my very best friend, is someone who has a lot more in her head than what she's going to wear to the next ball, or who she should flirt with to make a good marriage for herself.'

My very best friend. Lilian was so touched by the words that foolish tears pricked at her eyes. She had to blink them away.

'We'll have great fun!' Prue declared emphatically. 'Norfolk here we come!'

They would have fun. In Lilian's eyes, there couldn't have been a more perfect posting. Firstly, they would still be together and, secondly, they would only be about five miles from Uncle Jack and Aunt Violet's farm. If they got hold of a couple of bikes, they could pay the farm a visit and be pampered by Aunt Violet.

'You'll love Norfolk,' she told Prue enthusiastically.

'Is it a bit quiet though?' Prue asked.

'I suppose it is.'

It was very quiet compared to Blackpool or Sunderland; then again Prue came from the Cotswolds. From what Lilian had gathered, her home was a couple of miles from Chipping Campden, right on the northern edge of the Cotswolds. Charlie's family, the nearest neighbours, lived half a mile away.

'You're a country girl,' she said. 'You'll love it.'

'I'm not a country girl,' Prue argued. 'I was born and raised in the country, true, but give me a bit of life any day.'

Lilian was surprised. Whenever Prue spoke of her life, it seemed like one roundabout of riding horses, usually with Charles, or long walks through the woods, usually with Charles.

'Charlie loves it,' Prue added, smiling fondly. 'He's passionate about the land. He loves every tree and every blade of grass. The thought of Hitler getting his hands on a square yard of British soil is more than

Charlie can bear. He'd fight the Germans single-handed if he could.'

'I know exactly how he feels,' Lilian said passionately. She thought briefly of Roy, and his reluctance to join up and fight. She wished he could have been more like Prue's Charlie. 'I couldn't bear the idea of our home belonging to someone else either. It's a terrible thought. Can you imagine it?'

'No, I can't,' Prue said emphatically. 'And I'm not even going to try!'

⌒⌒

Lilian felt the excitement race through her veins as she walked round the Norfolk RAF station. She knew the area fairly well thanks to holidays spent with her aunt and uncle, but walking round the airfield was something else. There were people everywhere, all rushing around and looking very important. There were planes lined up ready to take off.

The atmosphere was one of efficiency, of readiness for anything, and she loved it. She walked taller, proud to be wearing her WAAF uniform. She felt a part of it all.

It was time to drive to the station to collect the mail and drop off the parcels. She'd have Jimmy with her, a cocky little private who made the WAAFs' lives a misery. It would mean a hand on her knee for the entire trip, Lilian thought grimly. Jimmy was harmless enough, she supposed – and hoped – but he was a nuisance.

Just for once, however, he was quiet as she drove to the station.

She was sitting in the truck, waiting while he collected the parcels, when she glimpsed an RAF sergeant. He had obviously just got off the train and was looking around him as he wedged his forage cap more firmly on his head. A suitcase and two kit bags were at his feet.

'Do you need a lift up to the camp, Sergeant?' she called out.

He turned around and, as Lilian looked straight into his smiling face, she felt something melt deep inside her. He walked over to the truck – she was struck by fair hair with a slight tinge of red and the most gorgeous green eyes she had ever seen. Smiling eyes, she thought.

'Thanks!' Those eyes twinkled with devilment. 'Are they all as pretty as you round here then?'

Lilian should have been used to the flirting by now, but his words made her blush. He really was gorgeous, and his accent told Lilian he came from Liverpool.

"Fraid not, Sarge,' she replied cheekily.

'Pity.'

Jimmy was walking back to the truck, loaded with boxes and parcels.

'It'll be a squeeze,' Lilian warned their passenger. She called to Jimmy, 'Put the sergeant's things in the back, Jimmy.'

Inside the cab, it was a squeeze – the perfect excuse for Jimmy to put his arm along the back of Lilian's seat and let his hand rest on her shoulders.

The truck jerked forward.

'Christ – women drivers!' Jimmy muttered, grinning in the sergeant's direction.

'If you'd learn to keep your hands to yourself, Jimmy,'

Lilian retorted, 'I might be able to concentrate on what I'm doing!'

He just laughed at her outburst, and kept his hand on her shoulder, making sarcastic comments every time she braked or cornered.

'You straight from the Operation Training Unit, Sarge?' he asked their companion.

'I am. And glad to be away from it. We had the most pompous Squadron Leader commanding our Flight. He'd served in training command, though, and everyone reckons that instructors like that are a damn sight more pernickety than the pilots from the operational squadrons.'

'You'll be all right here,' Jimmy said. 'They look after you chaps well.'

They were in sight of the camp.

'We'll let you off at the Guardroom, Sarge,' Jimmy said, 'and drop off your kit at the sergeants' Mess.'

'Thanks.'

Lilian stopped the truck at the Guardroom and he jumped out.

'Thanks for the lift,' he said, smiling at Lilian.

'Pleasure, Sergeant.' She was blushing again.

Instead of driving on, she gazed after him, but when he turned round and caught her watching him, she wished she hadn't. She was shaking, she realized.

For the rest of the day, she couldn't get him out of her mind for a single second.

That evening, when she managed to spend five minutes with Prue in the canteen known as the NAAFI and run by the Navy, Army and Air Force Institutes, she told her all about him.

'Have you seen him yet?' she asked eagerly.

'Lil! In case you haven't noticed, there are hundreds of good-looking men in this place.'

'Yes, but –'

'I know. He was so handsome that I couldn't help but notice him – right?'

'Yes!' Lilian laughed at herself. 'I'm sure you'd have noticed him though, Prue. His hair is very fair, but it has the slightest tinge of red to it. And his eyes – honestly, Prue, I've never seen eyes like them. A really dark shade of green they were.'

'Polished emeralds no doubt, just like yours,' Prue said with a splutter of laughter.

'As a matter of fact –'

Prue groaned. 'Shut up, Lil!'

Lilian did, but she couldn't stop thinking about him. No matter what she did, or what she tried to think about, he was lurking at the back of her mind.

She collapsed into bed exhausted that night, but after a few moments she was wide awake again and remembering those green eyes. His smiling face was clear in her mind when she eventually fell into a restless sleep...

∽◌∽

The following morning, Lilian was sent to the officers' mess where she had instructions to meet a Pilot Officer Benson and drive him to Cambridge.

He tried to disguise it, but his face fell as soon as he saw her. Lilian suspected he'd been expecting a car and a male driver. Instead, he had Lilian and a Commer truck full of armaments. The thought amused her briefly. But only briefly. His demeanour made her nervous. She gained the impression that he had a low opinion of women, an even lower opinion of women who drove trucks, and that he was fully expecting her to crash the Commer.

He was handsome in a somewhat severe sort of way. Tall and erect, slim, dark hair, tidy moustache –

He wasn't exactly watching her as she drove, he was staring intently at the passing countryside, but Lilian knew, without a doubt, that he was aware of her every move. Conversation was kept to a very bare minimum; he asked about journey times and roads, and Lilian replied with polite but monosyllabic answers. Her father would have called him a 'real toff'. Clearly well-educated, he had one of those voices you always heard on the radio.

Despite getting held up by the biggest, slowest moving flock of sheep Lilian had ever seen, and despite having to deliver the armaments on the way, she got him to Cambridge in plenty of time for his appointment and was given instructions to wait for him.

Half an hour later, Lilian was still waiting, and becoming more and more resentful. She could have been looking around Cambridge instead of waiting in her vehicle with her stomach rumbling every thirty seconds.

His business, whatever it was, took him more than two hours. If she'd known, she would have sneaked off to a café for something to eat. She had to admit that he seemed slightly more cheerful when he eventually returned – or perhaps he'd merely resigned himself to a female driver.

'Sorry,' he greeted her. 'I had no idea it would take so long. You must be starving.'

Lilian blushed, wondering if he could hear her stomach grumbling away.

'I'm fine, thank you, Sir,' she replied awkwardly.

'Mmm.' He wasn't convinced. 'We'll stop for a bite to eat on the way back. I noticed a nice looking pub that advertised good food. It's only about ten miles away from here.'

'Right, Sir.'

Lilian still felt uncomfortable, and the thought of sitting down and eating with him was not a pleasant one. But she was really hungry.

'I think it was along here,' he said after a while.

'A large black and white building, Sir?' she asked, grateful that the noise of the Commer drowned out the noise of her stomach.

'That's the one.'

Lilian had noticed it too. It had looked welcoming.

She pulled into the car park, managed with great difficulty to park the Commer, and switched off the engine. Her companion jumped out.

They walked inside the building. It was as welcoming inside as it was out, and the landlord greeted them with a broad smile.

Pilot Officer Benson ordered a pint of beer for himself and, not knowing quite what to say when asked what she would like, Lilian asked for a small port and lemon. She'd seen some of the more sophisticated girls drinking it, but had never tried it.

'They're on me,' the landlord said, nodding at their uniforms. 'Both my sons are in the RAF. May God watch over you all.'

Lilian was extremely touched by the gesture, and by his words. Her companion clearly was too and the two men were soon engrossed in a conversation about the strength of Britain's air power versus that of the Germans. While they chatted, Lilian nodded politely in the right places. They clearly didn't want or expect her opinion so she studied the menu chalked up on a board. Her stomach rumbled loudly at the thought of hot food.

This time, when Benson asked what she would like to eat, she didn't hesitate.

'Cottage pie, please, Sir.'

'Good idea.' He smiled at the landlord. 'Cottage pie twice, please.'

When the landlord left them, Lilian watched her unwanted companion stroll over to a table near the crackling log fire. She was uncertain – should she follow him and sit down, should she stay at the bar, or should she sit at another table? She was still trying to decide when he looked at her questioningly.

'Is this table all right for you?' he asked.

'Yes. Thank you, Sir.' Lilian picked up her as yet untouched drink and walked over to him.

'You can drop the 'Sir' – I'm David,' he said, as she sat next to him. 'And you are?'

'Lilian. Lilian Penrose, Sir.' His eyebrows rose as if he thought he'd been stuck with a complete idiot. 'Er – David,' she mumbled lamely. Well, what did he expect for heaven's sake? It was hardly usual for her to be on first-name terms with someone of his rank.

'So what made you decide to volunteer for the WAAF?'

She guessed he wasn't really interested, but they couldn't sit in silence and his rank said that he must be the one to make conversation.

'Several reasons, Sir – David,' she replied awkwardly. 'I worked in a solicitor's office, which was boring, so I wanted to leave that. And my father's quite strict. I wanted some freedom.'

He didn't approve. All he said was 'I see', but his voice was heavy with a mixture of disapproval and sarcasm.

'And naturally,' Lilian pushed on, wishing the landlord would hurry with their food, 'I wanted to do something useful, something to help the war effort.'

'Naturally,' he murmured, his voice still laden with sarcasm. 'And are you enjoying your taste of freedom?'

The man was infuriating! He'd taken it completely the wrong way.

'Yes. Thank you, Sir.' He could jolly well whistle if he expected her to use his first name. He was the last person on earth she wanted to be friendly with. And another thing, Lilian doubted if he had a better reason for being in the RAF. 'I assume you're here because you enjoy flying planes?' she murmured, giving him a sickly sweet smile.

'I suppose I am,' he replied dryly.

Lilian waited for a host of noble reasons for his joining the RAF, but none were forthcoming. She didn't care because the landlord was walking towards them carrying two plates. Simply seeing the steam rising from them made her mouth water, and the smell was wonderful.

'I'm ready for this,' David said, tucking in hungrily.

Lilian was too, and after the first few delicious mouthfuls, she felt her mood soften slightly. The two of them were chalk and cheese so there was no way they would get along, but he had put in some effort after all, and he was buying her lunch.

'Do you come from Norfolk, Sir?' she ventured politely.

'No, Lilian.' He emphasised her Christian name in his sarcastic fashion. 'I'm from London. What about you?'

'Oh, I'm from Sunderland,' she replied, 'although I have an aunt and uncle who live five miles from the camp.'

'Really? That's handy. Have you seen much of them?'

'Nothing yet,' Lilian admitted. 'A friend and I are hoping to cycle over there one weekend.'

'I see.'

They lapsed into silence once more and Lilian concentrated on her food. Every mouthful was delicious, and she was enjoying her first taste of port and lemon.

She hoped that she and Prue would be able to get bikes for the weekend. It would be fun to introduce Prue to Uncle Jack and Aunt Violet. It was at times like this that Prue missed her car, but after the embarrassment of arriving at the depot in it, the vehicle was safely garaged in the Cotswolds.

'Have you had enough?' David asked.

Lilian's plate was wiped clean. She wondered for a moment if he was mocking her healthy appetite, but she didn't think he was.

'Yes. Thank you very much.' It was easier, she decided, not to call him anything.

'Shall we go then?'

Lilian rose to her feet and, when they'd paid their compliments to the landlord and received his best wishes, they went outside to the Commer.

The journey back to camp was slightly, but only

slightly, less uncomfortable than the journey to Cambridge, but Lilian was relieved when she finally stopped the truck at the officers' mess.

'Thank you for a pleasant day, Lilian,' he said, taking her completely by surprise.

'I – well, thank you, Sir,' she stammered.

She forced the Commer into gear and was about to pull away when the breath caught in her throat. It was him – the man with those beautiful green eyes. Her skin tingled at the sight of him.

He didn't see her; but walked over to David and spoke to him. He looked serious and amused by turns. David simply looked serious. Lilian had no idea what was being said, of course, but David changed direction and the two men walked towards the runway.

Only when they were lost from her view did Lilian drive off to the military transport yard. She wished he had seen her, but then she wondered if he would even have remembered the girl who had given him a lift from the station. Probably not. They had only exchanged half a dozen words. She didn't even know his name.

~~~

David Benson lay in his bed that night and remembered a brilliant summer's day in 1937 at the annual RAF display at Hendon. He had been at RAF flying training school in Lincolnshire at the time and he recalled thinking that the Hawker Furys he saw that day could take on the world at anything. How wrong he had been! In fact, if the war had not been staved off for a year as a result of Prime Minister Chamberlain's

Munich agreement with Hitler, the RAF would never have had the time to re-equip their ailing fighter squadrons with the faster Hurricanes and Spitfires.

The fighter pilots were still the glory boys, David mused. Even more so now the war was for real. Those in Bomber Command like David were considered second-class by comparison.

How carefree he had felt that summer. And how quickly it had all changed. Those long, hot days had been idyllic. The laughter, the fun, the parties, the girls.

One day, a group of them had spent all afternoon by the river – chatting, drinking, laughing. David had been with Eve. He could see her now – petite, blonde, pretty, full of life and always trying to persuade them to take her up in a plane. If he closed his eyes, he could almost feel the tickling sensation as she teased his face with a long blade of grass. He'd been lying on his back, eyes closed, enjoying the sun on his face, and she'd thought he was asleep. He could hear her shriek of laughter as he'd suddenly grabbed her and pulled her into his arms.

His best friend, Tom, had been with Ruth. Jacob had been trying to convince Kate that she had to marry him...

That day by the river would always live on in his memory.

The next day, Tom and Jacob had been on a routine training exercise. Against all regulations – they'd all believed then that rules existed merely to be broken – they had made Eve's dream come true and sneaked her on the plane with them. To this day, David didn't know how they had managed that.

No one knew what went wrong. It should have been a routine flight. But an hour later, Eve, Tom and Jacob were dead.

His friends were gone, and with them, they'd taken David's spirit, his innocence...

From early in 1939, his days had been spent at air drill and as the glorious summer rolled on, it simply became a question of not whether there would be a war, but when it would start. And the closer it came, the more they heard about the staggering numbers of superbly equipped German bomber and fighter squadrons.

Those numbers, and the knowledge that the odds were stacked so highly against them, had been uppermost in his mind that Sunday morning when they had gathered in the mess at eleven-fifteen to hear Prime Minister Chamberlain say: 'This country is at war with Germany...'

The first weeks had been tense. Time had been spent standing-by, not knowing what they were supposed to be doing, and expecting to be bombed at any moment. Everyone was tense but then, when nothing happened, everyone at home seemed to relax. Everyone except David it seemed. He couldn't relax.

He didn't think he would ever relax again. He knew the facts. He still worried about the might of the German air force. He knew, without doubt, that many, many pilots – maybe even himself – would be killed before this war was over.

He linked his hands beneath his head and stared into the darkness. He wondered what had put him in such a thoughtful mood. Perhaps it was spending the day with Lilian Penrose. Just to have female company made a refreshing change. But no, it was more than that. She was happy and carefree, just as he had been in that summer of 1937. She reminded him of the man he'd once been, and the man he had become – lonely, detached. He was slightly envious of Lilian, just as he was a little envious of his companions, but he couldn't be like them. Not now. He'd lost too much. Friends, the ability to be carefree, a part of himself…

∽ *Chapter Five* ∽

JUNE 1940

Lilian pouted at her reflection in the broken piece of mirror. Her skin was dry and there was no make-up to be had anywhere. She needed colour on her lips and her cheeks. It was all right for Prue; she had natural spots of colour in her face. Lilian didn't.

'Present for you,' Prue announced.

Lilian spun round.

'Nylon stockings!' She picked up the beautifully sheer stockings in utter disbelief. 'Where on earth did you get these from?'

'I have friends in high places,' Prue said with a grin. 'Actually, I have a cousin in America and she sent me a parcel this week.'

Lilian had seen the parcel arrive, but Prue always got lots of mail so she'd paid it no attention.

'I wanted to surprise you. Here –' Prue delved in her cupboard and brought out a wealth of treasures. 'None of it is what I'd choose,' she said, 'but beggars can't be choosers.'

Lilian felt like a child at Christmas. There were four pairs of stockings, a tub of rouge, three lipsticks, two hair slides and a small bottle of scent.

'The scent's awful,' Prue said, pulling a face, 'but it's marginally better than diesel.'

Lilian grinned. No matter how hard they scrubbed,

they couldn't seem to rid themselves of the smell of engine oil.

'Oh, but these stockings!' she said happily. 'After these horrid regulation WAAF things – oh, and lipstick. The colours are a bit strange admittedly, but at least it's colour.'

They spent the next half hour trying out lipsticks, scrubbing them off, then settling on the first one they'd tried. When Lilian next looked in the mirror, she felt much better. Her lips and cheeks had colour in them, and she still had a minute amount of make-up for her eyes. When she added the final touch – beautiful, smooth stockings – she felt like royalty.

Prue, generous to a fault, soon had half a dozen girls gathered round borrowing lipsticks.

By the time they set off to catch the bus into the village, Lilian felt wonderful. She loved the dances anyway, but for once she felt almost glamorous. It was amazing what a pair of fashionable stockings could do for a girl.

'Are the seams straight?' she asked Prue as they walked inside the village hall.

'Perfect,' Prue replied. 'You look wonderful, Lil. You always do. That's why all the men are looking at you.'

Lilian looked about them. It was true; a few men were looking at her. She couldn't understand it, not when she was walking next to Prue who was far prettier.

One thing was certain, Lilian was never short of a dancing partner. She loved it. No matter how long and tiring the day had been, she always felt that she could happily dance until dawn.

For all that, after eight consecutive dances, she was pleased to have a break to get a drink. She was about to be served, and was looking round for Prue.

'May I get you a drink, Lilian?'

The voice startled her, but it was a familiar one. She turned her head and gave Pilot Officer David Benson a polite smile.

'Thank you, Sir.'

'David,' he reminded her.

He was served far more quickly than Lilian would have been, and they stood uncomfortably with their drinks. At least, Lilian felt uncomfortable. David Benson was a puzzle to her. On the one hand, he seemed correct to the point of stuffiness and downright disapproving of her. On the other hand, he asked her to use his Christian name – hardly conventional behaviour.

'I imagine you enjoy the dances, Lilian,' he remarked.

'Very much,' she nodded. 'It's wonderful to have fun, and not have to report my every movement to my parents.'

'I'm sure they don't feel the same,' he replied dryly. 'They must worry about you.'

'Well – I don't know. I don't think so. I haven't really thought about it.'

'No. I don't suppose you have.' Smiling, he picked up his glass. 'Excuse me.'

With a growing sense of indignation, Lilian watched him walk away. The cheek of it. He saw her as a flighty, uncaring, waste of time. No matter that she was driving trucks and thus freeing men for the important work. In his eyes, she was just a nuisance. Not that Lilian cared what he thought. He was the stuffiest, dullest person she had ever met. He was more suited to working in the offices of a boring solicitor than he was to flying planes.

The other pilots seemed far more fun. In fact, she was only surprised that he had bothered to come at all. She would bet her life that he didn't actually ask anyone to dance.

Within seconds of his departure, a young man asked Lilian to dance and she gladly accepted. She put David Benson firmly from her mind.

When the music ended, Lilian was about to find Prue when yet another man touched her arm.

'May I?'

Lilian was speechless. All she could do was nod. She had been searching the room all evening, hoping to catch a glimpse of her handsome sergeant, and suddenly he was taking her by the hand and leading her to the centre of the dance floor. She could hardly believe it.

'So, Lilian,' he said, 'how are you enjoying the dance?'

She was enjoying it far more now.

'I – how do you know my name?' Prue could scoff all she liked but his eyes really were beautiful.

'I asked,' he replied, smiling. 'I gather you drove David Benson to Cambridge.'

She nodded, still unable to believe she was with him, touching him.

'I'm Ben,' he introduced himself. 'Sergeant Ben McAllister.' He gave a small bow and she laughed.

'Lilian Penrose. Delighted to meet you.'

They danced and talked and laughed. Lilian had never been happier. Never!

'Where's home, Lilian Penrose?' he asked.

The music ended and they walked over to get a drink.

'Sunderland,' she told him, 'with Mam, Dad, sister, nephew and niece. What about you?'

'Liverpool,' he answered, proving her original theory right. 'And is there a boyfriend in Sunderland?'

'No one.' She shook her head.

She longed to know if there was someone special waiting for him in Liverpool, but she didn't know how to phrase the question without sounding forward.

'I'm glad,' he said softly, making her heart turn over.

She danced with no one but Ben for the rest of the evening, and she felt as if she was floating on air. His devil-may-care attitude made her laugh, and he had a knack of seeing the funny side of everything.

When they'd had the last dance, and the last note had faded away, Ben slipped his arms around her waist and kissed her. His lips were gentle yet insistent on hers. Lilian's arms snaked around his neck as she responded eagerly.

'Can you meet me tomorrow night?' he asked, setting her back from him, but still keeping his arms round her waist.

'Yes.' She didn't even stop to think.

'We could go along to the pub for a drink and a bite to eat.'

'I'd like that, Ben.'

Ben. She loved the sound of his name on her lips.

'If I'm on Ops, I'll let you know somehow,' he said. 'If not, I'll see you about seven. OK?'

'Fine.'

Fine? It was wonderful! She knew she would be counting the seconds.

And then he kissed her again. Lilian had never experienced anything like it. Every nerve ending in her body exploded into life and her heart raced erratically.

She had no recollection of getting to her bed that

night. Her mind was totally filled with Ben. Usually, she was asleep within seconds of her head hitting the pillow, but not tonight. She relived every magical moment of the evening – well, from the moment Ben had appeared at her side. From then on, he hadn't left her for a second. She went over every word he'd said, every gesture, every expression that had flitted across his handsome face.

That he wanted to see her again was unbelievable. He was so handsome, so self-assured, and such good company that he could take his pick of the WAAFs. Why on earth had he singled her out?

The why didn't matter, she told herself. He had seen something in her that attracted him and that was all that mattered.

And the way he had kissed her –

For a moment, her mind flitted back to Roy and the disappointment of her first kiss. She wished Ben had been the first to kiss her.

And tomorrow night, he would kiss her again. Oh, she hoped so…

∽◦∾

The next day, Ben thought about the time he'd spent with Lilian. He liked her. She was very pretty, outspoken and shy by turns – and unless he was very much mistaken, as hungry for him as he was for her. He hadn't liked to push things last night, in case she had scruples about going too far on a first date, but she'd held nothing back when she kissed him.

He'd see how things went that evening and, if she seemed willing – he smiled to himself.

The words leapt off the Notice Board at him:
OPS TONIGHT. BRIEFING IN OPS ROOM 1430
HOURS.

'Yes!'

At last! For the first time, he would be flying for real.
In his excitement, Lilian was forgotten. Or if not
forgotten, pushed to the back of his mind. She'd wait for
him, and if she didn't, there were plenty more pretty
WAAFs around.

After lunch, he took his cup of tea to the ante-room
and joined the others. His first posting to Ops could
have been a lot worse. They were a friendly lot and Skip
was great at letting him take control of the plane.

When he'd finished his tea and smoked a couple of
cigarettes, he went back to his room for a rest. Sleep
was impossible. He was far too excited about that
night's raid to rest, and was at the Flying Operations
Centre just after 1400.

By 1415, the briefing room was already half full.
Chairs had been set out in rows and three blackboards
stood on easels. Pinned on one was a large-scale map,
on another were several recent air photographs of the
target, and the third held sheets giving meteorological
reports, the latest anti-aircraft fire reports and other
items of interest.

He found Terry, the gunner, and Jock, the navigator,
and sat in a vacant seat by them.

Right on the dot of 1430, in walked a Squadron
Leader, Group Captain, a Wing Commander, the Met
Officer, a WAAF Officer and a Senior Intelligence
Officer. Ben watched the Intelligence Officer put his
pile of papers and small target maps on the table.

'Right,' he said, 'it's Bremerhaven tonight. Now, you

haven't been too successful, have you? Nothing's been on target – it's been a shambles. We want results this time – OK? It'll be a dark take-off, so you'll go at three-minute intervals...'

'Bloody idiot,' Ben heard someone mutter behind him. 'He'd get lost going to soddin' Kings Lynn!'

'...failing that, your target will be any self evident military objective, or a military objective previously attacked...'

Ben found there was a lot to take in. The first aircraft off would be carrying incendiaries to raise fires which would hopefully help them to see their bomb targets. Two would be carrying cameras and the rest would be carrying high explosive bombs. Leaflets were to be dropped immediately after bombing.

The Intelligence Officer handed over to the Met Officer, whose opening comments on the sort of weather they could expect was met by peals of derisive laughter.

'We'll be clear when you return – just a light wind.'

Ben shifted restlessly in his chair. He wanted to get on with it.

Finally, the Group Captain addressed them.

'Above all,' he said, 'get back safely.'

Ben was quite touched until he added, 'It costs a lot of time and money to train you – we can't afford to lose experienced men.'

Thanks, Ben thought with an inner grin.

When they'd left, Ben joined the others to look at the photographs and other papers pinned to the boards.

'Ben –' David Benson came over to him '– all ready for your first Ops?'

'Certainly am, Skip!'

'Anything back there you weren't too sure about?'

'I don't think so.' A lot of it had been confusing, but Ben guessed he'd get the hang of it once they were there. He didn't want to appear stupid in front of David Benson.

'Good.' David looked around to see everyone dispersing. 'They'll be serving us early tea around 1600 hours – I expect you'll find everyone in the mess ante-room.'

Ben did find them there, but they were quiet. As soon as tea was over, they all went back to their rooms. With nothing better to do, Ben did the same.

He smoked half a dozen cigarettes, then remembered the Intelligence Officer's instructions to make sure there was nothing on his person which could be useful as a source of information to the enemy.

Finally, it was time to leave. Only then did he remember that he was supposed to have got in touch with Lilian about that evening. Oh, well – too late now.

Ben was putting on his flying gear when he heard the Flight Commander telling them the bus would be outside to take them to their planes at 1900 hours.

It was a dark bus ride and Ben was glad that theirs was the second stop.

He'd started to feel a little apprehensive but as soon as his head and shoulders squeezed through the flight hatch and he saw the array of instruments glowing green in the dark cockpit, his excitement returned. David was already in the pilot's seat and Ben assisted with the checks.

A truck was in front of the aircraft carrying an aldis lamp showing green. They were clear to go.

'Ever done a fully laden take-off, Ben?' David asked

through the intercom.

Ben admitted he hadn't.

'Then watch carefully,' David said. 'You need to get the gear up at 100 feet. She climbs very, very slowly.'

Ben soon realized that the aircraft was much slower to accelerate than she'd been when he'd flown her, and was very reluctant to take off. Three times she was airborne and three times she sank to the ground again. Finally, she managed to just scrape over the boundary fence.

Ben was amazed, but David seemed to consider it normal.

'Altimeter!' David said, and Ben cursed beneath his breath. He'd forgotten to get the gear up.

'Gear's up, Skip,' he said.

They were climbing at just over 100 miles per hour and Ben realized that it was going to be a very long night.

Ben poured himself a coffee from his flask, drank it, then refilled the cup and handed it to David.

'Thanks. I've got my own, but we can share that on the way back.'

'ETA Bremerhaven twenty minutes, Skip,' the navigator announced.

Before David could answer, there was a clatter from the starboard engine. Ben, looking at the tachometer, saw that the revs had dropped very low.

'Now what?' David muttered.

The revs were down, the cause was untraceable, and the engine was still making worrying noises.

'OK – we're turning back,' David said. 'Jock, radio base and tell them we're on our way back.'

The navigator did as instructed.

'All I need is a bombs-on landing,' he muttered.

They flew on with the engine sounding more unhealthy by the minute. If he'd been in control tonight, he would have taken a gamble and kept going. He was disappointed to be turning back without seeing any action.

'Is a bombs-on landing very tricky, Skip?' he asked.

'It's not too bad, although there's a lot of weight so we can't bounce her. The bombs are safe so long as you don't land heavily. If you do that, the extra weight can push the gear up through the wings and with a heavy fuel load, she'd be an inferno.'

They radioed base – emergency landing, bombs-on, Chance light needed.

They lined up on the runway. Ben switched on the navigation lights and the downward identification light so that they could be seen. As soon as David gave the word, he switched on the landing lights. Below them, the Chance light bathed the runway with bright light and David landed the plane smoothly. Ben was surprised at how difficult it was to stop the plane with so much weight on. Headlights from a truck coming towards them were masked but still visible, and they taxied after it.

After the normal shut-down procedure the crew climbed down. They informed the fitter about the engine problems, threw their gear in the truck and drove back to the crew room to take off their flying gear and put away their chutes. Then it was back to the Ops room for debriefing.

Ben was bitterly disappointed and even the special Ops breakfast of double egg and bacon was no consolation. His first Ops and it had been a fiasco. He wished he'd spent the evening with the lovely Lilian instead.

'Oh, well – we've been on Ops so we can have a lie-in,' Jock said cheerfully.

No one answered him. They ate their breakfast and went to their beds. It wasn't even midnight.

∽∾∾

Lilian had been disappointed not to see Ben the previous night. She'd thought he might have found a way to let her know he couldn't make it. But that was silly of her. He wouldn't have had time. He would have had far more important matters on his mind.

Anyway, he was worth the wait.

They caught the bus into the village and walked along to the Black Horse. The pub was packed with servicemen and women, all in high spirits. Lilian loved the atmosphere. She loved the chatter, the noise and the laughter.

Ben looked even more handsome than ever. There was a tiny scar by his left eye that she hadn't noticed before, and now that she'd spotted it, she couldn't stop looking at it. It added to his rakish appearance.

His arm rarely strayed from her waist, giving her a sensation of being cherished. She felt that Ben wanted to tell the world she was his girl. He introduced her to a member of his crew, a young navigator who had them in gales of laughter with his tall stories. At least, Lilian hoped they were tall stories or they would never win this war!

Then, to her dismay, David Benson came in and made straight for them. The atmosphere changed immediately. He was in a fairly light-hearted mood, but all the fun and laughter became a little restrained.

'Still busy enjoying yourself, Miss Penrose?' he asked in what she could only assume was his naturally sarcastic manner.

'Yes, thank you, Sir,' she replied coolly. Confound the man. Why shouldn't she enjoy herself? It wasn't a crime. 'You?'

He simply smiled a patronising sort of smile, nodded, and struck up a conversation with Ben.

Fortunately, he only stayed for half an hour or so.

'He disapproves of me,' Lilian confided, 'in case you didn't notice. He thinks I'm a useless female who should be at home looking after my parents.'

'He's OK,' Ben said, sipping from his glass. 'He takes life a bit seriously, but he's fair and he's a damn good pilot.'

'He is,' Jock agreed. 'He's one of the best.' He took a swallow of beer. 'War's a serious business,' he added, his voice such a perfect imitation of David Benson's that they burst into laughter once more.

Ben bought more drinks and then suggested a game of cards. Before she knew what was happening, Lilian was being taught the rudiments of poker. Her father would have a fit if he knew. They were playing for cigarettes, not money, but it would still be gambling in Dad's eyes. He would be horrified.

'You'd do a lot better, Lil,' Ben pointed out with a grin, 'if you didn't keep flashing your cards around for everyone to see.'

'I do not!' In her indignation, she dropped her cards on the table and they landed face up for anyone to see. 'Oh! Now look what you've made me do!'

Again, they were helpless with laughter.

Lilian knew she would never make a good poker player, but she didn't care. It was great fun, and she was sorry when the evening was over.

She and Ben stepped outside, ready to catch the bus back to camp, into a brilliant moonlit night.

'Oh!' It was perfect. 'Doesn't the blackout make you appreciate the moonlight,' Lilian said softly. 'It's beautiful.'

'So are you, Lilian Penrose.' Ben reached for her hand, entwined his fingers through hers and put their hands in the pocket of his greatcoat. 'You're right, though. It's a lovely night. Perfect for flying.'

'Do you enjoy flying, Ben?'

'Love it!' There was no hesitation and the passion he felt was plain to hear.

'What's it like?'

'Wonderful. There's a sense of freedom that you just can't imagine. To see the rivers and the fields – oh, you'd love it, Lil.'

Lilian suspected she might. She would love to experience it for herself.

'I'm not so sure about flying over the sea,' she said, shivering in the night air.

'There's not much of a view,' he replied.

Lilian hadn't been thinking of the view, or lack of view. She had been thinking of crashing into the sea. But then thinking about it, if a plane crashed, it wouldn't make much difference if it was over land or sea. But she didn't want to think about such things; the night was too perfect. The moonlight was wonderfully romantic, and it made a refreshing change to be able to walk without stumbling along in the darkness.

Her hand was lovely and warm in Ben's pocket. Only her nose was cold. Not that she was complaining. She could have walked with Ben till dawn.

When they reached the camp and the point of parting, Ben pulled her collar up around her neck and, still holding the lapels, kissed her very slowly and very expertly. He drew back, smiled deep into her eyes, and kissed her again until she was breathless.

'Goodnight, Lil. I'll see you around,' he murmured.

Her heart dropped like a weight at his words. 'See you around' sounded very couldn't-care-less.

'If I don't see you tomorrow, I'll catch you on Thursday,' he added.

'OK.' Her heart was soaring once more.

And then he kissed her again...

∽✺∾

Maud looked at the packed suitcases with a feeling of dread. She adored Uncle Jack and Aunt Violet, and it was very generous of them to offer her and the children a home, but deep in her heart she didn't want to go. She didn't want to leave her parents, and all that was familiar. She had delayed it for as long as she could, hoping that some miracle might happen and the war would be over.

The children would love it in Norfolk, she guessed. John was already talking of feeding the animals, and Rose wanted to collect eggs for breakfast. They would love being spoilt by Aunt Violet, and they would be spoilt. Aunt Violet adored children. She hadn't been able to have any of her own and she seemed to make up for it by lavishing her love and time on other people's.

It would be fine, Maud told herself for the hundredth time. The children would be safe and happy, Joe would worry about them less, and there was the added advantage that Lilian was only about five miles away. If that was an advantage, Maud thought with an inner smile. Lilian infuriated her beyond words at times, but she needed some of her sister's cheerful optimism. They all did.

'Is that everything?'

Maud turned at the sound of her mother's voice and smiled bravely. 'I think so. It will have to be – I can't carry any more.'

Dorothy came into the bedroom and sat on the bed beside her daughter.

'How do you feel?'

If anyone else had asked, Maud would have lied and said she was looking forward to the move. However, she knew she couldn't fool her mother.

'I know it's for the best,' she answered slowly. 'You do think so, don't you, Mam?'

'Yes. Yes, I do, pet. The children will love it, and it will be so much better for them.'

'I know.' Maud nodded.

'You'll be fine, love.' Dorothy patted her daughter's arm.

'I know,' Maud said again. 'And it won't be for ever.'

'Of course it won't.'

Both women wished they knew just how long it would be for though.

'And you'll be able to see our Lilian,' Dorothy added. 'Who knows –' she chuckled '– perhaps she'll take you for a drive.'

'Not on your life!' Maud retorted. 'I wouldn't let Lilian

drive me to the end of our street.'

'She can't be that bad,' Dorothy laughed.

'Mmmm.' Maud didn't want to comment on that. Lilian's mind jumped from one thing to another like a yo-yo and Maud couldn't imagine her being able to concentrate on anything for more than five minutes at a stretch. That was all well and good – well, safe at any rate – if Lilian was filing at Singleton's, but not when she was behind the wheel of a truck. Maud shuddered at the thought.

'You can always come home if you don't like it, pet,' Dorothy reminded her gently.

'I suppose so, but I know Joe will feel a lot happier when he knows we're there. No – until this war is over, I'll have to stay there. I hope Uncle Jack and Aunt Violet haven't changed,' she added worriedly. 'I haven't seen them for – what will it be, Mam? – about seven years?'

'Aye, it must be. But don't worry, pet. Violet will never change. She never has and she never will. She's a bit of a worrier, but she has a heart as big as a horse. Jack's never changed, either. He loves his farm, his animals, and Violet. And probably in that order,' she added with a laugh. 'Thinking about it –' her mother was serious now '– Violet and me were always a bit like you and our Lilian. Violet was very much like you, and I suppose I was as daft as your sister. We drove each other mad as kids.'

'I know the feeling,' Maud put in dryly.

'But we loved each other dearly,' Dorothy said softly. 'I missed her terribly – still do.'

Just as she missed Lilian, Maud supposed.

'I'll write and tell you all the gossip,' her mother said, changing the subject.

'Thanks.' A sudden lump wedged itself in Maud's throat. 'And I'll write and tell you about life on the farm. I'll tell you what the bairns are up to, and let you know when I've heard from Joe.'

Her mother nodded.

'I'll drop Joe a few lines now and again,' she said. 'I won't have much to tell him, but I can let him know we're thinking about him. Besides, it must cheer them up to get news from home.'

'Yes, it does.' The lump in Maud's throat changed to a stinging sensation in her eyes. For two pins, she could have thrown her arms round her mother and burst into tears. She hated this damn war. Although she knew she was better off than a lot of people, she couldn't shake off her self-pity. She wanted Joe home, she wanted them to be a real family again, and the very last thing she wanted was to live in Norfolk.

∽∾

∿ *Chapter Six* ∿

AUGUST 1940

David could feel himself frowning as he watched Ben walking towards the plane, slinging his flying helmet round his neck by its intercom leads. Ben was a good pilot, or could be. He seemed keen, a little too keen at times perhaps, but eager to learn. He was a friendly sort too, easy to get along with. The other members of the crew had taken to him immediately. David couldn't really fault him, and yet something about his attitude irritated him. Was he a bit careless?

They didn't yet know if they were on Ops or not that night, the weather was a bit worrying, so more night-flying tests were on the agenda for now.

All they needed was an Irvine jacket, parachute and helmet, and they wore the lot. Flying in a Wellington aircraft, a chap needed all the warmth he could get, and it was never enough.

David decided he'd let Ben fly today. Although Ben had the makings of a good pilot, David had found that they rarely taught pilots how to weave at the operational training units. They quickly learnt, as soon as they came under enemy fire, but in David's view that was too late. Taking violent evasive action was a must, and the trick was to take this action inside the attacking curve of the fighter and force him to steepen his turn in order to try and aim his fire where he expected the bomber to be when the bullets and shells got there.

Ben would be second pilot with David until he'd got some experience under his belt, and then he'd either take David's place when David's tour was over and get a second pilot of his own, or he'd get another crew when the other captain had finished his tour. In David's opinion, Ben still had a lot to learn before he captained his own crew.

For now David forgot Ben and chatted to the ground crew. A corporal and two mechanics were standing by, ready to start the engines. He took the form from the corporal and initialled it, ready to sign on his return, and climbed up the ladder under the plane's nose.

The gunners were already on board, Jock was seated at the navigation table and Ben stood waiting instructions as David moved into the pilot's seat. He remembered his decision to let Ben fly and got out of the seat.

'You may as well do this, Ben.'

'Smashing! Thanks, Skip.' He turned his head slightly to call out to the crew. 'You lot ready for an expert at the controls?'

'Let's take it seriously, shall we?' As soon as the words were out, David regretted them. He'd sounded pompous.

Not in the least bothered by the reprimand, Ben began the cockpit check, made sure the brakes were on and slid back the small window.

'Clear the props,' he shouted to the corporal.

'Props clear,' came the response.

David adjusted the port throttle lever until it was idling smoothly, then they went through the same procedure for the starboard engine.

Ben then checked that the intercom was working.

'Pilot to rear gunner – OK?'

'OK, Ben.'

'Pilot to front gunner – OK?'

'Yes, Ben. OK.'

'Pilot to navigator – OK?'

'Yep – loud and clear.'

'Pilot to wireless operator – OK?'

'OK, Ben.'

'Pilot to –'

David simply nodded to say that his intercom was working fine. Ben was taking him at his word and doing everything by the book.

It was when Ben heard the cool, clear voice of a WAAF from flying control that David's irritation returned. Ben couldn't resist flirting with her.

'Do an operational take-off, Ben,' he snapped.

'Wilco, Skip.'

They usually used the night flying tests as excuses for a little low flying. So long as there was no one around to take the plane's letters, it broke the monotony, and David considered it good training. What with one thing and another, they'd done little real flying lately and needed all the training they could get.

'Take her down to 200 feet,' David said, and Ben grinned appreciatively.

All went smoothly. No incidents, no problems – just a very competent performance from Ben.

When they landed and returned to the crew room, the first thing they saw was a notice telling them they weren't on Ops that night and could stand down. They stowed away their flying gear and parachutes, and David was about to head to the mess for lunch when something stopped him.

'Do I take it that you and Lilian Penrose are courting?' He had to ask.

'You do.' Ben grinned like a schoolboy. 'She's the best-looking WAAF here, wouldn't you say?'

Lilian was eye-catching, there was no denying it. She wasn't beautiful in the accepted sense of the word, but there was something about her that drew attention. As soon as she walked into a room, it was as if no one else existed. Perhaps it was her height that commanded interest, or the way she was always laughing at something or other. Yes, she was certainly eye-catching.

'And is that what you want, Ben? To be seen with the best-looking WAAF?'

'Don't you?' Ben chuckled.

'No.' David thought for a moment about what he would want. 'I'd rather be with someone I could talk to, someone who thought the same way as I did. It wouldn't matter what she looked like.'

Not that David was looking for anyone. Until this war was won – and he hoped to God they could win it – any meaningful relationship was out of the question.

'It wouldn't matter what she looked like?' Ben said incredulously. He laughed suddenly. 'You can have the fat, ugly ones then, Skip.'

David dismissed that.

'Nothing can come of it,' he reminded Ben. 'You – or Lilian for that matter – could be posted to the other side of the country tomorrow. Then what would you do? Find the next best-looking WAAF?'

'Probably.' Ben nodded. 'As you say, Skip, none of us knows what to expect next. We have to live our lives one day at a time.' He lit a cigarette, exhaling the smoke very slowly. 'But I'm more than happy with Lilian for the time being. I'm the envy of the camp.'

David bit back the retort that sprang to his lips. What was the point? Ben was right. A lot of men would give all they had to be in Ben's shoes and have the lovely Lilian dangling from his arm. There was a time when David would have enjoyed having fun with Lilian, or any girl like her.

A sense of isolation swept over him. He felt different, separate from the rest, and it saddened him. How he wished he could be less awkward in his manner. There were times when he sounded so stuffy – but that's the way he was and, whether he liked it or not, he couldn't change…

∽◌∾

Maud hadn't walked alone for years and she should have been enjoying herself. It was a round trip of four miles from Uncle Jack and Aunt Violet's farm into the village, and it was a lovely route.

She'd left John and Rose helping, or hindering, Aunt Violet in the kitchen. Violet was having a mammoth baking session and she was more than happy to let the children join in.

She was a lovely woman, Maud thought fondly. Like her mother in a lot of ways, but more practical and more serious. Uncle Jack was the one who provided all the laughter in the house. He refused to worry about anything, and the children worshipped him.

The farm was warm and cosy, and at times it was difficult to believe there was a war on. How different life was for those in the country. They seemed to have plenty. There were fresh eggs for breakfast, as well as thick rashers of bacon; Aunt Violet made the cheese and butter; the milk couldn't have been fresher.

With so much going on around them, the children were in their element. The night before Maud had made them sit and draw pictures of the farm to put with her letter to Joe, but they didn't seem to have had time to miss him.

Maud supposed she should be grateful. It would be dreadfully upsetting if they didn't settle. She wished she could stop thinking about him, but she couldn't. She missed him more every day. It was difficult knowing what to say in her letters. With the move to the farm, there had been dozens of things to mention, but now she'd told him everything. She wanted to reassure him that they were all well and happy, but found it increasingly difficult to sound happy when life was so pointless. The children were no trouble; they were happy to be with Uncle Jack or Aunt Violet. Aunt Violet neither wanted nor needed help around the farm so there was little for Maud to do.

Or perhaps she was simply feeling sorry for herself. Before their lives had been thrown into total disarray by this awful war, Maud had been proud of the work she'd been doing – keeping Joe and the children well-fed and smart, making their house a real home that was a pleasure to be in. Now, she had no home of her own, Joe was being fed and clothed by the army, and the children were being fed – very well-fed – by Aunt Violet. Maud felt useless.

She was outside the church and, to pass time more than anything else, she stepped inside, letting the heavy oak door close with a deep thud behind her.

It was a plain building, but beautiful nevertheless. Shafts of sunlight streamed through the stained glass windows making rainbow-coloured ladder patterns on the pews and floor.

She had assumed she was alone and was taken by surprise when the vicar rose from the front pew.

'It's a grand day,' he remarked, smiling. 'It's just a pity the warmth doesn't penetrate the building.'

She smiled. It was much colder inside the church than outside.

'It is a nice day, which is why I've come out for a walk. I'm staying with my aunt and uncle – Jack and Violet Appleby. I assume you know them?'

'I certainly do. Very well indeed. So you must be Maud? And you have two children – let me think – John and Rose. Am I right?'

'You are! Gosh, am I the talk of the village?'

'Not at all, my dear. Your aunt was so pleased you were coming to stay, she felt she had to tell everyone. I think – well, I could be wrong, but I had the feeling she felt she was pampered on the farm, as if she was doing nothing for the war effort. Looking after you and the children has given her a purpose. I do hope she isn't fussing too much,' he added knowingly.

'She is,' Maud replied with a smile, 'but I love her dearly for it.'

Maud sat down in the front pew and was pleased when he sat beside her. She was grateful to have someone to talk to and he seemed a kind, understanding type. He must be seventy, she thought, but he stood tall and erect, and his shock of grey, almost white, hair gave him a very distinguished, knowledgeable air.

'Do you have a family?' she asked.

'My wife, Anna,' he replied, smiling fondly, 'who has been meaning to pay you a visit ever since you arrived. You'd better look out. Before you know where you are she'll persuade you to start knitting blankets and goodness knows what else. And we have a son – oh, silly me,' he said suddenly. 'Why don't you come round to the vicarage now? Do you have the time? I know Anna would love to meet you.'

'I'd like that. Thank you – er –'

'William,' he said, offering his hand. 'William Partridge.'

They shook hands and walked out into the sunshine.

The vicarage was only a short walk away, an old square building in need of a coat of paint, Maud couldn't help noticing.

Anna was younger, and about a foot shorter than William, but just as friendly. Her welcome was very warm.

'I've been meaning to call at the farm,' Anna told Maud, 'but my sister's been ill and I've been in Cambridge with her. Sit yourself down, lass – the kettle's on the boil. So you're Maud. You don't have the children with you?'

'Er – no.' She was a delightful woman, but it was difficult to keep up with her. 'They're helping Aunt Violet in the kitchen.'

'I'm glad.' Like a bird, Anna darted from one side of the kitchen to the other for cups and saucers. 'She'll be glad to feel she's helping out in some way.'

When the tea was on the table in front of them, Anna said worriedly, 'I hope William hasn't been pestering you. He does tend to press gang his flock.'

'Oh, no. Not at all,' Maud said quickly. 'I wandered into the church for a look round and your husband – William – knew who I was and kindly invited me here to meet you.'

Anna and William were good company and they chatted about all sorts of things. Maud discovered they had a son, Alfred, who was an army chaplain.

'He's not fighting, like your husband,' Anna said, a worried frown marring her features, 'but, of course, he has to go where the men need him most. It's a worry.'

Maud understood perfectly.

'If you want company,' Anna said, 'you're welcome here any time. Also, I've organised a knitting circle. We meet on Tuesday and Thursday evenings. It gives us women a chance to chat while we knit. We knit blankets, socks, anything we can that will help. With their menfolk away, a lot of women are struggling to clothe their children.'

Maud couldn't help wondering, however, if that was as good as it got – knitting socks? She could just imagine what reaction folk would get from Lilian if they suggested she filled her time doing that! Still, at least she would be doing something useful instead of just sitting around.

Maud hadn't told anyone, not even her mother, about the strange feelings she'd had at the station the day she waved Joe off. She hadn't intended to tell William and Anna but suddenly the words were tumbling from her lips.

'I was convinced, just for a second, that I'd never see him again,' she tried to explain. 'Does that make any sense?'

'A lot of sense,' William said thoughtfully. 'Saying goodbye to a loved one in such circumstances is very traumatic. I think the mind automatically thinks "what if?". It's bound to make you panic.'

'It's dreadful,' Anna agreed. 'It really is. It tears me in two having to say goodbye to Alfred and not knowing when I'll see him again.'

'I suppose that's it,' Maud said softly. 'As I said, the feeling only lasted a second. It was so clear though. For that split second, I was quite convinced I'd never see him again.'

'Pay it no heed,' William said. 'None of us can see the future. That's in God's hands, not ours.'

'Try to put it from your mind, lass,' Anna suggested. 'It's hard, I know, but don't go thinking you've had a glimpse of the future. None of us have that.'

'I know.' Maud smiled, feeling much better for having talked about it. 'I was just being fanciful. It was probably a mixture of fear and exhaustion. I didn't sleep well when he was home. It seemed a shame to squander my time with him. Oh, and it was bliss just to lie awake and watch him sleep.'

Anna and William laughed, but they understood only too well. Everyone understood, Maud realized. Everyone had someone to worry about, someone to miss, and someone to pray for.

∽◦∾

The sun was beating down on their backs as Lilian and Prue pedalled towards Uncle Jack and Aunt Violet's farm. Fortunately, the land was flat and the going was easy.

It was the first time Lilian had been to the farm since her posting; life had been too hectic and the summer was flying by. She couldn't wait to see them all, especially Maud and the children. It surprised her just how excited she was at the prospect of seeing the sister she hadn't been able to get away from quickly enough.

'Are you sure this is a short cut?' Prue asked doubtfully.

'Yes. I remember it well.' It did look different, Lilian thought, and it had been several years since she'd been in this part of the world.

The heat didn't bother Lilian and she had so much energy, she could have cycled for miles. Just like the blue sky above them, there wasn't a cloud in her life. This evening, with luck, she would be dancing in Ben's arms again.

'How do you know if you're in love?' she asked Prue.

'Bells ring, doves sing – you just know, idiot!'

'Are you in love with Charlie?'

Prue was silent for a long time.

'I love him,' she answered at last, 'but I don't think I'm in love with him.'

'There's a difference?' Sometimes Prue could be exasperating.

'Of course. You can love a person because they're good, kind, thoughtful and things like that. And you can be in love with someone who is a real cad. He can be thoughtless and deceitful, and yet you can still fall in love with him just because he's handsome and fun.'

Lilian, too confused to argue, decided to drop the subject. It was far too beautiful a day for one of Prue's philosophical discussions.

Ben was handsome and fun, but he was also kind and thoughtful. So did Lilian love him, or was she in love with him? And was there really any difference between the two?

She didn't care. All she knew was that she longed to feel his arms around her and to taste his lips on hers again. And, more than anything, she longed to hear him say 'I love you'.

'Here it is – we turn left here, and I reckon the farm is about a mile down this road,' Lilian said confidently.

'Thank goodness,' Prue replied. 'I can't wait for this promised glass of lemonade.'

'Don't get too excited,' Lilian warned her. 'Aunt Violet might not make it these days. Perhaps she just made it for us when we were kids.'

Lilian could still remember the taste of her aunt's lemonade. It always reminded her of long, hot, happy days on the farm. Funny, but she couldn't remember it ever raining at Home Farm –

Four airmen drove past in a Hillman, calling out and whistling at them. Both Lilian and Prue managed to maintain their balance, and their dignity, until the car was out of sight, when they both disintegrated into helpless laughter and had to get off their bikes before they ended up in the hedge.

'Now that chap in the back,' Prue said, 'the one with the dark hair and moustache, I could fall in love with him. He could be the biggest rogue on the planet, but any girl could fall in love with him.'

Lilian hadn't even spotted the man Prue was talking about. All she had seen were four men dressed in RAF uniform. She'd been too embarrassed by the shouts and whistles, and too busy trying to keep her balance to pay more attention.

Was Prue implying that Ben, who was handsome and good fun, was the type a girl could fall in love with, but not the type she could love? Oh – it was just too complicated for Lilian.

'There –' She stopped so suddenly that Prue had to swerve to avoid her. 'Sorry, but that's it. That's the farm.'

It was about half a mile away, a small square redbrick building with the sun catching the windows, and ivy clambering over the west gable. Scattered untidily around it were various outbuildings. Cows grazed in the fields.

'It looks lovely,' Prue said. 'I can almost taste the lemonade.'

Lilian laughed.

'Are you sure they won't mind me tagging along?' Prue added.

'Quite sure. They'll be thrilled to meet you.'

Lilian was confident of that. Aunt Violet, she knew, would welcome the whole camp if Lilian decided to invite it.

As they pedalled along, Lilian couldn't take her eyes off the farmhouse. Those childhood holidays suddenly seemed a lifetime ago. She could remember strolling through the fields and wondering what life had in store for her. Never would she have guessed that the country would be at war, that she would be stationed nearby wearing the uniform of the WAAF and in love with a handsome young pilot from Liverpool.

Two small figures suddenly emerged from the door and Lilian pedalled as fast as she could towards them with tears of emotion pricking at her eyes.

'John and Rose,' she called to Prue who was trying to catch up with her.

When she was close to them, Lilian jumped off her bike, threw it to the ground for Prue to avoid, and ran the last couple of yards to gather the children in her arms. She almost squeezed the breath from their bodies.

'Just look at you!' She ruffled their dark curls. 'You're positively glowing with health. And I swear you've grown again.'

They laughed happily and planted wet kisses on her face. Rose was a little shy when Lilian introduced them to Prue, but then Uncle Jack, Aunt Violet and Maud joined in and, during the pandemonium that followed, Rose came out of her shell. Soon she was shouting to make herself heard.

'You look well, Maud,' Lilian told her sister later. 'Better than the last time I saw you.'

'I'm fine,' Maud replied. 'I like it here on the farm, and I've made friends with people from the village. And, of course, the kids are thriving.' She looked at Lilian and smiled. 'You look the same as ever, Lil. Still sailing through life without a worry in the world.'

'There's no point worrying,' Lilian replied with a shrug. 'Since when did that help anything?'

Maud rolled her eyes. 'How do you put up with her, Prue?'

'I ask myself that question fifty times a day, Maud.'

Lilian thumped her and, laughing, they continued their tour of the farm.

'What's Joe doing?' Lilian asked. 'I haven't had a letter from him for ages.'

'He's still in Palestine.'

Lilian decided not to push it. Maud was clearly worried about him. But that was Maud – never happy unless she had something to worry about.

She wanted to tell her sister about Ben, but it was such a perfect day and the two of them were getting along so well that she didn't want to spoil things. Why telling her sister about Ben should spoil things, she didn't know. She simply felt that it would. Maud was sure to find something to disapprove of. Just as David Benson did. Thinking about it, Maud and David Benson would make an ideal couple. The idea had her stifling a giggle.

Today, though, Maud was a perfect companion and the two sisters chatted on to Prue about their antics on the farm as children. Every sentence started with 'Do you remember…' and it was as if they had always been the best of friends. They hadn't of course; in fact they had fought like tigers at times, but on this stunning summer's day it was difficult to remember why. Perhaps, Lilian thought, it had been because of the six-year gap in their ages. That gap seemed nothing now, but it had been a lot when they were children.

When the three of them went back inside, Aunt Violet, the dear woman, gave them hot scones filled with thick strawberry jam and, to Prue's delight, tall glasses of tangy lemonade. Those in the country were so lucky. It seemed as if there were no shortages, nothing they couldn't grow or make. Lilian and Prue polished off the scones as if they hadn't eaten for days.

'We'll come again,' Lilian promised when it was time to leave, 'just as soon as we can escape for the day.'

Aunt Violet loaded them up with food – 'a few treats' – the children gave them more wet kisses, and they set off for the camp. Lilian was quiet as they cycled. She was happy, relaxed and tired. It had been a perfect day. And she still had the dance that evening to look forward to.

They were almost at the camp when they both stopped. Plane after plane was roaring down the runway and taking off.

'So much for tonight,' Prue said. 'There'll be no men left.'

Lilian's spirits sank to her feet. She had so been looking forward to the dance...

∽◌∾

David heard the planes taking off, too. From his sick bed, it took a few moments to realize what the deep rumbling sound was, and then he simply rolled onto his side and closed his eyes again. He was dog tired and couldn't stop shivering.

'Flu,' the medical officer had told him.

'It doesn't feel like flu,' David had retorted.

Flu didn't make you pass out, did it? He'd been feeling as right as rain one minute, and the next he'd collapsed in the mess. Every bone in his body ached; even his teeth ached. One minute he was shivering, the next he was sweating. And who the devil caught flu in August?

'It's flu,' the medical officer said confidently. 'Fortunately it's only a mild strain – it's knocking you bods out for 48 hours and then you're fighting fit again. Enjoy the rest.'

It was impossible to enjoy the rest. He either felt too ill to move, or he felt as if he was perfectly capable of flying. He would far rather be where he belonged, in his plane with his crew. The ambition of every crew member, and David was no exception, was to complete his tour of 30 Ops. Then they would send him to an operational training unit. He wouldn't complete his tour by lying in this confounded bed...

The next day, he felt much better. The medical officer was right; it was nasty while it lasted but, thankfully, it didn't seem to last long.

'We'll have you back on the job tomorrow,' the medical officer promised him.

So David spent another night in sick bay, listening to the roar of planes taking off. That was two Ops he'd missed now...

He felt a bit groggy the following morning, but he kept quiet about it. Another day in bed would send him mad. He was sure he'd feel better once he got back into his routine. David was on his way to the mess room when he heard a voice that stopped him in his tracks.

'Rotten bloody shame about Jock – he was only three away from finishing his tour too...'

Jock?

'What's that?' David asked.

The lad spun round and saluted. He was clearly embarrassed.

'Sorry, Sir, didn't realize you were there.' He looked to his pal, but there was no help there. 'Your plane didn't make it back last night. Haven't you been told?'

David shook his head. He couldn't take it in, and was shivering again. His plane gone? His crew?

'Sorry, Sir,' the lad said again.

'All gone?' David said, dazed.

'Yes – shot down, I'm afraid, Sir. George Farnborough

had taken your place as captain, and Jim Kelly took the second dickey's seat.'

'Second –?'

'Ben McAllister is in sick bay, Sir. He's gone down with this flu bug. Lucky for him he has, Sir.'

'Yes – thank you.'

David strode away from them, convinced he was going to be sick. Ben was safe, thank God, but the rest of them – gone.

They'd been through so much together and now they were gone. David could hear their voices – the banter, the laughter, the leg-pulling.

A depression settled around him and he couldn't shake it off. There seemed no sense to anything. He couldn't believe he'd never hear the voices of his crew again.

He felt he ought to go and see Ben, but he couldn't face it. In any case, someone else was sure to have told him the news, and they would make a far better job of it than David could. There was nothing he could say to make the loss any more palatable.

He spent the rest of the day wandering aimlessly around the camp. He had no plane, no crew, no purpose – nothing.

He didn't sleep that night. He hadn't just lost his crew, he'd lost his very good friends. They had flown together, faced the enemy together, faced possible death together – it hurt that he hadn't been with them. God, he hoped it had been quick and painless…

The next morning he had instructions to see the Flight Commander.

'Good morning, Pilot Officer,' the Flight Commander welcomed him with a broad smile. 'I trust you're feeling fully recovered.'

David nodded, not sure how he was feeling. Depressed, furious, sad, shocked –

'Bad luck losing your crew like that,' the Flight Commander went on briskly, 'but that's war. Now, we're transferring you to –'

That's war? That was all he had to say on the matter? Those men had lost their lives and all he could say was "that's war"?

David could feel his heart pounding with fury as the Flight Commander told him he was to take command of another crew.

'Their captain's just completed his tour. Their second pilot's in hospital – broken legs – so McAllister can take his place.'

David took some comfort from the knowledge that Ben would be flying with him, but the prospect of taking on a new crew was daunting. It only needed one misfit and the crew couldn't become a cohesive unit. His own crew had got along so well, too.

He wondered if the top brass had any idea of what it was like to be part of a crew. Probably not. It was expected that an NCO would salute an officer in his crew the first time he saw him, then, for the rest of the day, rank would be ignored. Even that was often ignored though – unless, of course, there was a senior officer around. Most crews were on first-name terms while flying, and most went to the pub and drank together, regardless of rank. A good crew couldn't be replaced.

He should have gone along and introduced himself to his new crew, he supposed, but he couldn't face that either. He walked out of the Flight Commander's office and, once in the fresh air, took out his temper on the wall. He kicked it hard...

He saw Lilian Penrose walking towards him. She was easy to spot, always in a hurry. It was as if life moved too slowly for her.

'Sorry to hear you haven't been well, Sir.'

'Thank you, Lilian. I'm fine now.'

She looked around them, and he got the impression that she was uncomfortable in his presence. He didn't feel particularly at ease in hers, either. He was surprised, and very touched, that she'd taken the time to ask after him, but he couldn't find a way of showing his appreciation.

'You heard our plane didn't get back, I assume?' he said.

Her expression was blank. She gazed back at him, and David knew she hadn't heard.

'The men were all killed, I'm afraid – the plane was shot down,' he explained.

Still she looked blank.

'But Ben's OK,' he added quickly, just in case she hadn't heard he was another victim of the flu bug. 'He's in the sick bay – flu.'

She nodded, stared at him for a while longer and, without another word, carried on her way.

David watched her go. He couldn't decide if she was selfish and uncaring – so long as Ben was OK it didn't matter that men had lost their lives – or if the horrors of life simply didn't register with her. It was almost as if she thought the war was being staged purely for her entertainment, as if no one had told her that men were being slaughtered.

She was a mystery to him. He couldn't make her out

at all. Dismissing her from his mind, he carried on walking towards the mess.

❧

Lilian had never felt so foolish in her life. David Benson must think her a complete idiot, a heartless one at that, but she had been so shocked to hear the crew had been lost, and to know that Ben and David could so easily have been killed with them, that she hadn't been able to offer sympathy or make any of the usual noises. Words seemed so pointless and empty.

The news shook her. It would hit her out of the blue and her eyes would fill with tears. Young men with their lives ahead of them – wiped out in a split second.

She and Prue caught the bus to the village and went to the pub that night. Inside, everyone was in high spirits, as if it was just another day. Lilian supposed it was. They all had to carry on with their lives.

She was hoping Ben would come along to the pub and join them. She'd heard he had left the sick bay, and she felt restless. She'd feel much better when she saw him. It had struck her lately just how unsure she was of his feelings for her. It was a horrid thought but she knew that as soon as she was with him, she would know he loved her just as much as she loved him.

The door opened and David Benson walked into the bar. Lilian was bitterly disappointed that Ben wasn't with him.

David was coming towards them. Lilian went to nudge Prue, but Prue was deep in conversation with a man she didn't recognise.

'Can I get you a drink, Lilian?' David asked.

Lilian knew his opinion of her must be at rock bottom, and she guessed he was only being polite. She looked at her empty glass with something approaching despair. She couldn't really refuse.

'Thank you, Sir.'

'David,' he reminded her, somewhat testily.

'Er, yes.' God, he made her nervous. And he was so – public school. However, she felt she should at least try and get on the right side of him if for no other reason than he'd just bought her a drink. Added to which, their paths kept colliding and it would make a refreshing change to meet without this tension between them. 'I – er – I was so sorry to hear about your crew. I was very fond of Jock,' she said, knowing the words were painfully inadequate. 'He plays –' she swallowed hard '– used to play shove halfpenny with Ben and me. His girlfriend, Pat, is very – well, I suppose you can imagine.' And now she was rambling.

'All too well, I'm afraid,' he said quietly.

He was about to say more but before he had a chance, a gang of four airmen Lilian didn't know came in and soon they had drinks lined up for him behind the bar. She could have crept away and joined Prue but was too fascinated to move. She gathered that this was David's new crew, and they considered him a lucky captain. They were delighted to have him take command.

Lilian sensed that he was uncomfortable with them. She'd always known he was different from the others, but for the first time, she gained the impression that he was aware of it too. For a moment, he seemed lonely. And isolated. He was clearly embarrassed by their praise.

The group left and David drank his beer while shifting

his weight awkwardly from one leg to the other.

'Perhaps you are a good luck charm,' Lilian said, uncertain as to what was expected of her.

He gave her one of his long, calculating looks before saying in a voice that was very quiet, 'I very much doubt it.'

'You were certainly lucky to catch the flu when you did.' He couldn't argue with that. 'Let's hope you manage to shoot down a few German planes and get your own back.'

A dark eyebrow rose at that.

'I doubt you'd say that if your father or brother was flying one of those planes.'

'Well – I – no,' she replied. 'But I said a German plane.'

'And German wives, mothers and sisters don't grieve as British ones do?'

'Of course they do.' Confound the blasted man! 'But it is what you fly for. The object of the exercise is to beat the Germans.' She, too, could be sarcastic when she wanted to.

'Indeed,' he agreed flatly. 'If we don't bomb their factories and homes, they'll bomb ours. If we don't shoot down their planes, they'll shoot down ours. You're right, Lilian. This time, I was lucky.' He took a large swallow of his beer. 'I still wish to God I'd been with my crew, though.'

His words shocked her so deeply that Lilian couldn't respond. There was a bleakness in his eyes that she could never hope to penetrate. Try as she might, she couldn't imagine how he must feel.

The door opened and Lilian felt her heart soar. The next minute, she was wrapped tightly in Ben's arms and it was as if she'd never been out of them.

'Have you missed me, Lilian Penrose?' he asked, kissing her forehead.

'Yes.' He would never know quite how much.

'Good!'

He ordered drinks and the fun and laughter began.

Only David, Lilian noticed, remained apart. He was with them, but he might have been a million miles away.

Looking back at him, she experienced an unexpected rush of sympathy. He looked unhappy. Given the deaths of his crew that wasn't surprising, but she thought she saw something else as well. There was a wistfulness in his expression, as if he wanted to join them, to be part of the crowd, yet couldn't...

∽∾∽

✦ *Chapter Seven* ✦

SEPTEMBER 1940

Dorothy Penrose opened the letter from her friend Jane and was immediately transported back to her time in London. She didn't miss those days, she was more than content with her life now, but they had been very happy. She and Jane had been young and ambitious, without a real care in the world. They'd too much time on their hands, she decided ruefully, rushing from rally to demonstration to rally, all in the cause of the suffragette movement.

Thinking about it now, her friendship with Jane must have been very like Lilian's friendship with Prue. Like Prue, Jane was very well-to-do. And like Prue, Jane had no airs and graces.

Dorothy and Jane had been equally passionate about the suffragette movement and had thought the same way about most things. All these years later, they still kept in touch.

Jane had showered Maud and Lilian with gifts when they were growing up, and now she did the same for John and Rose.

She'd never married, despite several love-affairs. She was a free spirit.

The air-raid warnings are a total bore, Jane wrote. We have so many that people are beginning to disregard them. I was strolling through Regent's Park yesterday when the warning sounded and at least half the people ignored it. Sometimes I forget whether the alarm is on or whether the All Clear has sounded. Honestly, Dorothy, it's too ridiculous for words. The alarm sounds over a wide area, when the German planes are only operating in a tiny part of it, so people are dragged from their sleep or their work for no reason. It will be a cry-wolf thing, I fear, because the impression is that all air-raid alarms are false. This could be terribly dangerous.

It's such a waste of time, I can't tell you. My social life is non-existent. Any promising evening always seems to end up in some awful shelter. And they are truly awful. I decided long ago that if I had to die, I would rather die in the open air than suffocate slowly with a lot of strangers.

The letter, so typical of Jane, said nothing of what concerned Dorothy most, except for a brief paragraph towards the end.

I can't, in all honesty, say my cough is any better, Jane wrote. If anything, it's worse. It makes me feel tired all the time. The doctors don't seem to know what they're doing...

Dorothy read that paragraph over and over. Jane's cough had been troubling her for some time, but she rarely mentioned it.

Dorothy sat back in her chair and faced the facts. She'd known, deep in her heart, for some time that Jane was seriously ill. It was no ordinary cough, they both knew that.

She wondered how Clive would feel about her spending three or four days in London. She didn't need to wonder though; she knew he would forbid it. Yet if she prepared plenty of food and made sure his clothes were ready, he would cope, and Ida, their next-door neighbour, would be sure to invite him round there for his evening meal, but even so, he wouldn't like it.

But was there any real need to go to London? Yes, she decided, there was. Jane was ill, she had been ill for some time. For all Dorothy knew, it might be the last time she would see her friend. She had to go...

'I had a letter from Jane today,' she told Clive as soon as they had eaten that evening.

'Oh? What did she have to say for herself?'

She took the letter from the table and handed it to him.

'Here – see for yourself.'

He was smiling as he read it, until he reached the part about Jane's cough.

'It's probably nothing,' he said, guessing at her thoughts. 'We all get coughs.'

'It's serious, Clive. I know it is. I've known for some time, you know I have.'

Jane was too independent to look for sympathy. With Jane, you had to read between the lines.

'I'd like to go to London,' she said urgently. 'I have to see her, Clive. I'd never forgive myself if –'

'Go to London? Oh, no! You can't just take off for London when the mood takes you. And where's the money coming from?'

'I'll find the money.' The last thing Dorothy cared about was the money. She'd go into debt if necessary. The more she thought about it, the more she knew she had to see Jane. And the more she thought about it, the more she knew it could be the last time she would see her.

'It's out of the question, Dorothy.'

'But, Clive – you don't understand –'

'I understand,' he said grimly, 'that you've got some idea in your head that she's very ill. If she was, she'd have told you. For heaven's sake, you're her best friend.'

'And that's exactly why she wouldn't tell me,' Dorothy said softly.

Clive looked at her, and she could see him slowly, reluctantly, accepting the truth behind those words.

'It will only be four days at the most,' she said, pleading now. 'And if I sort everything out before I go, you'll cope.'

'It's not a question of me coping,' he retorted. 'God knows, Dorothy, I know what you're like – you think nothing of setting off for London. But you're no longer eighteen years old. There's a war on, money's tight – and, well, damn it, Dorothy, it's dangerous!'

'I have to go, Clive,' she said simply. 'I know it sounds rash and irresponsible, but I have to go.'

He was silent.

'I think,' she said softly, 'that it may be the last time I'll see her.'

'Then you must go. But don't,' he added harshly, 'think that you're going with my blessing because you're not! Things are getting serious. Can't you see that? The Germans attacked London, so the RAF bombed Berlin – it's not safe anywhere!'

The tension in the room was unbearable as Dorothy cleared away the plates. There was nothing she could say. She didn't want to go against his wishes, but she knew she wouldn't live with herself if she didn't see Jane.

'I've often wondered,' Clive said later, his mood

slightly better now that he'd resigned himself to the fact that she was going, 'if you miss that life – all the friends you had in London.'

'No! You know I don't miss it. I love my life here, you know that. You and the children mean everything to me. Everything. Yes, I enjoyed my time in London but I was just a child – our Lilian's age.'

'I know, pet. I know.' He gazed at her for a long time. 'I'd hate to think you'd given up all the fun in your life just to marry me.'

'Clive!' She rose to her feet and went to stand behind him, her arms linked loosely around his neck. 'I gave up my fun, as you call it, because I felt it was time to go home. Yes, I had fun in London, but I was glad to get home and back to a normal life. When I met you, I knew very quickly that I wanted to spend the rest of my life with you. I have no regrets. Far from it. I love you so much, Clive.'

She felt some of the tension leave his body.

'Aye, I know, pet. I love you too, Dorothy. So very much.'

'I'm not going to London because I want to go,' she tried to explain. 'I'm going because I have to. I have to see Jane...'

⤷⤶

Early on the afternoon of 7 September, Dorothy was in Kensington catching up on the news with Jane. No sooner had she arrived, it seemed, than London's air-raid sirens went off and they had to make their way to the shelter. Dorothy looked at her friend. Jane, always so elegant and poised, seemed small and frail. Her skin had an unhealthy grey tinge to it. And that cough –

'This sounds serious,' Jane said. 'Hark at all those planes – however many can there be?'

'We'll be safe enough here,' Dorothy murmured.

'Let's hope so,' Jane replied. 'Hitler warned us that a decisive blow was about to fall. Do you think this could be it?'

Dorothy didn't know what to think. It sounded as if there were hundreds of planes overhead. In broad daylight, too!

At least the shelter was fairly comfortable, crammed as it was with rugs and cushions. There were a few chairs but a bed would have been impossible. So would sleep, Dorothy thought, because the noise would surely prevent that.

The All Clear sounded at six that evening but, two hours later, the night raiders arrived to inflict yet more damage on the city. It went on and on, hour after hour. London had been bombed in August, so had many other towns and cities, but the country hadn't known anything on this scale. The noise was terrifying – the bombs, the planes, the guns, the wail of sirens.

Dorothy was trembling. She dreaded to think what Clive would have to say about it. Had he been right after all? Should she have stayed in Sunderland?

From the moment war had been declared, people had lived in fear of something like this happening. Very little had happened though, and everyone had started to relax. After tonight, it would be a long time before they relaxed again...

The sound of the guns was strangely comforting, but oh, those bombs. Dorothy felt relatively safe in the shelter, half-buried in the ground, but she wished she could stop shaking. The night went on. The bombs seemed to drop constantly and a couple were very near – far too near for comfort.

'Portobello perhaps,' Jane said quietly, looking visibly shaken, 'or perhaps Chepstow Villas. Oh, I don't know – it could be anywhere. Is the All Clear never going to sound?'

'I hope so,' Dorothy prayed. It was already four in the morning.

'God, I'm so tired,' Jane murmured.

Dorothy, too, was exhausted, although sleep was out of the question. However, she knew that Jane's fatigue had little to do with the bombs going off all around them.

It was a huge relief to hear the steady two-minute blast on the siren which signified the All Clear. They crawled out of the shelter, totally dishevelled and dizzy with exhaustion. But at least they were alive.

'If the city can survive that,' Jane said grimly, 'it can survive anything.'

Only later, when they had grabbed a couple of hours sleep, and when Jane's friend Ivan paid them a visit, did they realize that parts of the city hadn't survived at all.

'The damage around the East End is dreadful,' Ivan told them. 'There are fires everywhere. Thousands of homes along the Thames have been destroyed. You can't believe all you hear, I know, but they reckon almost four hundred German bombers came up the Thames. The fires are still blazing. The worst of it was that the daylight bombers meant they had to bring out fire appliances from every part of London. Then came the night raiders. A lot of men were lost as they tried to put out the fires apparently.'

'It's too awful,' Dorothy said, hardly able to believe that highly civilised people could inflict such damage. And what of Sunderland? Had Sunderland been bombed? Could they expect Sunderland to take a hammering like last night's?

'It is,' Ivan agreed. 'You know how these stories spread, but I heard that more than four hundred folk were killed last night and more than one and a half thousand people seriously injured.' He shook his head. 'You just can't take it in, can you?'

Ivan was a likeable man, and his feelings for Jane were plain to see. Whether he had ever been more than a friend, Dorothy didn't know, but she could see that every time Jane coughed – a hoarse, painful cough that left her breathless for a long time afterwards – it tore his heart in two. Just as it did Dorothy's...

The following nights were just as bad. The Germans came every night, trying to bomb the life out of the city.

When it was time for Dorothy to leave London, she had mixed feelings. Part of her was desperate to get back to the relative safety of Sunderland, but part of her couldn't bear to leave Jane.

'Come with me,' she urged her friend. 'Come and stay with us until the Germans have done their worst on London. If it keeps on like this, there will be nothing left of this city.'

'No one,' Jane said indignantly, 'especially a power-crazed German, is going to force me out of my home. Don't worry, Dorothy, I'll be fine. Thank you, but I really couldn't leave – not now. Do you understand?'

'Yes, I understand.'

'Don't worry, Dorothy.' Jane gave her a weak smile. 'We survived the last war – we'll survive this one.'

But would they? The war, it seemed, had begun in real earnest, and it promised to be every bit as bad, if not worse, than everyone had feared at the outset. It wasn't only the conflict Jane had to survive though...

'We've had some fun in our time, haven't we?' Jane said softly.

'We have.' Dorothy couldn't say more; she was too choked with emotion.

'And when this war is over,' Jane added, 'we'll have some more.'

Dorothy smiled, and nodded, just as Jane wanted – needed – her to, but they both knew the truth. Jane had her own battle to fight, a battle she had no hope of winning...

∽∾∾

It was good to have an afternoon with Maud. Lilian had been busy lately, they all had, and it made a change to relax and catch up on the news with her sister.

They had agreed to meet in the village at the tea rooms and it was crowded with servicemen and women.

'Good grief,' Maud said with a sigh, picking up a teaspoon that had been tied down. 'Are folk so desperate they're stealing teaspoons now?'

'It wouldn't surprise me.'

Over tea and sandwiches, they talked about the news from home. Neither could quite take in the fact that their own mother had almost been blown up while visiting her friend in London. Maud was fairly matter-of-fact, Lilian thought, whereas she took it personally. She was filled with angry indignation. How dare they try and bomb London, especially when her mother was there?

Trust her to visit London, to arrive on the very day the Phoney War had ended and London took its first heavy bombing.

Their mother hadn't said much about it in her letter, but Lilian guessed she would have been frightened out of her wits to hear bombs dropping all around her. Everyone had been saying from the start how Sunderland was a prime target, and Lilian only hoped that Hitler wasn't building up to give it the same battering that London was getting. The Germans' attack on the capital was relentless – night after night they bombed the city.

Thinking about it, however, their mother had said very little about anything in her letter. She certainly hadn't given any reason as to why she'd suddenly taken off to London to see Jane. Lilian was surprised their father had allowed it...

'So how are things on the camp?' Maud asked, changing the subject.

'Fine.' Lilian thought about it. 'But we are losing a lot of planes.' She always said that – they were losing planes. She couldn't bear to think about the men they were losing. 'It's become a habit now. We count the planes as they leave and we count them when they return. I can't describe the sense of relief when they all return safely.'

Sitting in the cosy tea rooms, with the immaculate white cloths on the tables, and a small flower arrangement in the centre, it was impossible to describe the way she almost willed those planes home.

'You OK, Lil?' Maud broke into her thoughts. 'You seem quiet.'

'Fine,' Lilian replied quickly. 'Tired. They have us working very hard, you know.'

'Quite right too.' Maud laughed.

They tucked into their sandwiches, lost in their own thoughts.

'I've heard nothing from Joe for ages,' Maud said, breaking the silence. 'I suppose it's just that his letters aren't getting through.'

'Yes, I'm sure that will be it.' Lilian hoped that was the reason. 'Roy Walker has joined up,' she added, remembering the news from her mother's letter. 'Well, he had no choice now he's the right age. I gather he wasn't too happy about it though.'

'I bet he wasn't. Mind you, it's the best place for him,' Maud retorted. 'Idle so-and-so that he is.'

Lilian thought back to the night of Grace's party, and how surprised she had been to realize that Roy wasn't rushing off to enlist. She supposed Maud was right; he was idle. He wanted the war won, they all did, but it seemed he didn't want to play any part in it himself. Selfishly, he wanted everyone else to win it for him. It was depressing to realize she had been taken in by his good looks alone. She had thought herself in love with him, and had longed for his kiss, and yet she hadn't really known him at all.

'And you're better away from him,' Maud added sharply. 'Don't think I don't know what was going on there.'

'Nothing was going on!' Lilian retorted.

'That's not what he says. He was boasting to me about kissing you, Lilian Penrose.'

Lilian felt her face flush with colour.

'He kissed me once, that's all,' she murmured.

'That was once too often,' Maud said grimly.

'You're right,' Lilian agreed, unable to resist smiling at the memory. 'Once was more than enough. It was a horrible kiss too.'

Maud burst out laughing.

'What did you see in him, Lil?'

'I thought he was nice,' Lilian said lamely.

'Roy Walker is a lot of things,' Maud told her, taking a sip of tea, 'but nice isn't one of them.'

Lilian had to laugh. She was glad now that she'd never got around to writing to him. It had been obvious he hadn't been bothered one way or the other and she was pleased that she'd let him think she hadn't cared either. At least it was true now; she didn't care.

'I'm seeing someone now anyway,' Lilian confided. She hadn't meant to tell Maud, but she couldn't keep it to herself. 'He's a pilot and his name's Ben.'

'What's he like?' Maud was curious. 'You've kept very quiet about him.'

'Yes, well – he's wonderful. He's from Liverpool. He's got the most amazing green eyes you've ever seen and lovely fair hair with bits of red in it. He's lovely. He makes me laugh a lot.'

Maud didn't say anything for a moment.

'And what does he think of you?' she asked at last.

'Well – I don't know. We haven't spoken about anything serious. But we spend all our spare time together. You'd like him, Maud, I'm sure you would.'

'So long as he's not another Roy Walker,' Maud replied. 'I hope he's not going round bragging about how easy it is to get a kiss from you, our Lilian.'

'Of course he isn't. It's not like that at all.' Lilian wished she hadn't mentioned him now.

'I hope not. You'll get a reputation if you're not careful.'

Honestly! Maud really was the limit. How the devil was she to get herself a reputation? She had been kissed by two men; one was Roy, a mistake that wouldn't have happened if Lilian had been given time to think, and the other was Ben. Some of the girls on the camp swapped boyfriends as often as they washed their hair, and it wasn't uncommon for them to have a boyfriend on the camp as well as one back at home, wherever that was.

Maud never changed, Lilian thought crossly. It was all right for her to fall in love and marry Joe, but heaven forbid Lilian should fall in love. There was one rule for Maud and another for her, and that was the way it had always been.

'There's nothing wrong with my having a boyfriend,' Lilian pointed out.

'No,' Maud agreed with a wry smile.

Lilian let the subject drop. As far as Maud was concerned, Lilian was a child, like John or Rose, who needed constant supervision and who couldn't be trusted to make her own friends. In Maud's eyes, she would never grow up. Maud would never understand her relationship with Ben. It was so special. It was the real thing – a true and lasting love.

'Are the children still liking it on the farm?' she asked, trying to keep all hint of impatience from her voice.

'They're loving it more each day,' Maud said, smiling. 'It's funny, but it's almost as if they've been born to that sort of life. John knows the name of every bird and every tree, and he's claiming that he's going to be a farmer when he grows up.'

'And does Rose like it?'

'She loves it. Every morning, she goes and collects the eggs. She takes the responsibility so seriously. She's named all the hens and knows each one – well, I think she does. I can't tell the horrid things apart so I have to take her word for it.' Maud laughed. 'You should see her bringing the eggs in. She's so careful with them.'

'It's good that they've settled well.' Lilian had thought they would miss their friends and would find life quiet on the farm. 'Don't they miss anything?'

'They don't seem to. They hardly ever mention Mam or Dad, or even Joe come to that.'

'Out of sight, out of mind,' Lilian said. 'Typical kids. Still, I suppose it's a good thing.'

They lingered over another cup of tea and then ventured out into the sunshine to walk through the village.

'Don't let me forget to post my letters,' Maud said.

They walked up the street and Maud surprised Lilian by stopping to chat with practically everyone they met.

'Uncle Jack and Aunt Violet are a very popular couple,' Maud explained. 'They know everyone and introduce me. It's the devil's own job trying to remember everyone's name but I think I'm getting there.'

A couple of men in RAF uniform were walking some way ahead of them with two young girls. One of the men reminded Lilian of Ben. It was the colour of his hair and the way he walked –

'Lilian! You haven't heard a word I've been saying.'

'Sorry?' Lilian's heart was beating loudly. The man didn't just look like Ben. It was Ben. 'Sorry, Maud. I thought I recognised someone but – er, no.'

Ben was with someone else. It might be his sister, although Lilian doubted it because he would have mentioned it if his sister was visiting. Whoever it was, Ben's arm was firmly linked through hers, just as it had been linked through Lilian's the night before. The girl was laughing happily into Ben's face.

Lilian felt sick. Her head was spinning, as if someone had slapped her across the face – hard.

'Do you know those girls?' Lilian asked her sister.

'No. I don't think so,' Maud replied. 'Why?'

'Oh, no reason. I thought I half-recognised one of them, but I may have been wrong.'

The foursome rounded the corner and were lost from their view. There was sure to be an obvious and innocent explanation, Lilian told herself. Ben was hardly likely to spend the evening with her, and then spend the afternoon with someone else. It must be his sister, or his sister's friend, or someone like that.

'So what were you saying?' Lilian asked, trying without success to push Ben and his mysterious companion from her mind.

'I was going to tell you about Joe,' Maud said. 'I know it sounds childish and fanciful, but when I waved him off at the station, I was convinced – honestly, Lil, I was absolutely convinced that I would never see him again. I knew at the time it was nonsense, but all the same…'

'How do you mean?' Lilian was still too dazed to make any sense of what Maud was talking about. 'What made you think you wouldn't see him again?'

'I honestly don't know.' They stepped off the pavement to avoid a group of young children. 'It was just a feeling I had. It was horrible, I can't deny it. I knew at the time I was just being silly, but I couldn't shake it off.'

'How strange.' Lilian couldn't help thinking that she had never heard a less Maud-like statement in her life. Maud was down-to-earth and practical. She wasn't the type to believe in premonitions. It must have been a very strong feeling for it to have affected her so deeply. 'Did you tell Joe about it?'

'No, I haven't told anyone. Well, I told the vicar and his wife, and now I've told you, but apart from that, I haven't mentioned it…'

It was soon time for Lilian to catch the bus back to the camp, and she wasn't sorry. She knew there was probably no reason for jealousy, but she was still shaken from seeing Ben like that.

'I must write to Joe,' she said. 'It's ages since I have.'

'Yes, do. He'd love that. He's always telling me how your letters cheer him up.'

'Really?' Lilian was pleased.

'Really!' Maud nodded. 'He says they make him smile. I think half the regiment reads them.'

'Then I shall have to write to him more often,' Lilian said. 'I'll have to dash, Maud, but I'll be in touch. And give John and Rose a great big hug for me.'

'I will.'

Lilian hugged her tight, then hurried off to catch her bus. As she walked, she looked out for Ben but there was no sign of him.

∾◡∾

She didn't see him until the following night. They'd arranged to meet up for a drink in the village, and he was his usual affectionate self. Lilian felt a little guilty about the dubious thoughts that had been chasing round her head ever since she'd seen him with that girl. She waited for him to mention his trip to the village and, when he didn't, she became even more convinced that there was nothing for her to worry about. He clearly didn't think it worth mentioning.

Lilian usually enjoyed the company of their friends but, tonight, she wanted time alone with Ben. She didn't get it however. They spent the whole evening in a group.

Lying in bed that night, she tried to decide if Ben had acted any differently. She didn't think that he had. He'd been his usual attentive, affectionate self and his goodnight kiss had been as warm and as passionate as ever. If anything, it had been a little too passionate. Or perhaps she was being prudish. Many girls on the camp were going a lot further than a few kisses. Those girls didn't see it as giving in; they wanted more than kisses. Perhaps it was only to be expected that Ben wouldn't be satisfied with a kiss. And if he wasn't satisfied, Lilian knew he'd have no problem finding girls eager to go further...

The following day, she was on her way to the transport yard when she spotted him strolling out towards the runway. She ran to catch him up.

'Hi!' He sounded surprised but pleased to see her. 'What are you doing?'

'I'm just on my way to the yard. I have to go and pick up the CO.' There was little time and she blurted it out. 'I was in the village on Monday with my sister. We saw you.'

'Oh?'

'Yes.' She wasn't sure what else to say and wished

she hadn't mentioned it. It would sound as if she didn't trust him. She did trust him; it was just that she would feel a whole lot better if he told her who the girl was.

'Why didn't you come and say hello?' he asked curiously.

'You were with some people,' she explained, feeling more and more foolish. 'I didn't want to intrude.'

'Oh.'

That was it. Just 'Oh'. Lilian didn't know what to think. From wishing she hadn't mentioned it, she now wanted to know every detail. She wanted to know exactly who that pretty girl was and she wanted to know why Ben's arm had been linked with hers. She simply didn't know how to phrase it. That 'Oh' had sounded guilty. Or had it? Surely she trusted Ben. Yes, of course she did. And yet –

'So who were you with?' she asked quietly.

'What? Well, I can't remember. I saw a lot of folk that day, Lil.'

'I see.' His casual, almost impatient reply brought tears to her eyes and she had to blink them away.

'If you'd had the sense to come and say hello,' he told her, his voice teasing now, 'I could have introduced you to whoever I was with, couldn't I?'

'I suppose so.' She nodded, and would have left it at that, but something made her push on. 'You were with a girl. Short with dark curly hair. Not in WAAF uniform.'

'Oh, that was probably Ellie. Her father owns The Pheasant – you know, the pub some of us visit.'

'You seemed quite friendly with her,' Lilian couldn't help remarking. 'The two of you were arm in arm.'

'For God's sake, Lil! What is this?' His expression was suddenly hard. 'Am I supposed to ignore my friends now – or the female ones at any rate? Is that what you're saying?'

'Of course not!' She felt very small and very petty. 'I just wondered, that's all.'

'I know her father,' Ben explained with exaggerated patience, 'and I know her through him. She's just a friend – not even that really. An acquaintance. Honestly, Lil, I didn't have you down as the possessive type.'

'I'm not!' At least, she hoped she wasn't. That girl had been very pretty though. 'I wondered who she was, that's all.'

'She's no one, no one special. She's not worth talking about.' His eyes were teasing again. 'You're my girl, Lilian Penrose, and don't you dare forget it.'

'I won't.' She smiled at him and he kissed her very briefly on the lips.

'Now go and get some work done,' he said, patting her on the bottom, 'before you land us both in trouble.'

'OK.'

'And the next time you see me out and about with strange women,' he said, still teasing her, 'for goodness sake come and say hello so I can show you off. Got that?'

'Yes.' She laughed happily. 'I'll see you later, Ben. I love you so much,' she added fervently.

'Good.'

He laughed, but he didn't tell her he loved her too. It didn't really matter though. He had told her she was his girl and that was enough for Lilian. Her heart was light as she walked quickly on to the yard.

~ *Chapter Eight* ~

OCTOBER 1940

Maud could feel herself growing more and more impatient with the children. If she had to tolerate any more bad behaviour, she would scream.

'You're not going out until you've eaten that,' she told John firmly, pointing at the cabbage he'd pushed to the side of his plate.

'Don't want it,' he muttered.

'You'll eat it,' she said sharply. 'Auntie Violet hasn't cooked it for you to waste it. Now eat up. You've never been a fussy eater and you're not going to start now. I'll not see it wasted, John.'

'Don't want it!' John insisted, his chin jutting out firmly.

Rose, always quick to copy her big brother, pushed her cabbage to the side of her plate.

'Rose, don't you dare start!' Maud cried. She stood at the table, hands on hips, chest rising and falling with anger. 'You will both eat your cabbage. Do you hear me? I don't care if we stand here into next week, but you'll eat it.'

'Shan't!' In a sudden fit of temper, John pushed his plate aside, threw back his chair so that it landed on the floor with a crash, and raced from the kitchen. Rose, with her bottom lip quivering, followed him.

Maud was all set to chase after them but she only got as far as the kitchen door before she burst into tears.

Aunt Violet was soon by her side, her arm round her shoulders.

'Come and sit down,' she suggested gently. 'I'll put the kettle on and you can tell me all about it.'

Maud sat at the table and cried until there were no tears left. She was wiping her face when Aunt Violet put a cup of hot tea in front of her.

'What is it, love?' Violet asked gently. 'It's not like you to get in a state with the children. And it's not like the children to play you up. You've been very edgy for days and I'm sure they're picking up on it. What is it, love?'

'Nothing,' Maud replied with a loud sigh. 'Oh, everything. I haven't heard from Joe for weeks. I'm worried to death.'

'I'm sure there's a perfectly good reason, love,' Violet said. 'He will have written, but I expect his letters are taking a long time to get here. They've got a long way to come. It's worrying, I know, but – well, I'm sure you'll hear from him soon.'

Maud wasn't. She knew it was fanciful nonsense, but she couldn't stop thinking about that feeling she'd had at the station. It was stupid, but it persisted.

'One day soon,' Uncle Jack said, 'you'll get a bathful of letters from him. They'll all arrive together. You mark my words.'

Perhaps Uncle Jack was right. Perhaps Joe's letters were simply piling up somewhere. Oh, she hoped so.

'I suppose so.' She gave her aunt a watery smile and got to her feet. 'I'd better go and find those children of mine.'

'Take the cabbage,' Uncle Jack suggested with a

chuckle. 'They can feed it to the pigs.'

Maud laughed and gave her uncle a quick hug.

'Thanks,' she murmured. 'Thanks for everything. For having us here, for being so patient with the children, and with me. We do appreciate everything you're doing for us.'

'Stuff and nonsense,' Aunt Violet said, embarrassed by her words. 'We love having you here, you know that.'

'I know. But thanks all the same.'

Maud scraped the cabbage onto one plate and carried it outside into the watery sunshine. Her spirits lifted immediately. Joe's letters hadn't arrived, that was all. It didn't mean anything. She couldn't go around behaving like a spoilt brat just because she hadn't heard from him.

She spotted the children playing on the tractor. Despite the sunshine it was bitterly cold, but they were laughing happily and her heart melted. She loved them so very much. She might not have Joe by her side, but she had his children and they meant everything to her.

'Come on, you two,' she said, smiling warmly as she walked over to them. 'Let's go and see if the pigs are fond of cabbage.'

Laughing, they raced across to where the pigs were snuffling the ground. The cabbage had soon vanished much to the children's delight. Maud's black mood had vanished too. It had been ridiculous to get into such a state over two helpings of cabbage.

∽∾∾

Lilian was grateful for the chance to go to the village

alone and sit in the pub for half an hour before work. The pub was quiet – it often was at lunch-time – and she was glad of that. She was so tired that all she wanted was to be left alone with her own thoughts.

Her mind was preoccupied with Ben. It had been a month now since she had seen him in the village with that girl – Ellie. A month. During that time, apart from the couple of weeks that Ben had been away from the station, she'd spent all her free time with him. Superficially, nothing had changed between them. She still loved him with all her heart. She still loved being with him. She still loved the thought of being his girl. And yet –

Something fundamental had changed, something she couldn't quite put her finger on, and it bothered her. In all honesty, she could no longer say she was happy.

A group of people walked in and Lilian looked up. Apart from David Benson, she didn't recognise any of the men. Although that wasn't unusual. New faces appeared at the station on an almost daily basis.

David got himself a drink, looked around, spotted her and walked over.

'May I?' He nodded at the chair beside hers.

'Of course.'

'You're looking very thoughtful,' he remarked.

'Sorry.' She smiled.

'Don't apologise. You don't have to be the life and soul of the party twenty-four hours a day, you know.'

'I know, but it's awful to sit with someone who's feeling gloomy.'

'Are you? Feeling gloomy, I mean?'

'A bit,' Lilian admitted truthfully.

'Any special reason?'

'No. Not really.'

They lapsed into silence.

'Where's Prue?' David asked eventually. 'I haven't seen her around.'

'In the hospital,' Lilian replied with a rueful smile. 'She has chicken pox and is feeling very sorry for herself.'

'I don't blame her.' David pulled a face. 'I remember having that. It's not pleasant.'

Lilian had to smile to herself. 'Bloody awful' was how Prue had defined her case of chicken pox. The poor girl was covered from head to toe in spots that she longed to scratch, and she was far from happy.

'She's almost better now,' she assured him.

'Good.'

Again, they lapsed into silence. It wasn't an uncomfortable silence though. In fact it made a nice change not to feel obliged to make conversation.

'Are you tired?' David asked curiously.

Lilian thought for a moment and decided she had been tired for months. Every night, she dropped into bed exhausted and was asleep within minutes, but she never seemed to wake up feeling rested and refreshed.

'Is there anyone on the station who isn't tired?' she asked with a wry smile.

'Probably not.' He laughed, but Lilian could see the weariness in his smile.

'What about you?' she asked. 'You've been busy lately. How are you coping with it?'

'As well as everyone else, I suppose,' he answered with a shrug. 'There's nothing else to do but cope.' He was thoughtful for a moment. 'The thing about a war is that most of us have no experience of it. We go into it with a hope and prayer, but no experience.'

'But how can you get experience?'

'That's just it. You can't.' He gave another shrug. 'By the time this is finally over, I expect we'll all know what it is we're supposed to be doing. Unfortunately, it will be too late then.'

'When this is over,' Lilian said with relish, 'I shall take to a nice comfortable bed for days, then spend another few days in a bath that is full to the brim. Heaven!'

'Such simple tastes.' He sounded amused.

They certainly were simple. But they were things Lilian felt sure she would never again take for granted.

'What will you do when it's over?' She was genuinely interested.

'I've no idea. I never allow myself to think that far ahead.'

His answer disappointed her, but she could understand how he felt. All anyone could do was live one day at a time.

'Mam was in London visiting a friend a month ago,' she told him. 'She arrived on the first night of the heavy bombings. It must have terrified her – and no wonder. I heard that more than five thousand people were killed in London during September. It's impossible to imagine such numbers, isn't it?'

He nodded.

'My home's in London. My mother lives there, and every time I hear from her, there seems to be less of London still standing.'

'What got to me most was when I heard Buckingham Palace had been hit – with the King and Queen inside. I could hardly believe it.'

'It's dreadful. I hate to think of my home city having

the heart bombed out of it. I sometimes wonder if anything of my old life will be left.'

'Is there nowhere else your mother could go?' Lilian asked. 'London can't be safe at the moment.'

'It isn't. And yes, there are dozens of places she could go. She's a very stubborn lady though, and it would take more than Hitler to make her budge.'

Lilian laughed.

'Mum's friend, Jane, said exactly the same. She's a lovely woman – a bit upper class – and she's used to a very active social life. She's really miffed with Hitler for putting a stop to her partying.' She emptied her glass. 'Mam tried to persuade her to stay with her and Dad in Sunderland but Jane wouldn't hear of it. They – Jane and Mam – were members of the suffragette movement when they were young –'

'The suffragettes? Good grief!'

'I know.' Lilian smiled. She was proud of her somewhat unconventional mother. 'That's how they met. I don't know much about it – it's only what my sister told me – but Mam was arrested when she was in London. She spent a night in jail.'

'I don't know why I'm so surprised.' David laughed. 'It's a case of like mother, like daughter, I suppose. I can easily imagine you chaining yourself to some railings.'

Lilian laughed, but he was right. She would have loved to have joined the suffragettes.

'They had fun – Mam and Jane.' Her laughter died abruptly. 'That doesn't mean they weren't serious about the suffragettes,' she added quickly, before he got the wrong impression.

'I'm sure it doesn't. What does your mother do now?'

He sounded genuinely interested.

'Looks after the house and family.' Lilian grinned suddenly. 'And takes off for London to visit her friend on the very day that Hitler decides to do his worst to the city.'

'Not the best timing in the world.' Smiling, he gestured to her empty glass. 'Would you like another?'

'I would. Yes, thanks.'

Lilian had intended to get the early bus back to the camp, but she was happy to relax for a while longer.

Watching him at the bar, she realized she had no idea whether or not he had a girlfriend waiting for him somewhere. In London, perhaps. She supposed he probably had. He was a few years older than she was, he was good looking, and, despite her earlier misgivings, she had to admit that he was a nice person. Now his disapproval of her seemed to have lessened, she found him easy to talk to. But perhaps it wasn't only that. Perhaps she was beginning to understand him a little. He was a complex character but beneath the slightly stiff exterior she sensed a warm, caring person. He was the sort, she decided, that you could trust with your life.

Unlike Ben.

The thought came from nowhere but it was difficult to ignore. The reason why she was no longer happy with Ben was because she no longer trusted him. It hurt her to accept the truth of that, but accept it she had to. She had no real grounds for this lack of trust, but for some reason, she no longer trusted him. Had she been a fool?

For all his faults, if David did have a girlfriend, that girl would know she could trust him. She would know

that David's feelings for her were real. She watched
him absently stroking his moustache as he spoke to
John at the bar. It was all very commendable being
serious about his girlfriend, Lilian thought as she
watched him, if indeed he had one. But surely there
was more to life than that. What about excitement and
passion?

∽∾

✀ *Chapter Nine* ✀

DECEMBER 1940

Maud didn't know if she was doing the right thing or not. If she were totally honest with herself, she suspected it was wrong to bring the children back to Sunderland for Christmas. The whole area was receiving regular bombing raids, and it was far safer on the farm. But she had to come home – if only for a week or so.

Uncle Jack and Aunt Violet had been sorry to see them leave, but they understood. It seemed so long since Maud had seen her parents.

It seemed even longer since she'd seen Joe, she thought miserably as the train trundled its way towards Sunderland. He was in Egypt now. Aunt Violet had been right; although he wrote regularly, the letters all came in batches so that she didn't hear anything for ages and then received several from him. She wrote to him every day, but she didn't know if or when he received her letters.

How she wished they were looking forward to another normal family Christmas. They would all gather at her parents' home – she and Joe, John and Rose, and Lilian. Their mother would make the house look pretty with sprigs of holly and mistletoe and John and Rose would make paper chains to hang from the ceiling. On Boxing Day, their parents' next-door neighbour, Ida, would spend the day with them and amuse them by getting tipsy on half a glass of sherry.

John and Rose had been so excited at the prospect of seeing their grandparents or – and more accurately, Maud thought with amusement – at the prospect of the train ride, that they hadn't slept the night before for excitement. Now, when they were on the train that had excited them so much, they were fast asleep.

'Let's hope the train gets through and nothing wakes them,' the man sharing their compartment remarked, nodding at their sleeping heads.

'I hope so.'

'And let's hope we get a quiet Christmas,' he added.

He was in his late fifties, Maud guessed, and looked a meek, friendly soul. She was glad of his company.

'Yes.' Maud, too, hoped that the Germans would take time off from bombing to celebrate Christmas. 'I'm taking the children home to Sunderland for the holiday.'

'It's a poor do when you can't spend Christmas with your family,' he said, understandingly. 'A lot of the evacuees are coming home too.'

'Christmas is a time for families.'

'It's funny,' he remarked suddenly, 'how folk cope, isn't it? I'm a special constable – Merseyside,' he explained, 'and one day, a woman whose house had been bombed came to me to borrow tuppence to ring up her husband. He was working a night-shift. She said to him "Don't come home to the house, Jack – it isn't there. Go to your mother's for breakfast." There's nowt so strange.'

Maud had to smile. He was right; it was amazing how folk seemed able to get on with their lives despite everything.

'My sister's boyfriend comes from Liverpool,' she

said. 'Has it been bad there?'

'It has.' He nodded grimly. 'Because all the incidents were fairly minor, everyone was unprepared for the big one at the end of November. By all accounts, there were five hundred and twenty-four raiders that night. It was the first experience we'd had of land mines and it wasn't pleasant, believe me. They come down by parachute so slowly and some of them ended up hanging from trees or rooftops.'

Maud shuddered at the thought of seeing a land mine hanging from the rooftop.

'There are barrage balloons floating from barges on the river,' he explained, 'and batteries of guns on each side, but still the Hun manage to get through. It makes you wonder what it'll take to stop them.'

'It does. I'm not too sure what the damage is in Sunderland. I get letters from Mam, of course, but I suspect she plays it down a bit.'

'I suspect she does. I don't know what's been happening in Sunderland, either. I'll bet it's getting its fair share though. Liverpool is our link with America which makes it a very important port. Sunderland is nicely sited on the north-east coast and I'm sure Hitler would like to put the place out of action. Who knows? All the towns and cities seem to be getting their fair share.'

'They do,' she agreed. 'Oh, well. We'll soon find out what Sunderland looks like,' she added as the train began to slow for the station.

John and Rose woke and rubbed their eyes.

'We're here,' Maud told them softly.

Their companion helped her with their luggage and they parted on the platform.

'Have a good Christmas,' he said. 'Let's hope we'll all have celebrated a victory by the time we're sitting down to our next Christmas lunch.'

'I hope so. Oh – Merry Christmas to you, too!'

She watched him walk away then looked around her. All she could remember was waving Joe off the last time she saw him. The memory made her shudder, but she refused to dwell on the feelings she had experienced that day. Far better to look forward to the day when she could stand on this platform and welcome him home...

～～～

Maud and the children spent their first night back in Sunderland in the recently acquired Anderson shelter. The two-minute rising and falling wail of the alert siren went off at 6.30pm and they dashed to the shelter. It was cramped with five of them in it, but their mother had made it quite comfortable. These days, she was well prepared and always had a flask of tea and sandwiches to take in there.

'Have you heard from Joe?' her mother asked.

'Not for nearly a fortnight,' Maud replied. 'I wrote and told him I was coming here for Christmas, and I don't know what he'll think of that. I doubt he'll be too happy about it – and if he'd seen the things I saw on my way from the station, he'd be even less happy.'

'It's been pretty grim,' her father agreed.

'It's the firemen and the ambulance drivers I feel so sorry for,' her mother said with a sigh. 'Well, I feel sorry for us all, but they get it bad. You know old Victor, the fireman? He was telling me about one night when the ack-ack guns hit one of the bombers. It came down on houses with all its bombs still on it. The fire killed everyone; they'd had no time to get to the shelter. Anyway, among the remains, they found the body of one of the German crew.' She glanced at her sleeping grandchildren. 'Still, we must keep cheerful. We'll win. We can overcome all this.'

But could they, Maud wondered. Could they really overcome all this?

∽∾

By Boxing Day, Maud knew she should have stayed in the relative safety of Norfolk. All they had done was dash to the shelter. They'd had a lovely Christmas Day though, despite everything. Her mother had stored up the necessary ingredients and had made a cake and a Christmas pudding. Not only that, she had made sure that both John and Rose found a silver threepenny piece in their portions.

'It's funny how little things cheer you up,' her mother said with amusement. 'I got quite excited when I heard we were getting extra sugar and tea rations for Christmas.'

Maud had to laugh. 'Well, don't use it all at once!'

It had been the custom for as long as Maud could remember for Ida to spend Boxing Day with them and this year was no exception. It was good to see her; her presence made it almost feel like old times.

'You'll be missing that man of yours at Christmas,' Ida declared sagely.

'Yes, I do.'

Maud wondered how Joe was spending Christmas Day. She knew he would be missing John and Rose desperately. They had very little money, but he had always managed to make Christmas a magical time for them.

'Well, as you know, my Bert, God rest his soul, has been gone for fifteen years now,' Ida said, 'and not a day passes when I don't think of him.'

Maud exchanged a knowing glance with her father. She only had a very dim recollection of Bert, but tales of the fights between him and Ida were known all over Sunderland. Many was the time Bert came home after a night's drinking session to find he'd been locked out. Once, so folk said, he'd had to spend a night in the infirmary after Ida had set about him with her rolling pin.

'We had our ups and downs,' Ida went on, 'but he was a good man. Wasn't he, Clive?'

'He was, Ida.' He winked at Maud before offering to top up Ida's glass of sherry. 'A drink at Christmas never hurt anyone,' he told their neighbour.

'You're right. Well, thank you, Clive. If you're sure…'

Maud felt certain Ida was the only person who had ever touched that bottle of sherry. Her mother put a spoonful in the Christmas trifle, and another in the Christmas cake, but apart from that, it was all Ida's. The bottle spent the rest of the year collecting dust at the back of the cupboard.

They played charades later, which the children loved. If only Joe could have been with them it would have been far more fun.

'Is Ida drunk?' John asked in a loud voice.

'Of course not,' Maud said sharply, stifling a giggle.

'Then why couldn't she get out of her chair on her own?'

Maud almost choked on a burst of laughter.

'Because – well, because she's getting older now,' she explained lamely.

Ida, she suspected, would need their father to escort her home. If she couldn't get out of her chair, there was no way she would make it up the front steps to her own door. She was on her third glass of sherry and her cheeks were getting more flushed by the mouthful.

'My Bert liked his beer,' she said, slurring her words. 'He knew when to stop, unlike some I could mention, but he did enjoy the odd glass.'

Maud caught her mother stifling her laughter. Bert had liked the odd several glasses by all accounts.

'Oh, I do miss him so,' Ida wailed suddenly.

'Now, now, Ida!' Clive spoke firmly. 'Don't go getting maudlin on us.'

'No, you're right,' she agreed, sniffing loudly. 'I shouldn't be thinking about my own problems when you've been so kind as to invite me. In any case, you've all got problems of your own. What with Joe in Egypt having to face the Lord knows what out there, and young Lilian driving those big trucks – where will it all end?'

No one had an answer to that one.

'Heaven alone knows how the children will turn out,' Ida remarked suddenly. 'All around us, they're playing war games. I saw a gang this afternoon with toy guns that someone must have made for them. One had a cork on a piece of string and this cork flew out of the gun like a bullet. The young lad who had been shot – he hadn't, of course, it was only a toy – but he clutched his stomach and fell to the ground groaning. Where will it all end?' she asked again.

'I suppose they have to find some way of amusing themselves,' Dorothy said. 'So many are left to their own devices these days, poor little mites. Their dads are away and the women too tired to pay them any heed.'

Maud was thankful her own children weren't being left to their own devices. Life on the farm was relatively quiet, and they were more inclined to play at being farmers than soldiers, thank goodness. The constant air raids fascinated John, and he loved hearing tales of how many planes had gone over, how many had been shot down, and how many buildings had been destroyed. Back on the farm, though, they were mostly untouched by it. He saw the RAF planes fly over and they fascinated him so much that Maud thought he might get ideas of becoming a pilot when he grew up. But no, he was still intent on becoming a farmer.

'It's nothing but air raids, running from shelter to shelter, rationing and darkness,' Ida complained. 'I'm sick to death of this war!'

Maud silently echoed that feeling. Her husband was in Egypt, the British forces were taking a terrific battering, there would soon be no towns left in England –

'Then all we can do is hope it will be over soon,' Clive said, attempting to put an end to such talk. 'We must keep our chins up and keep going.'

'Indeed,' Dorothy agreed. 'Now then, who's for another slice of Christmas cake?'

No one refused the offer.

'Oh, I did have a good evening in the shelter last week though,' Ida chipped in as she nibbled at her Christmas cake. 'I was on the bus during an air raid and it got so bad that it had to stop at the nearest shelter. Some people were sleeping on the floor, and a few men were playing cards, and then some bright spark started a singsong. The bus driver was singing and the clippie was there with her money-bag round her neck. Oh, it was grand. Then the warden came down, told us the All Clear had gone and off we went, back on the bus. We were still singing on the bus.'

Maud smiled at her story. It was remarkable how everyone could remain so cheerful when bombs were dropping all around them. Some of those involved in the singsong may not have had a home left to go to.

When Ida decided it was time to go home, Maud chuckled to herself as her father offered his services. He helped Ida out of her chair again, then kept a tight grip on her arm as he escorted her out of the house.

'She'll sleep well tonight.' He was grinning broadly when he returned.

'She will,' Dorothy replied with a chuckle. 'She likes the odd glass of sherry, just as her Bert liked the odd glass of beer.'

'The odd glass my eye,' Clive said, and they were soon helpless with laughter...

༄

Maud was tired when she got into bed that night. It would be heaven to sleep well, but she rarely did these days.

This night was no exception. Uncharacteristically, not only did she dream, but when she woke the memory of it was crystal clear. Joe had been wearing his uniform and he'd asked her to marry him.

The following night, she had exactly the same dream. It was a summer's day and they were standing on the top of a high hill looking down on buildings below them. The buildings hadn't been touched by the war. Joe was wearing a red rose in his button hole.

'Marry me, Maud,' he had pleaded urgently.

'Yes, Joe. Yes, I'll marry you.'

Laughing, they had raced down the hill, hand in hand, with the breeze on their faces and in their hair.

Considering the years they'd been married, it was an odd dream. But then, Maud supposed, all dreams were odd. For all that, it had been strangely comforting. Joe had seemed so real. When she woke, she imagined that if she just reached out, she would be able to touch him...

A week later, Maud had packed their suitcases again and was ready for the trip back to Norfolk. It was a cold day, heavy with frost, but the sky was blue and the sun was doing its best to shine. Maud was in good spirits.

The telegram arrived shortly after 9am. It was addressed to her parents' home, and had her name on it.

All she saw were the words 'Killed in action...' before she fainted.

∾ *Chapter Ten* ∾

JANUARY 1941

Lilian was grateful to have been granted leave, but as the bus trundled through the familiar, if greatly changed streets of Sunderland, she was dreading getting home. She didn't know how she would face Maud. She wasn't even sure that Maud would want to see her. Knowing her sister, she would probably prefer to be alone with her grief.

Lilian had hardly been able to take in the news of Joe's death so she couldn't begin to imagine how Maud was feeling. No matter how hard she tried, she simply could not believe that Joe would never be coming home. She couldn't imagine how John and Rose were supposed to cope without their father. Joe had never hurt anyone in his life. He was – had been, she reminded herself – a wonderful father and husband, totally devoted to Maud and the children. He'd been the type who would have given away his last penny with a smile. God, it was unfair. Unfair and unbearably cruel.

She walked slowly from the bus stop, in no hurry to reach the house. Her uniform attracted a few glances – it always did – but she paid it no heed. She was numb.

It was getting dark when she walked down the back path and pushed open the kitchen door. Her mother was standing at the sink, her hands in a bowl of soapy water as she washed up. Red hands, Lilian noticed.

They were always red because she had the water far too hot. No one else in the family could put their hands in such hot water, not even their father.

'Oh, our Lilian!' Wiping her hands on her apron, her mother rushed forward and threw her arms round her. 'I'm so glad you're here. What are we to do with our Maud?' She sniffed loudly. 'She's having a lie down. The bairns are playing with Edna O'Connor's lot.'

'How is she, Mam?' Lilian asked, grateful that she wouldn't have to face Maud for a little while longer.

'She fainted when the telegram came.' She pushed Lilian into the chair by the stove. 'Then, when she came round, I couldn't stop her screaming. Terrible screams, Lilian. I truly thought she was going mad. I had to slap her across the face to stop her, God help me.'

Lilian paled at the thought. Maud wasn't prone to hysterics.

'Since then,' her mother went on, 'she's hardly said a word to anyone. She walks around the rooms, picking things up and putting them down, but she says nothing. I don't know what to do with her.'

Lilian couldn't sit still. She got to her feet and fetched two cups from their hooks.

'I need a cup of tea, Mam.' The kettle, as always, was on the boil. 'Has she told John and Rose?'

'No. It's as if she's managed to push it from her mind.'

That didn't sound like Maud, either.

'What if someone else tells them?' Lilian asked worriedly. 'News travels fast round here and I expect everyone's heard by now.'

'I know. She'll have to tell them. I hardly dare mention it though. And I think they're safe – this is the first time they've been out of the house. What's even worse perhaps is that she hardly speaks to those poor bairns. She's just withdrawn into her own little world somehow. I'll be honest, Lil, it's frightening me.'

It was frightening Lilian, too. If her mother couldn't cope with Maud, how on earth was she supposed to? Suddenly, she felt terribly young.

'Did she tell you about the day she waved Joe off at the station?' she asked and her mother shook her head, frowning.

Lilian poured them tea and sat back by the stove.

'She told me about it when we met up in the village one day,' Lilian explained. 'It was odd but she was saying something about having a strange feeling at the station. Just for a minute, she said, she was sure she'd never see Joe again. Of course, I thought she was just being daft. Mind you, Maud thought she was just being daft too. Well, she was right as it's turned out. That day at the station was the last time she would ever see him.'

'She never whispered a word about it. Oh, that poor lass.'

'What does Dad say?'

'He's at a loss. We none of us can believe it could happen to Joe so it's no wonder it's knocked Maud for six. She's hated this war right from the start. All she wanted was a quiet life with Joe and the kids. That's not much to ask, is it? It's so unfair.'

It was. That was the hardest part; trying to accept the unfairness of it. It was the same for a lot of people though. It is just that it only really hit home when it was family. And Lord, did it hit home hard.

'They are sure?' Lilian asked. 'I mean, that he's – dead. He couldn't be missing or just presumed dead?'

'They're sure. She had a letter from his Commanding Officer this morning. She read it, said nothing and left it lying on the table there.' She nodded at the table. 'When she went for a lie down, I read it. It was a lovely letter, explaining how Joe had died and saying how sorry he was. He said that Maud could be proud of her husband. Aye, it was a nice letter. One day, she'll be glad to have it. But yes, there's no doubt. Joe is dead.'

Lilian had a sudden recollection of the day she was bridesmaid at their wedding. Joe had told her she was the prettiest bridesmaid he had ever seen. 'You're almost as pretty as the bride,' he'd said, as he danced her around the room, telling her all the while that he was the happiest man alive. He'd been so happy and proud that day. Almost as happy, she thought, as he was the day John was born. Anyone could have been forgiven for thinking that no man alive had ever produced a son before. Then, when Rose was born, he hadn't been able to believe that anyone could have such a beautiful daughter. He had loved those children so much. Maud, John and Rose – they had been his life.

'If we survive this war at all,' Lilian said fiercely, 'it will have sent us all insane! I hate it!'

'So do I, love. So do I.'

They sat in silence in the warmth from the stove until a sharp hammering on the door and an irate voice reminded them that it was dark and they hadn't drawn the curtains.

'Dratted blackout,' Dorothy muttered as she pulled the curtains closed, making sure that no chink of light escaped.

They sat quietly and drank their tea, both thinking of Maud upstairs.

'Go up and see her,' her mother suggested quietly. She must have seen the panic in Lilian's eyes, because she smiled in an understanding way. 'She's your sister, love. She's not changed. She's the one you've fought with all your life. Just be yourself, Lilian.'

But she had changed. The Maud she had fought with didn't withdraw into a world of her own, or have strange premonitions. Lilian wasn't sure she understood this Maud. She didn't know how to deal with her.

'You don't even have to say anything,' her mother went on. 'Just give her a hug, love. That's all we can do – let her know we love her. Let her know we're here for her.'

It was awful to dread seeing your own sister, but dread it Lilian did. However, she knew it had to be faced sometime and she knew it wouldn't get any easier.

She walked slowly up the stairs to her old bedroom, tapped on the door and stepped inside. Maud was standing by the window, in complete darkness, gazing out at the blackness. She turned round when Lilian walked in and gave her a smile.

'Hello, Lil. It's good to see you.'

That was all it took.

'Oh, Maud!' Lilian rushed forward and hugged her tight. She didn't speak, couldn't speak, but she held her close.

They stood, not saying anything, just holding each other for what seemed like hours.

'Come on,' Lilian said at last. 'Let's get the curtains drawn and put the light on. We've already had stern words from the warden tonight.'

She pulled the curtains closed, made sure they were light-tight, then fumbled for the light. At last she could actually see Maud. There was no sign of tears, no red, swollen eyes as Lilian had expected. She looked almost – well, serene. There was a half-smile on her face and it made Lilian shudder.

'Mam's worried about you,' Lilian told her. 'She's worried about John and Rose too. You've got to tell them, Maud.'

'Yes, I must.' Maud sat on the bed and patted the space beside her. 'How long are you home for?'

Lilian sat down on the bed.

'I have to be back on Thursday night.' Her mother was right, Lilian thought. Maud was deliberately pushing it from her mind. 'When will you tell John and Rose?'

'I haven't decided yet.' She stood up, walked to the dresser, picked up her hairbrush and began to brush her hair.

They heard the back door open and close.

'That'll be Dad home for his dinner,' Lilian said. 'Let's go down and eat, Maud. John and Rose will be back any minute.'

'OK.' Like an obedient child, she put down the hairbrush. 'Actually I'm quite hungry.'

Despite that statement, Maud swallowed about two mouthfuls. Their mother had always insisted that the family sat down together for the evening meal – she said it gave them each the opportunity to talk about their day – but this occasion was a very quiet, tense affair. Even the children were unusually quiet. Lilian guessed that Maud's strange behaviour, and that was the best way she could describe it, was upsetting them. John especially kept looking at his mother, waiting perhaps for some sign of life. Lilian watched her mother look from Maud to the children, a worried frown marring her features. Their father ate his food slowly without looking at anyone but Lilian could tell he was equally worried.

∽◌∾

Afterwards, when the children had gone to bed, the rest of the family sat around the fire, saying very little, just watching the sparks dancing in the hearth. Lilian thought of several things she wanted to tell them but the atmosphere was even more tense without the children around to lighten it. Finally, she could hold back no longer.

'Maud,' she began carefully, 'if you don't feel able to tell the children about Joe, perhaps you should let Mam or Dad do it.' She gave her parents an apologetic glance, realizing belatedly that she should have spoken to them first. 'Or I could do it,' she added, desperately hoping she wouldn't have to. 'They have to be told, though. It's not fair to keep it from them.'

'Lilian's right.' Clive Penrose got to his feet and stood with his back to the fire. 'Like it or not, Maud, we have to face facts, love. The little ones know something's wrong. I'll tell them tomorrow morning, with your mam. She'll see they're all right. Don't you worry, love. We'll deal with it.'

Maud looked at him for several moments as if he was speaking a foreign language. Then she shrugged.

'As you like. I'm going to bed now. Goodnight, all.'

The three of them chorused their goodnights and watched her leave the room. They listened to her slow steps on the stairs and heard her padding around the bedroom above them.

'Sorry if I spoke out of turn, Dad,' Lilian said in a lowered voice.

'You were right to speak, Lilian.' He sat back down in his chair by the side of the fire. 'Those poor children have to know, it's only right.'

'We'll tell them,' her mother assured Lilian. 'Although the Lord alone knows how they'll take it. But they're young and resilient. They have a loving family, thank God. We'll get them through it between us.' She smiled at Lilian. 'It'll be a help having you here, love.'

Lilian was touched by her mother's words, but she didn't imagine she was going to be of much use. She simply couldn't accept it. She couldn't grasp the fact that Joe was lost to them…

For once, it took Lilian a long time to fall asleep that night. Maud, she could tell, wasn't sleeping either. In the past, Lilian would have chattered long into the night, but she simply lay in the darkness wishing there was something she could do or say that might help Maud. But she guessed that only time could help Maud now.

It was almost dawn when she awoke and she couldn't decide if Maud was asleep or merely pretending to sleep, so she dressed quietly and crept out of the bedroom leaving her sister to rest.

John and Rose were already sitting at the kitchen table. They looked very small and very vulnerable, Lilian thought sadly. Her mother, standing at the sink, looked at Lilian and gave a brief nod.

The poor things, Lilian thought, her heart aching for them. How she wished she could gather them in her arms, wave a magic wand and bring their father walking through the door with that huge smile on his face…

❦

Between them, she and her mother kept up a conversation that was as normal as they could make it. It was when Lilian was eating a slice of toast that John spoke.

'Dad's dead.' His voice was completely devoid of emotion.

'I know, sweetheart.' Lilian's throat was tight with emotion. 'Your dad has gone to heaven. A lot of dads have gone to heaven because of this war. One day though, when this war is over, you'll be able to tell everyone that your dad was a very brave man who helped us to win.'

'I want to see him now,' Rose piped up. 'I want to tell him about my hens.'

'Then I know what we'll do,' Lilian said briskly, her voice tight with emotion, 'we'll get those photographs – you know the ones that were taken when he came home in his new uniform? We'll go to the shops and buy two frames. You can have a photograph each, to keep safely, and then you'll be able to tell him things whenever you want to.'

'Can we go now?' John asked eagerly.

'As soon as I've had my breakfast,' Lilian promised.

Much to Lilian's surprise and relief, the two children chatted happily as they walked around the shops. Lilian dreaded an air raid but they were lucky. The children chose the frames for their photographs and then they trooped into the café for a cake and a drink. It was a treat for them and it gave Lilian a rest. Yesterday she had felt very young: today she felt extremely old.

In the café it was business as usual although two windows had been blown out and hastily boarded up, and a few panes were cracked. Not for the first time, Lilian wondered if there would be a building still standing at the end of the war. Although by all accounts, the RAF were giving Berlin, Hamburg and other German cities the same treatment.

It was early afternoon when they got back home.

'Maud's in bed,' her mother spoke in a hushed voice. 'Claims she has a headache.'

Lilian nodded.

'And your Aunt Violet's written,' she added worriedly. 'Three letters arrived from Joe and she's put them in the envelope.'

'Oh, no.' Lilian groaned.

'Who knows, perhaps they'll help.'

Perhaps they would. Then again, perhaps they wouldn't.

They busied themselves putting the photographs of Joe into the frames. It hurt Lilian to see him with his usual broad smile but the children seemed to gain some comfort from the pictures. When asked if they wanted to visit Ida with their grandmother, they both insisted on taking their photographs.

Lilian read through Aunt Violet's letter then took the letters from Joe up to Maud. Her sister was sitting on the bed, staring out of the window at the buildings opposite.

'Mam's taken John and Rose next door to see Ida,' Lilian said.

'That's nice.'

'I took them shopping this morning,' she added. 'We bought a couple of photograph frames so they could each have a picture of their dad.'

Maud simply nodded.

'It seems to help them,' Lilian pushed on. 'They need to remember Joe, Maud. They can't just pretend he never existed.' You can't either, she added silently.

'Of course,' Maud agreed, not seeming to care one way or the other.

Lilian sat down on the bed opposite, not sure her legs could support her for much longer. The letters were clutched to her chest.

'And – er – Aunt Violet wrote. Three letters went to the farm for you – from Joe. They're here.'

'From Joe?' Maud's eyes were suddenly bright, dangerously bright.

'Yes.' Lilian's hand shook as she passed her the letters.

Maud looked at the official stamps on the letters and put them in date order. Then she stared at Joe's handwriting on each letter in turn.

Very slowly, Maud opened the first envelope. She read the letter carefully, with no flicker of emotion on her face. She read the second letter in exactly the same way, and then the third. Without saying a word, she returned the letters to their envelopes. Lilian sought desperately for something to say, then realized there was nothing. She couldn't imagine how it must feel to read words written by the man you loved, and to know you would never see him again. She got to her feet, thinking Maud might prefer to be left alone, when a huge shuddering sob stopped her in her tracks. She spun round to see Maud with her hands covering her face and painful sobs wracking her body.

'Maud, I'm so sorry. So very, very sorry.' Lilian threw herself down on the bed beside her and held her sister close.

Maud's sobs were silent, but they were shaking her whole body. Then with a loud, despairing cry, the tears came. There was nothing Lilian could do but hold her close. Maud cried and cried, almost choking as she said Joe's name over and over again.

'Have a good cry,' Lilian said gently, stroking her sister's hair as she held her. 'Joe was worth our tears.'

Maud cried until there were no tears left.

'I can't go on, Lil,' she gasped. 'I can't go on, not without Joe. I don't even want to. I don't want to face a whole lifetime without him. I just can't do it.'

'You can, Maud.'

Poor Maud was always so strong, so down-to-earth, so practical. Now she seemed like a child.

'You have to,' Lilian said soothingly. 'And you will. We'll all help you. Mam, Dad, me – we'll get you through it. You must go on, Maud, for Joe's sake. You have to be strong for him – take care of his children for him.'

'I can't,' Maud wailed, shaking her head.

'You can.'

'But I'm so frightened, Lil.'

Lilian could hardly believe this was Maud talking, Maud who had never been frightened of anything in her life. She was frightened now. She looked small and vulnerable, and Lilian knew that for the first time in their lives, she was going to have to be the one to look out for Maud, and not the other way round.

'I know, so am I, but you'll manage. I know you will.'

Lilian gazed at Joe's familiar handwriting on the envelopes. 'Joe died trying to make sure that you, John and Rose had a good future. You have to give his children that life, Maud. You owe him that much.'

Maud looked at her and wiped the remaining tears from her cheeks with the back of her hands.

'Since when did you get so wise, our Lilian?' she asked with a weak smile.

'Wise? No, not me. I'm as angry as hell. I can't bear to think of young men losing their lives and I'm damned if I'll see those lives lost in vain. We'll win this war, Maud. We'll win it for Joe, we'll win it for John and Rose – we will damn well win it!'

❧

~ *Chapter Eleven* ~

FEBRUARY 1941

Back at camp, Lilian threw herself into her work. It wasn't a conscious decision; she simply had to work to keep herself sane. When she wasn't busy, her mind insisted on dwelling on Joe, the state poor Maud was in, and the way her niece and nephew had to face life without their father. It was all too much for her. She hadn't cried. She couldn't cry; she was far too angry for tears.

She had a free afternoon. Normally, even a free hour was precious but she didn't know what to do with a whole afternoon. There was nowhere she wanted to go, and no one she wanted to see. She could write a letter to her mother or Sarah, she supposed, but the thought didn't appeal, mainly because she knew that when she looked at her writing pad, she would find the half-finished letter to Joe that would never be sent.

'Are you coming along to the NAAFI?' Prue asked, when Lilian went back to the hut.

'No, I don't feel like the canteen.' She didn't want company, not even Prue's.

'Come on, Lil,' Prue coaxed. 'We'll have a laugh. It will cheer you up.'

It wouldn't. Lilian didn't want to laugh; she only wanted to be left alone to try and make sense of a world where men like Joe were being killed every day.

He had been just twenty-five years old with his whole life ahead of him. It was so unfair.

'Thanks, Prue, but no. I'll catch up with you later.'

Before Prue could argue, Lilian grabbed her greatcoat and set off for the camp gates. She had no idea where she was going, but she had to get away from the camp and all her well-meaning friends who were determined to cheer her up. She appreciated their efforts, and certainly didn't want to alienate them by being such poor company but, just for a few days, she wanted to be left alone.

She saw Ben and David walking towards the gates from the other direction and her heart sank. At the moment, she didn't even want to see Ben.

'Lil!' He clasped her in his arms and all she could do was stand there like a statue. 'Coming to the NAAFI?'

'Maybe later.' She forced a bright smile. 'I'm going for a walk first.' In case he suggested accompanying her, she added quickly, 'I need some time alone.' Immediately the words were out, she wished she hadn't spoken.

'Lilian Penrose, you're getting to be a bore!'

She was about to apologise, then reminded herself that it hadn't been his brother-in-law who'd been killed...

'I'll see you later then.' He gave her a quick kiss on the cheek and strode off.

Later, Lilian decided that perhaps he had a point. When he'd accused her of being a bore, she had thought she'd detected something almost nasty in his tone, but she could see now that it had been his usual light-hearted teasing. True, Ben wasn't the one who'd lost his brother-in-law, but he'd lost friends – they all had. No matter how low they were feeling, they had to put on a cheerful face for the sake of everyone else.

By the time she met him in the pub that night, she was feeling better about things. He could always make her smile. It was what she needed, that and to feel special, which is how Ben made her feel.

As it turned out, he didn't make her smile. He spent most of the time playing cards, and Lilian joined a group of WAAFs.

'Let's walk back to the camp,' he suggested later. 'I've hardly seen anything of you all night.'

Lilian was delighted. She'd imagined they would join the others on the bus and have no time at all together.

It was a cold night, but it was clear, and a half moon helped them see where they were going. They said little as they walked but Ben had his arm tight around her waist.

'I'm glad we're not going on the bus with the others,' Lilian said.

'Me too. Two's company, and any more than that is a damn nuisance. I haven't had nearly enough of your company lately.' He stopped walking to kiss her. 'We've got plenty of time before you have to be back. Let's walk by the towpath.'

'In the dark?' Lilian protested, laughing. 'And what about the tunnel? It's creepy!'

'I'll hold you very tight,' he promised, grabbing her hand.

Her laughter hid her blushes. She would put up with the tunnel willingly so long as Ben held her close. She loved to feel his arms around her, to feel his lips on hers. She always had.

Ben walked quickly along the towpath, too quickly

for Lilian. A couple of times she tripped. Fortunately, he slowed to a more sensible pace when they reached the tunnel. Lilian vowed to keep very close to him.

They were in the middle when Ben stopped and spun her round so that her back was pressed again the wall. Her laughter echoed through the length of the tunnel.

'It's warmer here,' Ben murmured, pausing between words to drop kisses on her neck. 'We're sheltered from the wind.'

'What wind?' Again, Lilian burst out laughing.

Ben put his hands on her waist, and pressed his body against hers. Lilian appreciated the extra warmth and didn't mind when he unfastened the buttons of her coat. It felt good to feel his hands on her waist through her shirt as he kissed her. She linked her hands at the back of his neck and responded eagerly to his kiss. His tongue pushed between her teeth – and all the while his body was pressed hard against hers.

She felt his hand move downwards. He lifted her skirt, and his fingers dug into her thigh.

'Ben!' She tried to laugh, tried to push him back.

'Come on, Lil.' His hand moved higher.

'Ben – no!' He was too strong for her and she was suddenly struggling to breathe. 'Ben! Stop it!'

His breathing was heavy as he tugged on her shirt. The material tore and Lilian felt real fear.

'Please!'

She was fighting him, pummelling ineffectually at his chest, shouting, crying –

When he began fumbling with his trousers, she screamed.

'Christ!' He stepped back from her and cursed

loudly. 'You bitch! You're nothing but a bloody tease!'

Lilian stumbled away from him, hand against the wall in the darkness.

'I've wasted enough time on you, Lilian Penrose!' Ben yelled after her. 'Go and lead some other bloke on, why don't you?'

Lilian tried to shut out the sound of his voice as she stumbled on. He wasn't following, thank God, but she was taking no chances. Once out of the tunnel, she began to run, fastening her coat as she went.

Her shirt was torn – yes, she would worry about that. Safer to think about her uniform and push everything else from her mind until later.

What a fool she'd been. She'd had no idea Ben had wanted –

But she would worry about her uniform. She'd been a fool, but she'd been a lucky fool...

∽∾∽

The next day, Lilian was off-duty. She was walking out of the camp and met David at the gates.

'Going anywhere exciting?' he asked, and she shook her head.

'Just walking.'

'Me too.' He looked awkward. 'I'll go in the opposite direction if you like.'

She had to smile. A few weeks ago she would have evaded any kind of contact with him but now she saw no reason to avoid him.

'There's no need for that.' She looked up at him. 'I'd be glad of your company if you'd like to come with me. I'm feeling a bit low.'

'You're sure you wouldn't rather be alone?'

'Quite sure. I just don't want to be with people who expect me to be great company,' she tried to explain. 'With you – well, you don't –' She was floundering. 'You're different,' she ended lamely, surprised to feel herself blush with embarrassment.

If David noticed her discomfort, he didn't comment.

'Then I'd love to walk with you,' he said. 'Which way shall we go?'

'Towards the village?'

'Fine.'

They set off along the road. There had been a hard frost overnight but the sun had shone since dawn and it was still shining. It was perfect for walking, although Lilian was glad of the warmth from her greatcoat.

David had been right all along, she thought. From the start, he'd seen her as a flighty, careless, thoughtless, empty-headed female. And that's exactly what she'd been.

'I was sorry to hear about your brother-in-law, Lilian,' David said after a while.

Throughout the long, sleepless night, Lilian hadn't spared her sister a thought. She'd been too wrapped up in her own problems. She'd been haunted by the events in the tunnel. Every time she had closed her eyes, she'd felt Ben's hands on her body, felt his hot breath on her face. But what she had gone through with Ben was nothing to what poor Maud was going through. Maud had done nothing to deserve such pain.

'How's your sister coping?' he asked.

Lilian wasn't sure how to answer that. The truth was, she wasn't sure that Maud was coping.

'When I got home she was in a dreadful state – she wasn't talking about it, she wasn't talking about anything, she was ignoring the children, she wasn't eating –'

'That's understandable, I suppose.'

'I guess so. It was very worrying though,' Lilian said. 'She's coming back to Norfolk, to Uncle Jack and Aunt Violet's farm in a couple of days. Perhaps that will help. I don't know. I think the only thing that can really help is time.'

'I'm sure it will.'

They walked slowly, listening to the sound of the birds against the distant drone of aircraft.

'My father was killed in the last war,' David remarked.

'Oh, I'm sorry. I had no idea.' She knew nothing of David's life.

'I never knew him,' he said. 'He was killed a couple of weeks before I was born.'

'Your poor mother.'

'Yes.' He nodded. 'She had a tough time bringing me up alone. Financially she was well provided for, but in other ways – the grief and heartache she suffered made it very difficult for her.'

'Did she marry again?' Lilian was curious.

'No.'

'So you have no brothers and sisters? That's a shame.'

He smiled at that.

'I have enough cousins to make up for it. My mother was the youngest of twelve children so there were always aunts and uncles to help when I was a child.'

'It's not the same though, is it?' Lilian said sadly,

thinking of John and Rose facing life without their father.

'No. It's not the same.'

'Did you miss your father?' she asked.

'They say you can't miss what you've never had,' he replied thoughtfully, 'but yes, I missed him. Or rather, I suppose I missed a father.' He kicked a stone from their path. 'I wasn't alone. A lot of children lost their fathers to the war. But I have to confess that I was very envious of those children who had fathers to play football or cricket with. Every boy wants to grow up just like his father, I guess, and uncles aren't quite the same.'

The thought came to Lilian that he would make a good father. Then she realized that for all she knew, he might already be a father. Until this afternoon, she had known nothing of his personal life. He didn't speak of it often.

'Is there anyone waiting for you, David?' she asked curiously. 'I mean a wife or girlfriend?'

'No, no one.' He smiled suddenly, and his whole face seemed softer. 'Do you realize that's the first time you've called me David without prompting?'

'Sorry.' She smiled a little self consciously, surprised that he seemed so pleased about it.

'There's no one in my life,' he went on seriously, 'because I couldn't bear to put anyone through what my mother went through. When my father was killed, her life ended. By all accounts, she was full of fun before then, but all I've known is a woman whose life had come to an end. Her life was empty, meaningless – over before it had really begun. She never remarried, never really recovered.'

Lilian shivered. Was that how it would be for Maud? Oh, she hoped not.

'Before this war is over, Lilian, there are going to be a lot more in the same position as your sister, I fear. The facts aren't pleasant, but they have to be faced. I may not be here tomorrow or next week so I can't afford to get involved with anyone.'

'But you can't live your life like that,' she argued. 'You don't plan to meet people or fall in love with them – it just happens.'

'Not if you don't allow it to.'

That's where they differed, Lilian supposed. David simply wouldn't let himself meet a girl and fall in love. His head would always rule his heart. Lilian knew she would always be ruled by her heart. Good or bad, right or wrong – and in view of what had happened last night, it was clearly wrong – that was the way she was.

Without thinking, they stopped at the entrance to a field and leaned on a wooden gate.

'Wouldn't you like someone to be with, though?' she asked. 'Someone to – well, just to be with?'

'Of course.' He lifted his leg to rest his foot on the bottom rung of the gate. 'It would be great to land my plane, after being through God knows what, and know that someone who cared for me was waiting. And yes, I'd love to plan the future, talk of hopes and dreams with someone who cared, someone who understood me. Who wouldn't?' He turned and faced her, looking a little self-conscious. 'But it's out of the question. I think of my mother, and I think of your sister – I couldn't put anyone through that.'

Lilian felt he was wrong; she knew he was wrong.

'I don't agree,' she said. 'I'm sure that Maud – I know

at the moment she probably wants to die – but I'm sure she wouldn't have had things any differently. She loved Joe. She wouldn't have traded the years she had with him for anything.'

'I'm sure my mother felt exactly the same about my father, but any girl who got involved with me might not have years. They might only have days.' He smiled suddenly. 'Anyway, it's all academic because there's no one special in my life.'

Nor in her own, Lilian thought sadly. First she had imagined herself in love with Roy Walker. Then she had fallen head over heels in love with Ben. She hadn't loved either of them, not really. She'd fallen for their good looks and their charm, and then discovered, too late, that Roy was a lazy good-for-nothing, and Ben – well, she knew all too well what Ben was like!

'We're almost at the village,' David remarked. 'If you can face walking the extra mile, I'll buy you tea. Now there's an offer you can't refuse.'

Lilian laughed.

'Thank you. I'm sure I can manage the extra mile. Oh, and I'll warn you, I'm starving.'

It was true. She'd hardly eaten anything since she had heard about Joe but, suddenly, she was hungry.

She had to forget last night. She'd been lucky to escape with only a torn shirt, but at least she'd escaped – and with her pride intact. No one, especially Ben, would take away her dignity or her pride. She'd learnt her lesson the hard way and now it was over. Best forgotten.

They walked on in a companionable silence into the village and to the tea rooms. It was the first time Lilian had been inside since she had gone there with Maud.

What a strange afternoon that had been – the same afternoon she had seen Ben with the pretty girl on his arm. It was also the afternoon that Maud had told her about the strange feeling she'd had at the station, when she'd waved Joe off and believed she would never see him again. That was too painful to think about now.

She tried to push her thoughts away as David ordered tea, sandwiches and cakes for them, but it wasn't easy. Visions of Maud and Joe at the station, saying what had turned out to be their final goodbye, haunted her. She wondered if Joe had had a similar feeling.

'I thought you were hungry,' David teased as she picked at a sandwich.

'Sorry. I was, but –' She shrugged.

'That's OK.' He looked at her pale face. 'Would you like to leave?'

'No.' Given the choice, she probably would, but she could see he was hungry and it didn't seem fair. She was touched he had asked though. 'No, I'm fine. Just not hungry.'

She finished her sandwich, drank her tea and ate a cake. She immediately wished she hadn't. It had a very odd taste due to the lack of butter and sugar, no doubt, and made her feel a little nauseous. Or perhaps it wasn't the cake; she hadn't felt right for days, well, not since Joe –

She was pleased when it was time to leave.

'Sorry I'm not very good company,' she remarked quietly as they walked out of the village and back towards the camp.

'No one would expect you to be. In fact,' he added

grimly, 'I'm surprised any of us are good company. These are difficult times, Lilian.'

She nodded. They were difficult. Until now, she simply hadn't realized just how difficult.

'I can't believe I was so naive,' she confessed. 'When I volunteered for the WAAF, it was a big adventure. I thought it would be great fun. I can't believe I was so stupid. I honestly never thought it would be like this. Every time I go home, someone else I know has been killed. Bombs are being dropped on the country every night –'

'Yes, I know.' He walked with his hands deep in the pockets of his greatcoat.

'I was in the middle of writing to Joe when – when I heard he'd been killed,' she said shakily. 'Maud told me he liked getting my letters, that they made him smile. I haven't looked at the letter again, but it's still there, half-written. It was full of nonsense – silly stories that I thought might amuse him.' She could feel her hands trembling in her pockets. 'I can't believe I'll never finish it, that he'll never read it, that he'll never come home.'

'I'm so sorry, Lilian.'

'It's Maud and the children I feel sorry for,' Lilian went on, her voice barely audible now. 'I took the children out shopping and bought them a photograph frame each so they could carry a picture of their father. I told them they could talk to him whenever they wanted. But they can't, can they? They can never talk to him again.'

A huge, gulping sob almost choked her and she put a hand to her mouth. She hadn't cried for Joe and she wasn't about to start now – not in front of David. It was unthinkable.

'I'm sorry –' She swallowed back another sob. 'I hate this war. God, I hate it so much!'

'I'm so sorry, Lilian,' he said again, but his voice sounded as if it was coming from a long way off.

'Not Joe,' she whispered brokenly. 'Not Joe. He was so – Oh, I just can't bear it.'

Her legs refused to support her and she dropped to her knees with her hands covering her face. The painful sobs shook through her body until she was struggling to breathe.

David went down on his knees so that his face was level with hers. She tried to speak, to apologise, if nothing else, but she was too choked up. His arms went round her and he gathered her close as she broke down completely. She cried and cried, a noisy display that she knew she would be ashamed of, but she could do nothing to stop it. It was as if some safety valve had been released and she had lost all control.

'It's OK, Lilian.' David's voice was soothing and there was no hint of embarrassment; it was as if he was quite used to women breaking down in front of him. 'Have a good cry. Let it all out and you'll feel better. I promise.'

Her tear-soaked face was buried inside his coat, and even when the tears had stopped she was far too embarrassed to move her head and look at him. She wished she could stay in the safety of his arms for ever.

He held her long after she had stopped crying, until the only sign of her distress was a deep shudder that ran through her body every now and again.

'Feeling better?' He lifted her head and used his fingers to brush away the last of her tears.

'I'm sorry. I don't usually –'

'Don't be,' he cut her off. 'It happens to us all – you're not alone.' He helped her to her feet. 'Do you feel able to walk?'

'Yes. Yes, of course.' But she couldn't look at him; she was far too ashamed.

'Come on then.' He took her hand and pulled her arm through his.

And that was how Lilian walked back to the camp, with her arm through David's and her fingers clinging to the fabric of his greatcoat...

∾◦∽

Ben and a crowd were playing cards that evening, but David didn't join them. Instead, he carried his drink to a table in the corner of the pub's lounge and sat alone. He couldn't face Ben; he felt too guilty about the time he'd spent with Lilian that afternoon. She was Ben's girl and he shouldn't have taken advantage of her vulnerability by asking her to have tea with him. She'd been embarrassed by her uncharacteristic display of emotion and David knew that Ben should have been the one to offer her comfort.

Not that he had been able to offer any comfort, David thought grimly. What could anyone possibly say? Nothing.

His heart had gone out to her though. At first, her determination to enjoy life had irritated him. He'd thought that, in Lilian's eyes, this war was just a laugh, something that enabled her to escape her somewhat humdrum everyday life. That's just what it had been, too. She had admitted as much that afternoon. She had great strengths though, and it was unfair that the harshness of life should have been brought home to her so drastically. She clearly came from a close family and anything that hurt the family hurt Lilian.

It pained David to see her struggling to cope with life. She was a hard worker, very conscientious, and always had a smile for everyone. It grieved him that the smile was no longer there. He only hoped she would be able to bounce back.

Ben wandered over to him and David wished he'd had the foresight to pretend he'd fallen asleep.

'Do you think we'll be on Ops tomorrow?' Ben asked, sitting down in the chair opposite.

'I've no idea,' David replied. 'All we can do is wait and see. The weather's supposed to improve but –' He shrugged.

'Fancy a game of cards?'

'No, thanks.'

'Did I see you go off with Lilian this afternoon?'

'Yes.' David felt uncomfortable. But there was no law against him going for a walk with Lilian.

'Where did you go?'

'Only into the village.'

'Did she say – well, was everything all right?'

'Yes.' David frowned. He wasn't at all sure what Ben was driving at. 'Well, she's upset about her brother-in-law, naturally.'

'I suppose so.' Ben seemed almost relieved. 'But it's more than that. She's changing. Even before her brother-in-law was killed, she'd changed. She might be the prettiest WAAF on the camp, but I want to have fun while I can.' He gave the cards another shuffle. 'Are you sure you don't want a game?'

'Quite sure,' David replied irritably. How the devil could Ben think of cards when Lilian was so upset?

David suspected Ben didn't really care about Lilian. He liked to be seen with the prettiest WAAF from the camp by his side, but he didn't really care about her feelings. Lilian deserved more than that. Any girl deserved more than that.

Ben went back to the crowd and David leaned back in his seat and closed his eyes. He thought of the afternoon, how it had felt to hold Lilian in his arms, and how it had felt to walk back to the camp with her hand clutching his sleeve.

His feelings disturbed him. Lilian was very vulnerable at the moment and would have reacted in exactly the same way no matter who she had been with. The fact that it had been him would have meant nothing to her. Just as it should mean nothing to him. Perhaps they were all feeling a little vulnerable at the moment...

∽∾

Lying in bed that night, Lilian could make no sense of anything at all. She kept thinking of the afternoon and none of it seemed very real. She'd enjoyed the walk into the village with David; it was only when they reached the tea rooms that she had started thinking about Joe. Why she had suddenly gone to pieces, in front of David of all people, she had no idea. She wasn't the type to get hysterical; she never had been. Any tears she had shed in her life had only been witnessed by the four walls of her room. Even now, the thought of her behaviour brought a glow of embarrassment to her face. Whatever must David have thought of her?

But it was no wonder she was behaving strangely. First Joe, then Ben –

Whatever David thought, however, she knew he would never make fun of her or tell anyone else. She knew, had known for some time, that he was a man who could be utterly trusted.

The thought flitted through her mind that perhaps it was because she'd been with David that she'd felt able to let down her guard. She felt safe with him these days, and had felt very safe indeed clasped in his arms. Not for the first time that evening, she shivered at the thought. Even now, she could still feel his warmth, could still smell him. The power of the memory shocked her.

She knew she wasn't behaving very rationally at the moment and, in the light of day, perhaps she would see things more clearly. But still she couldn't stop thinking about David. Not that there was much to think about. She knew nothing of his background. Oh, she could tell from the way he talked that his upbringing had been very different to her own. Ben had once said something about David going to Cambridge University. Perhaps his father had been wealthy; perhaps his mother was wealthy. Whatever – Lilian came from a very different walk of life. She forced David from her mind and thought instead of Maud. How was she feeling? In the same situation, Lilian didn't think she would cope at all.

Her mind leapt back to the days when Joe and Maud had been courting. The whole family had taken to Joe immediately because he'd fitted in so easily. He'd shown their father plenty of respect, had flattered their mother, and positively doted on Maud.

The memories brought tears to her eyes and she let them fall...

∽✌∽

~ *Chapter Twelve* ~

MARCH 1941

Lilian got ready for the dance, and tried to straighten the seams of her stockings without letting her rough fingers damage them. She thought back to that other dance when she'd spent the evening with Ben for the very first time. It shocked her to look back. It was difficult to believe they were into the spring of 1941, and it was even more difficult to believe just how much she'd changed in that time.

Thinking back even further, she remembered her excitement at going to the WAAF recruitment office. The most important thing on her mind then had been escaping the watchful eye of her parents and not having to share a bedroom with Maud. Since then, she thought with amusement, she had shared bedrooms or huts with girls from every walk of life. These days, it would be a taste of heaven to crawl into a warm, comfortable bed and chat to Maud.

Following that visit to the recruitment office, she had learned how to make a bed, fill in endless forms, and salute everyone just in case they were important. She had learned how to drive, could recite the daily vehicle inspection by heart and knew the number of every military transport form. She had thought herself in love with Ben, danced with him till dawn – and learned the truth about him. Friends had been made and lost. She had lost her brother-in-law and seen the effect that had had on her sister. She had seen the damage done to her home town by German bombers...

It was no wonder she had changed.

Strangely, however, no one else seemed to have changed. Prue was exactly the same girl who had driven up to the camp gates in her car, and Ben was the same happy-go-lucky man she had been drawn to.

'I'm ready,' she declared. 'Shall we go, Prue?'

'Sorry?'

'You're miles away,' Lilian told her. 'Again!'

'I know. Sorry.'

'Is something wrong?' Lilian asked curiously. On the surface, Prue was as bright and bubbly as ever, but Lilian had spoken to her several times during the day only to have to repeat herself because Prue had drifted off into a world of her own. 'Is something bothering you, Prue?'

'Not really. Well –' She shrugged. 'I don't know, Lil. I had a letter from Charlie's parents. He's been wounded – he's in hospital in Portsmouth.'

'Wounded? How bad is he?'

'That's just it,' Prue told her. 'I don't know. According to his parents, he didn't want me to be told about it.' She looked at Lilian, her eyes full of hurt. 'Why would he say that, Lil?'

'I've no idea. I suppose he didn't want you worrying. That means it can't be too bad, doesn't it? Presumably, if he didn't want you to be told, he's going to be fit again soon and back with his regiment. If it was bad, he wouldn't be able to keep it from you, would he?'

'I suppose you're right.' But Prue was worried.

'What exactly did his parents say?' Lilian asked.

Prue took the letter from her coat pocket.

'It's from his mother. She says "My dearest Prue. Bad news I'm afraid. Charlie has been wounded and flown to a hospital in Portsmouth. We've heard from him but he was very vague about his injuries. He said he didn't want us to tell you but, having thought things through, I didn't think that was fair. I hope he will forgive me. His father and I are going to visit him this weekend and I'll be able to tell you more then." That's it. She goes on to talk about life at home.' Prue folded the sheet of paper and returned it to the envelope. 'Why wouldn't he want me told, Lil?'

'Because he knows you'd worry,' Lilian said firmly, 'which is exactly what you are doing. If he can write to his parents, he can't be too bad, can he? Try not to worry, Prue. You'll soon know more.'

Prue nodded, but didn't look. Lilian wasn't surprised. It seemed very strange indeed that Charlie didn't want her told. If, however, he planned to be back in action soon, there would be no point in worrying Prue unnecessarily. Yes, Lilian was sure that was it.

'Come on – let's go,' she said brightly.

The village hall was crowded when they arrived. Lilian couldn't help smiling to herself as she saw a crowd of WAAFs trying to attract the attention of three airmen. The WAAFs, Lilian knew, had spent an age trying to make themselves look presentable, and it wasn't easy – with no make-up to be had, women were having to be very inventive. The WAAFs' lips were red with beetroot juice and there was more gravy browning on their legs than there was in the canteen.

Already, the music was loud and couples were dancing. Times were difficult and everyone seemed to have someone to worry about, but given the opportunity, people still knew how to enjoy themselves.

She spotted Ben in the centre of the dance floor, a tall brunette draped all over him. When the music ended, he came over to Lilian.

It was obvious he'd already had a lot to drink.

'Well, well, well.' He swayed on his feet. 'If it's not the lovely Lilian. Looking for some other sucker, are you?'

His voice was loud; everyone would hear him.

'We've nothing to say to each other, Ben.' Lilian spoke quietly and calmly, but her face was hot with embarrassment.

'You might not. I've got plenty!'

Refusing to have a scene in public, Lilian started to walk away.

'Girls like you deserve all they get,' he shouted after her. 'You're nothing but a tease. One of these days, you'll find yourself stringing along the wrong kind of bloke!'

Lilian kept walking. She was aware that every pair of eyes in the place was on her, but she walked with her head held high, till she was in front of David. It had felt natural to go to him, as if he was the only person she could go to, but she turned her gaze to his, suddenly uncertain of his reaction. Was he going to tell her what he thought of her? Would he say she deserved all she got?

'Let's get a drink.' He took her arm and, as they walked to the bar, people carried on with whatever they'd been doing before Ben's outburst had claimed their attention.

He ordered their drinks and Lilian knew there would be no comment from David. He was willing to accept her for what she was. And she was fine. She felt dangerously close to tears, but that was due more to David's quiet acceptance than anything Ben had said.

'Come on,' David said, picking up their drinks. 'There are a couple of free seats over there.'

Lilian was grateful to sit down. David sat beside her and took a drink from his glass.

'Did you get that car going this afternoon?'

Lilian's heart swelled with gratitude. He wasn't even going to mention the scene with Ben.

'Eventually.' She smiled. 'I'm afraid my language wasn't very ladylike when you walked past. I had to collect the CO in it and I thought the confounded thing would never start. I took him into town and didn't dare stop the engine.'

He laughed.

'You never have much luck with the CO, do you?'

'I don't, do I? Prue, the lucky devil, never seems to get landed with him.' She was thoughtful for a moment. 'David, I probably shouldn't tell you this but Prue's had a letter from her boyfriend's mother.' She told him exactly what the woman had written. 'What do you think that can mean? Why wouldn't Charlie want Prue to know he'd been wounded?'

'Well, I don't know. I suppose it would depend on what his injuries were. If he's been disfigured for instance –'

Lilian shuddered at his words. She hadn't thought of that.

'I honestly couldn't say, Lilian.'

'I know. I was just curious as to what you thought. It's a bit of a puzzle and it's worrying Prue to death.'

'I'm sure it is.' He ran a finger thoughtfully along his moustache. 'I suppose he simply doesn't want her to be upset. And if that's the case, his injuries can't be too bad – he'll probably be better before she knows anything more about it.'

'Yes. That's what I thought.'

Ben walked past them, but thankfully, his mind was no longer on Lilian. He had his arm round the waist of a blonde. All Lilian felt was sympathy for the girl...

~~~

Maud was looking forward to seeing Lilian. She was curious, too. Lilian had telephoned from the camp but she hadn't given much away – only that a friend, David, had offered her a lift. Maud had asked if David had stepped into Ben's shoes. But Lilian had simply laughed and said, 'Don't you start. No, David's just a friend.' Maud was still curious.

The children were excited about seeing Lilian too, which was why they and their mother were walking along the road to meet her.

It had rained continuously for what seemed like weeks but had in fact only been three days, but today the sun was warm on their backs. The ground, flooded yesterday, was already drying out. Everything looked fresh and green; everything smelt fresh too. Joe would have liked it on the farm, Maud thought. He might have been brought up in Newcastle-upon-Tyne, on the edge of the big river, but he'd always hankered for the countryside. The peace and quiet would have suited him. He'd never been the ambitious type and would have been happy to grow their food, keep a few animals and live a simple life.

Sometimes she felt he was with them, walking along

the tree-shaded lanes. How she wished he was. The pain had receded now, and even the numbness was beginning to wear off, but Maud doubted if she would ever know real happiness again. She'd been lucky, she supposed. At least she and Joe had spent a few years together and she did have two wonderful children from their marriage. But when they had said 'till death us do part', neither of them had realized just how soon they would be parted...

John was first to hear the approaching car and the three of them stepped onto the verge and waited for it to appear. It was a large, black car and, sure enough, it slowed to a stop beside them. The door was flung open and out jumped Lilian with hugs for them all.

The driver was a handsome, smiling man, Maud noticed.

'Oh, sorry,' Lilian said belatedly. 'This is David. David – my sister, Maud, my beautiful niece, Rose, and this little horror is my nephew, John.'

'I'm very pleased to meet you,' David said, and Maud was quite taken aback by the posh accent. 'I've heard a lot about you.'

John, his manners completely forgotten, said eagerly, 'Can we have a ride?'

'John!' Maud scolded, embarrassed.

David simply laughed.

'Of course you may. So long as your mother agrees.' He looked to Maud.

'Well, yes, if you don't mind.' Heavens, he was well-spoken. First Prue, now David – it seemed her sister had a knack for befriending the well-to-do.

They piled in. John sat in the front alongside David while Maud, Lilian and Rose sat in the back.

'Fancy you being able to drive, our Lilian.' Maud still couldn't quite believe that.

'Lilian drives huge trucks,' David pointed out with amusement, 'so this is very small-fry to her. And,' he added with a chuckle, 'if this breaks down, she'll know how to fix it.'

'I wouldn't count on that!' Lilian laughed.

Maud was more intrigued than ever. Lilian and David might be just friends but they seemed to have a very easy relationship.

John loved cars and was enjoying himself thoroughly. This would be the third ride he'd had in his life, Maud calculated. Rose wasn't so sure; she said she liked cars simply because she had to go along with whatever John said, but Maud could tell she wasn't too keen. She suspected Rose would be happy when they reached the farm.

Maud wasn't sorry when their journey came to an end either; it was hot and a bit cramped inside the car.

'Come and meet everyone,' Lilian suggested to David when he switched off the engine.

'Oh, no,' he protested. 'I couldn't possibly intrude.'

'You won't be,' Maud assured him. 'Aunt Violet was hoping you'd call in.' Maud wasn't the only one who wanted to see Lilian's 'friend'. 'She's prepared sandwiches and scones especially for the occasion.'

'Come on, David,' Lilian insisted. 'You don't have anything better to do, do you?'

'Well, no. I had the chance of a vehicle and thought you'd appreciate the lift, that's all. If you're sure I won't be a nuisance –'

'Quite sure,' Lilian said emphatically.

Uncle Jack was visiting a neighbour's farm but Aunt

Violet was in her element, Maud realized with amusement. She loved fussing over children and tended to treat any male visitors in exactly the same manner. Even had he wanted to, and Maud suspected he didn't, David wouldn't have been allowed to refuse the scones with butter and thick strawberry jam. Nor would he have been allowed to refuse Aunt Violet's legendary lemonade.

Both Lilian and David tucked in hungrily and Maud thought again how lucky she was to live on the farm where food was fresh and fairly plentiful.

'Come and show me these hens of yours, Rose,' Lilian suggested when she had cleared the plates away.

Rose was delighted. The hens were definitely her responsibility and she loved it when people showed an interest. They left Aunt Violet in the kitchen and set off.

John chattered to David the whole time, and Maud couldn't help wondering if he missed having a man in his life, although, even if Joe had been alive, he would have been many miles away from his son.

'John,' she said at last. 'Give David a rest. You're talking far too much.'

'Not at all,' David said. 'He's a very bright boy,' he added. 'You should be proud of him.'

Maud smiled at the compliment. She was proud of John; she was proud of both children.

Later, when Lilian and the children were chasing a hen, Maud found herself alone with David.

'I was so sorry to hear about your husband,' he said quietly. 'Lilian told me all about it.'

'Thank you.' There was little else she could say, although she was touched he'd said anything, and that he had waited until the children were out of earshot.

'There are a lot of women in my position though.'

'Yes,' he agreed sadly, 'but I'm sure that thought is of little consolation.'

'None at all.'

She knew she was luckier than a lot of women – she had Joe's children, she could stay on the farm for as long as she chose, she ate well – but at the moment none of that was any consolation. If she could spend just one more night in Joe's arms…

'I gather you and Lilian are very close,' David remarked, and Maud had to laugh.

'I'm not so sure about that. As children we fought like cat and dog – we still do sometimes. Lilian has driven me mad many, many times. We're like chalk and cheese – and I suppose the six-year gap in our ages hasn't helped. She's always seemed very young and immature to me. But lately – yes, we have grown close.'

She had to ask.

'What about you and Lilian?' She feigned interest in the grass at their feet. 'Are you close?'

He was so long in answering that she looked up at him, wondering if the question had annoyed him.

'I don't know how to answer that,' he said at last. 'Lilian has driven me mad on occasion, too. Lately, though –' his gaze strayed to where Lilian was laughing at the children's antics '– yes, we have become good friends.'

Maud didn't quite know what to make of that. David sounded as if he hadn't thought about his relationship with her sister until now. He sounded almost surprised to think of them as good friends. And yet they seemed so easy with each other.

'Lilian would drive a saint mad,' was all she said, and

he laughed.

Maud would have liked some time to quiz her sister, but there was no opportunity. She wanted to know how Lilian felt about David, and where Ben figured in the grand scheme of things, if at all.

Given their two very different personalities and backgrounds, Maud would have thought David and Lilian's an unlikely friendship, but there was no denying that they appeared extremely relaxed in each other's company. Maud hoped they were – or would become – more than friends. She liked David. The children liked him too. Rose didn't normally take to strangers easily but she was soon at ease with him. John thought he was wonderful; he was always fascinated to see the planes flying overhead and it thrilled him to think that now, when he waved at them, David might be waving back at him. Even as he came to terms with his father's death, John was too young to realize the dangers involved. Maud could see that David was acutely aware of those dangers and, unless she was mistaken, even Lilian was beginning to realize that this was no game they were playing.

∽∾∽

David was thoughtful as he drove them back to the camp. He had thanked Violet for her hospitality and thanked Maud and the children for their company, but he hadn't been able to express just how delightful it had been.

'I really enjoyed the afternoon,' David remarked.

'So you said.' She yawned lazily. 'I'm glad you enjoyed it.'

'I did – thoroughly.' He still couldn't find the words.

For the first time in what seemed an age, he hadn't felt awkward and out of place. He had almost felt like part of the family. 'Thanks again for inviting me.'

'Thank you – you saved me a bike ride.'

'Maud's fine – don't you think?'

'I do.' Lilian smiled at him. 'I was proud of her. The thought of Joe is with her all the time – I know that because it's with me all the time – and it would be so easy for her to feel sorry for herself. She was good company, wasn't she, all things considered?'

'She was.'

'And she's marvellous with the children.' Lilian chuckled to herself. 'Even when she's been at her most awful, and believe me, over the years she's been unbearable at times, I've always marvelled at what a good mother she is. Far better than I would ever be.'

David smiled at that. He couldn't imagine Lilian as a mother. Her poor child would probably be taken to a shop and forgotten as something more pressing caught her attention. Any child would be lucky to survive.

'What are you smiling at?' she asked curiously.

'The thought of you as a mother.'

'Frightening, isn't it.' She grinned at him.

'Terrifying!'

As they laughed together, David couldn't help thinking about Maud's question. He and Lilian had somehow, and David wasn't sure how, become friends. They weren't close, David wouldn't allow it, but he had to confess that he looked forward to spending time in her company. It was clear Maud had been hoping to hear they were more than friends, too.

'What time do you have to be back, David?'

'Mmmm? Oh, I've another hour yet. You?'

'A couple of hours. Do you fancy a walk?'

'Well, yes.' The question surprised him, but the idea of a walk was appealing. He was in no rush to get back. It was bliss to pretend, for a little while longer, that it was just another sunny Sunday and the country was at peace. 'Yes, I'd like that.'

He found a lay-by and parked the car. Before he'd even switched off the engine, Lilian was out of the car and marching along the road towards a small wood. He had to stride out quickly to catch her up.

'I wonder if this path goes right through the wood,' she said, racing on ahead. 'Oh, look – buttercups!'

He smiled at her childlike delight.

'We don't see many buttercups in Sunderland,' she told him apologetically.

'It's a beautiful spot.'

'It is.' She bent to pick a flower. 'What's that game –' She lifted the buttercup and held it beneath his chin. 'Oh, you like butter.'

'I do.' He laughed. 'But how can you tell?'

'Don't they say that if you can see the yellow reflected on the skin, that person likes butter?'

'I've no idea!'

'I've probably got it wrong.' She walked on, twirling the buttercup in her fingers.

For a while, David stopped pretending. It wasn't just another sunny Sunday; the country was at war, people were getting slaughtered and the country was being bombed to the ground. But if they hadn't been at war –

He wondered how he would have felt then. He wondered what he would have said. He wondered what he would have done. Would he have watched Lilian race ahead of him with her buttercup? Or would he have chased after her, reached for her hand and held it tightly in his own? Would he have kissed her beneath the shade of the tall chestnut trees?

His thoughts shocked him and he tried to push them aside. If there hadn't been a war on, he wouldn't even have met Lilian given the differences in their backgrounds.

But he had met her. And the more time he spent with her, the more she invaded his thoughts when he wasn't with her. He would love to be able to take her hand, to kiss her on the lips, and to tell her he loved her –

'Damn and blast!'

Lilian turned around at his outburst.

'Are you all right, David?'

'Yes – fine, thanks. I just tripped on this bramble. Sorry.'

She chuckled and carried on walking.

Tell her he loved her indeed! He didn't love her, couldn't possibly love her. It was out of the question.

∽✦∽

❧ *Chapter Thirteen* ❧

MAY 1941

Dorothy could hardly wait for the train to pull into the station. It seemed an age since she'd seen Lilian. They'd exchanged lots of letters, and it never failed to amaze Dorothy what a good letter writer her daughter was, but words on paper were a poor substitute.

When the train finally arrived, dozens of people got off. Dorothy hadn't told Lilian she would meet the train and had visions of them missing each other. Then she saw her and her heart melted. Lilian looked so grown-up, and far too attractive for her own good in her WAAF uniform. Had she grown up, Dorothy wondered, or was it just the uniform? Men, both young and old, couldn't resist looking at her daughter.

'Lilian!' Dorothy called out, waving her arms.

A huge grin lit up Lilian's face and she ran, dodging the crowd, to give Dorothy a rib-crushing hug.

'Oh, it's good to be home, Mam!'

'It's good to have you home. I really miss having you girls about.' Dorothy held her at arm's length. 'You do look smart in your uniform, our Lilian.'

'It's improving,' Lilian said with a wry smile, 'but the underwear – you have never seen anything like it. The harvest festivals – well!'

'Harvest what?'

'That's what the thick winter knickers have been

nicknamed. Harvest festivals – all is safely gathered in.'

'Lilian!' With a splutter of outraged laughter, Dorothy slipped her arm through Lilian's and they walked out of the station. It was good to have her home; she could always be relied on to raise a smile. Dorothy had a loving mother-daughter relationship with Maud, whereas she and Lilian were more like best friends.

'Have you seen Maud, love?'

'Yes. I called at the farm with a friend – she's fine, Mam. She's coping well. Honestly.'

Dorothy was relieved. Maud had sounded reasonably settled in her letters but Dorothy didn't trust them. It was far too easy to put on a brave face in a letter. Maud's were different to Lilian's – like well-written essays, whereas Lilian's were like a chat.

'Who was the friend? Prue?'

'No. One of the pilots – David.' Lilian shifted her kit bag, making it easier to carry. 'So what's the news from here, Mam?'

Dorothy was far more interested in hearing about this David, but she didn't press the point. If there was one thing Lilian couldn't do, it was keep quiet about things. Dorothy guessed she would hear all about him in time.

'None of it's good, love,' Dorothy replied thoughtfully. 'Sometimes it seems that every family will have to lose someone before this war is over. You know Elsie Blackwell? She works in the tobacconist's. Well, she's lost two sons now. Her husband died a few years back. Oh, and Roy Walker – you'd have been at school with him, wouldn't you?'

'Roy? What's happened to him?'

Dorothy noted the pallor in her daughter's face and cursed her own stupidity. It wasn't easy for anyone to hear about all these deaths. It would be doubly difficult for Lilian to hear about the deaths of young lads she'd been at school with.

'He's dead, love,' Dorothy said gently. 'Killed in action – his mam got the same telegram Maud had.'

Lilian said nothing but unless Dorothy was very much mistaken, there was a shimmer of tears in her eyes as she stared determinedly at the buildings they were walking past. Dorothy was surprised; she hadn't even been sure Lilian knew Roy Walker, so she couldn't have known that Lilian had been specially fond of the lad. Perhaps it was simply too much to hear of yet another boy of her own age being killed.

'How were the children when you saw Maud?' Dorothy asked, swiftly changing the subject.

'Fine.' There was a slight catch in Lilian's voice. 'No – they were better than fine. They seem as happy as Larry, Mam. I don't suppose they can really take in what's happened to their dad.'

'That's probably just as well.'

'Yes.'

They caught the bus and Dorothy noticed that Lilian was unusually quiet. She couldn't help thinking that the news of young Roy Walker had shaken her. The newspapers were full of reports telling them the enemy casualties were much higher than their own, but that didn't help. It didn't bring back Joe, or Roy Walker, or any of the other young lads this war had claimed. It wasn't the done thing to sympathise, but Dorothy knew that German wives and mothers must be grieving just the same and, just like John and Rose, German children were having to face life without their fathers.

'At least we're home before the blackout,' Dorothy

remarked as they walked up to the house.

'Yes.' Lilian smiled at that. 'Any more casualties of the blackout, Mam?'

'No, but Fred Lampitt seems to get home quicker in the dark.'

They both laughed. Fred Lampitt was fond of a drink and the family had watched him weaving his way along the road – one step forward followed by three steps back – many times. It was fortunate that he was a good-natured drunk because all the children hooted with laughter when they saw him staggering along.

It was a relief to get home. At least the house was still standing, Dorothy thought. Several houses in the next street had had their windows shattered by bombs. So far, they'd been lucky.

She made a cup of tea and was pleased to see Lilian looking more relaxed.

'Any news from Jane?' Lilian asked.

'I had a letter from her the day before yesterday.' Dorothy reached up and took it from the shelf. 'Here – read it for yourself. Her letters always make entertaining reading.'

That was a lie. Lately, her friend's letters had been far from entertaining. But that was only when you read between the lines and sensed the pain and fear.

Lilian read the letter, a smile on her face. When she laughed aloud, Dorothy guessed she'd reached the part where Jane had written exactly what she would like to do to Hitler.

'She's such fun, isn't she?' Lilian said. 'She's not going to let the war get her down?'

No – it wasn't the war that was getting her friend down.

'She's always loved some cause to fight, and she'll enjoy planning her revenge on Hitler. In any case, she's always been a softie for a man in uniform and she seems to see plenty of those.'

'Mam!' Lilian exploded into laughter.

It was good to hear Lilian laugh. Not so long ago, it had been an almost constant sound in the house, like background noise, and Dorothy missed it.

'Your dad's really looking forward to seeing you,' Dorothy said. 'You'll cheer him up.'

'Does he need cheering up?' Lilian's face filled with concern.

'No – no more than the rest of us. But he's tired, Lil. He's not getting any younger and he's finding it a strain working such long hours seven days a week.'

There was no point in worrying Lilian unnecessarily, but Dorothy was concerned about Clive. There was nothing she could put her finger on – he simply seemed out of sorts. He was constantly tired, but it was more than that. He was edgy and tended to snap at her for no good reason. Dorothy tried to put it down to the long hours he was working, but she wasn't convinced. But there was no point mentioning anything to Lilian, and having his youngest daughter in the house again, if only briefly, would work wonders.

'How's life on the camp?' she asked Lilian. 'You haven't managed to crash any of those trucks yet?'

'Not yet.' Lilian grinned impishly. 'But I almost put the Commanding Officer in the ditch.'

'No!'

'Yes! I was rounding a corner – probably going too fast – and I met a tractor taking up most of the road. I swerved to avoid it and skidded on a muddy verge. It was touch and go for a moment.' She laughed. 'The CO said "That was a close call" and off we went again.'

While Dorothy prepared the vegetables for the evening meal, Lilian told her dozens of similar stories from the camp. Dorothy loved to hear of their antics. She guessed she was getting a very colourful view of life, and knew there was a lot of hard, dirty work involved, but Lilian only seemed to remember the amusing incidents.

'Prue had some bad news though,' Lilian said seriously. 'Her boyfriend, Charlie – have I told you about Charlie?'

'Several times.' Dorothy nodded.

'Well, she heard from his mother that he'd been wounded. Apparently, Charlie had said he didn't want Prue told about it. How he thought he could keep it from her, I don't know. Anyway, it turns out that the poor man's had to have a leg amputated.'

'Oh, no. Poor, poor man!'

'I know. And he seems such a nice, friendly soul who wouldn't hurt a fly.'

'Is Prue serious about him?'

'I don't know really. I think she is. This has taken the wind from her sails, but she still cares for him as much as ever. In fact, I think it's brought out her maternal instincts,' Lilian told her, smiling. 'She enjoys fussing over him. Mind you, she enjoys bossing him around too.'

Dorothy's heart went out to them, to all the young people. Maud had to face the rest of her life without Joe. John and Rose would grow up barely remembering their father. Prue would have to decide if she could face life with a disabled man. Poor Charlie would have to adapt to a whole new way of life. Young people should be enjoying themselves. They should be falling in love and looking forward to a long and happy life with their chosen partner. They should raise children, grow old together, play with their grandchildren. Instead, too many of them were facing heartache.

'It's so sad,' Lilian said softly. 'Charlie is a real outdoor type. He loves walking and riding – he goes hunting, too. Or he did.'

'It's dreadful, love.'

'Some good news would make a nice change, wouldn't it?' Lilian said with the ghost of a smile.

They had all despaired of Lilian growing up. She had grown up now though, Dorothy thought, and not in the way any of them would have wanted. She hoped this war didn't rob her daughter of all that sparkle and spirit...

They ate as soon as Clive came home, and it was almost like old times. Best of all, there was no air raid to interrupt their meal.

Dorothy watched Clive laughing with Lilian and thought perhaps she'd been worrying unnecessarily. Heaven knows, this war was getting them all down. What with the long hours spent at the factory, the rationing, the constant darkness, his son-in-law dead, his eldest daughter grieving, his grandchildren fatherless – it was no wonder he was edgy.

He was a good man, Dorothy thought fondly. His family had always been the pivot of his existence and it hurt him terribly to see them suffer.

∽∾

Lilian had enjoyed her week's leave, but she was glad to be back on the camp. She felt more useful there, and had less time to dwell on things. It was easy to concentrate on her routine, like the daily inspection – check the radiator; check the contents of the fuel tank; check the oil level in the engine sump and top up as necessary with oil stores; examine the engine, gearbox and fuel system for leaks; start the engine and ensure the carburettor starting control wasn't sticking; check the oil pressure indicator was operating properly; check the speedometer wasn't damaged; test the tyre pressure; test the operation of the handbrake; test the horn, lights, headlamps, dipping system, traffic indicators, windscreen wipers, stop light and all switches. Then sign the Maintenance Book – Form 656.

She could do it in her sleep, but at least it was something to do with her hands.

There were half a dozen air raids that day and everyone was tense.

Everyone except Harry, Lilian thought with a smile, when she met her friend in the NAAFI early that evening.

'Well if it's not the gorgeous Lilian,' he greeted her. 'Where have you been hiding? I haven't seen you for ages.'

'I've been busy, Harry. And I've been on leave.'

'The place wasn't the same without you!'

Lilian laughed. She knew full well he hadn't even noticed her absence.

She liked Harry. He had a thick mop of red hair, and a smiling face permanently covered in freckles. He was twenty years old and had been married to Anne for over a year. It was rare that he stopped talking about her – he was still besotted. He was equally besotted with the planes.

Harry had become a rigger but, for extra pay, about sixpence a day, ground crew could volunteer for occasional flying duties, and Harry was first in the queue. After training on the drum-fed Lewis guns, he qualified to wear the brass-winged bullet of an air gunner on his arm – and he wore it with great pride.

'Fancy a game of poker then?' he asked.

His passion for life was refreshing, he was always ready with a joke and a smile, and Lilian enjoyed his company.

'It will have to be a quick one.'

'It never takes me long to beat you, Lil!'

This time he was wrong. Lilian actually won a game of poker. Her talent for poker playing, or lack of it, was well known on the camp and news of her win would be round the NAAFI in no time.

'I have to get back to work. Thanks for letting me beat you, Harry.'

'Consider yourself lucky. It won't happen again!'

She was outside when she saw David walking towards the NAAFI.

'Hello, Lilian. How did you enjoy your leave?'

'It was fine, thanks.' She pulled a face. 'No, it wasn't actually. I'll tell you about it sometime, but I must dash.'

'Are you all right?' he asked.

'Fine, thanks. Better than that actually – I've just beaten Harry at poker.' She gave him a short laugh. 'I'll catch up with you later, David.'

It seemed that at least half of the WAAFs had taken to their beds with some mysterious bug that was going around. They were suffering from nausea, headaches and other flu-like symptoms. While Lilian was grateful to have escaped it to date, she would be pleased when they were better. It left the rest of them with far more work to do.

Her feet hardly touched the ground for the rest of the day and she crawled into her bed exhausted. For once, she fell asleep quickly and slept deeply, without any of the dreams that had been haunting her lately…

∽∾

David woke early, and felt uneasy all day for some reason. Everything seemed to go wrong. They were on Ops that night and Chunky, their Canadian rear gunner, had vanished despite the consequences: being Absent Without Leave was a serious crime. Still nursing a hangover – or a blonde – from the night before, David suspected. Harry was delighted to take his place. His smile was enormous as he swung himself into the rear turret.

It was a clear night as David moved the plane forward across the grass. Ben was sitting in the second pilot's seat alongside David.

'What's going on, Skip?' Harry's voice came across the intercom.

'We're on our way to put the Luftwaffe out of action,' David replied grimly. 'Well – one of their main airfields at any rate.'

'Really?'

David shared a smile with Ben at the excitement in Harry's voice. He just wished he could feel excited about it.

'The airfield that's home to German fighter planes,' Ben shouted to Harry, 'in aircraft that are much, much slower. And knowing the powers that be,' he added for good measure, 'they'll have made a courtesy phone call to Hitler to let him know what time we'll be arriving!'

David almost smiled at the sarcasm in Ben's voice. Unfortunately, it was too close to comfort to be amusing.

For the most part, they were silent as they kept formation on the long haul across the North Sea. Harry tested his twin guns and Vic, the wireless operator/gunner, fired a few rounds from the front turret.

'There's no need for me to show off my superb navigation skills,' Ben remarked, yawning. 'Looks like it'll be a case of follow-my-leader.'

'It does. Let's hope it's a case of follow-my-leader, drop our bombs, and follow-my-leader home again.'

'Yep. Who knows – perhaps Adolf and his chums are taking the day off.'

If only!

It really was a clear night, David thought with concern. Conditions were ideal for the enemy to spot them and intercept. And spot them they did. When they were within sight of the German coast, three long hours out from Norfolk, six planes – Messerschmitt – came within range. David's throat was dry as he feared the worst. But thankfully, and ironically, the Germans saved them. Just as the fighters were about to attack them, the German anti-aircraft batteries opened a furious bombardment and the fighters had to pull back.

'Thank Christ for that. And thank Christ we're too high for the anti-aircraft fire,' Ben remarked grimly.

They flew on, but it almost seemed that Ben had been right, that Hitler had been given advance warning of their arrival. German fighter planes appeared from every angle.

In the end, orders came to bomb Wilhelmshaven and head for home.

'Bloody good job,' Ben muttered.

They went in and dropped their bombs, but it was difficult to assess how much damage was done – they were too busy turning towards the North Sea. The anti-aircraft fire was still splashing all around them, but it always felt better when they had a large number of planes in the formation.

And then the trouble really started. Within minutes, they were facing a crippling assault from Messerschmitt 109s and 110s. A twin-engined Messerschmitt 110 dived at lightning pace across the formation and the plane flying number three was hit. There was an explosion at the rear of the cockpit and the plane fell away from the rest and plunged headlong into the sea.

'I didn't see any parachutes,' Ben said, peering out.

David hadn't either.

It was clear to David that the German pilots knew exactly what they were doing. They knew the vulnerable spots. In aiming for the fuel tanks, they knew they could transform the planes into flying infernos. Even if the tanks didn't explode, the pilots would lose too much fuel to make the long journey home. Either way, the result was the same. A Messerschmitt 109 was shot down, caught in a web of machine-gun fire but there was no reason to celebrate. The formation was crumbling before their eyes.

'We're like bloody sitting ducks!' Ben cursed furiously.

And that's exactly what it felt like. To avoid the worst of the attack, David flew lower and lower until the plane was alone. They were very low over the sea – too low.

'109s!' Harry shouted.

This is it, David thought. We've had it. He clung to the waves and knew there was nothing they could do but hope and pray, as they were hit repeatedly in the fuselage.

'Jesus!' Harry shouted in amazement.

The wing tip of a German plane had touched the water and, in a second, it had vanished beneath the waves. To their astonishment, and immense relief, the other fighter broke away from them. But their relief was short-lived. Another fighter appeared from nowhere to take its place, and they suffered yet more hits to the rear.

'Christ Almighty!' Ben cried as they were hit again. 'That was one hell of a bang. I'll go and have a look.'

The fighter broke away and David silently prayed they could make it back to Norfolk. He was still flying almost at sea-level – so low he could virtually taste the salt. God alone knew what state the plane was in.

Ben returned to his seat, white-faced and trembling.

'Harry was hit!'

David looked at him and Ben shook his head. There was no need for words – Harry was dead.

For a split second David wished he could ditch the plane in the sea and put an end to it all. But the moment passed. He knew he had to get the rest of the crew back. He had to get Harry's body home.

'What state's the plane in?' he asked.

'You don't want to know.' Ben's voice was still shaking.

'Can we make it back?'

'I wouldn't bet a day's pay on it.'

They flew on in silence, precious fuel leaking into the sea. David knew that if they did make it back, he would never forget that night.

And then they saw it – home. The coastline had never

looked so good.

'We'll make it,' Ben said, sagging with the release of tension.

They were surprised to find they were the first to land back at base. An ambulance was waiting by the runway, and David prayed that Lilian wasn't driving it. She was very fond of Harry – they all were – and it would be too much for her. Fortunately, she wasn't.

After a half-hearted debriefing, there was nothing to do but wait for the rest of the aircraft to return. David couldn't settle, he couldn't stop shaking. One thing was certain, he couldn't take much more of this. But he wouldn't have to, he reminded himself. Only another three Ops before his tour was over. If he survived that, he would be classed as 'tour expired', trained as an instructor and sent to a training unit. Then, after a six months rest, he would begin another tour of twenty operations...

Early that evening, he saw Prue.

'Is Lilian around?' he asked her.

'She's delivering something somewhere.' Prue was her usual vague self, and David just nodded. He wasn't really sure why he'd asked.

By the end of the day, they knew the worst. Five planes had been lost. As far as they knew, three crews were lost and two might have been lucky enough – if one could call it luck, David thought grimly – to have been taken prisoner by the Germans.

❧

David couldn't sleep that night. Every time he closed his eyes, he saw the waves and heard the bangs. He saw planes hit the water in flames. He heard the screams of the airmen. And he still had the taste of salt water in his mouth.

The first person he saw the next morning was Ben.

'We've got the big noises from Air Ministry paying us a visit,' Ben greeted him. 'They want to know exactly what went wrong yesterday.'

'That should be interesting,' David answered dryly.

'Indeed,' Ben agreed, heading off for his breakfast. 'I'll be only too happy to tell them!'

The second person David saw was Lilian.

As soon as she spotted him, she ran towards him. She didn't stop running either. She ran straight into his arms, almost knocking him over. For long moments, her arms were tight around his neck.

'Are you all right?' she asked, the words muffled by his jacket.

'Yes.' Except he wasn't – not really. 'No.'

She lifted her face.

'You have to be, David,' she said urgently, as if it really mattered to her.

His heart was beating quickly in his chest as he experienced a whole host of emotions – most of them born from surprise at having her in his arms.

'I didn't get back till late last night,' she said, her arms still around his neck. 'I only heard about it this morning. God, poor Harry. Poor Anne. How will she cope?' She touched his face. 'Was it very bad, David?'

'Yes.' There was nothing to be gained by lying.

Then, as if surprised to find that her arms were around his neck, she dropped them to her sides. Reluctantly, David released the hold he'd had on her waist. She was the only thing that made any sense to him at the moment.

'I have to meet half of Air Ministry and bring them here,' she told him, her face full of colour.

'Yes, I heard they were visiting.'

'Was it a total disaster?' she asked.

'It was horrific,' he said flatly. 'Although we did claim four certain kills and two probables among the German fighters. I suppose that's something.'

She was no more convinced than David was.

'Were you on your way to breakfast?' she asked.

'No. I couldn't face it.'

'Me neither.'

They fell into step, walking aimlessly. They said nothing, but David suspected they were both thinking about the way she had thrown herself into his arms. It would have been a heat of the moment thing, he guessed. He would forget it; so would Lilian.

David's hands were still shaking.

'You were going to tell me about your leave,' he reminded her.

'Oh, that. It hardly seems very important now.'

'Tell me anyway.'

'You don't want to hear all my moans,' she said with the ghost of a smile.

'I do.' It was the truth; he wanted her to talk – about anything. If she talked, maybe he would be able to put the memories of the previous day out of his mind for a few minutes.

'There was a boy,' she began and for some inexplicable reason his heart sank. 'Roy Walker,' she continued. 'I never knew him well, although we went to the same school. But I thought was in love with him.'

His eyebrows rose at that.

'Before I joined the WAAF, a girlfriend had a birthday party and I was there with Roy. I remember being so disappointed in him because he wasn't keen to be in the war.'

David could understand that. Lilian took this war personally. She was fiercely patriotic and thought everyone should be doing their bit for the country.

'He was the same age as me, so when they lowered the age of conscription, he had to join up.' She sighed heavily, her gaze resting on the planes dotted around the airfield. 'When I went home on leave, I heard he'd been killed.'

'I'm sorry,' David murmured.

'Yes. So am I.' She sighed loudly. 'I was so quick to condemn him because he didn't want to go and fight. He went to fight and that's it – his life is over. What was the point? How has his death helped anything? How can anything we do help?' She pushed a stray strand of hair back from her face.

They walked on slowly, watching people rushing around.

'Your friend's death, your brother-in-law's death, Harry's death – it does seem pointless, Lilian. A lot of it is pointless. But we have to cling on. That's all we can do. We have to keep going, no matter how bad things get. We've got to see it through.'

'I know.' She rubbed her face wearily. 'Sometimes, though, it seems there's nothing left worth fighting for – as if there won't be any men left, or any buildings still standing.'

David knew exactly how she felt; he felt the same on occasion. Every day, there was more bad news – a friend had been killed or someone's home had been destroyed.

'There's plenty to fight for,' he reminded her. 'A quiet drink in a quiet pub. A game of cricket on a Sunday afternoon. A stroll through a park. Long, lazy summer days.'

He wondered if she would mock such simple pleasures, but she just nodded and smiled her understanding. They were simple pleasures, but what bliss to enjoy them without air raids, without thinking of death and destruction all the time.

'How was the rest of your leave?' he asked.

'It was OK, I suppose,' she said thoughtfully, 'but Dad's not himself. He seems to age ten years every time I go home.'

'What does he do?' David was curious about her home life. With her mother a suffragette, there was no guessing what kind of man her father was.

'He's a shop floor manager – the factory's been turned over for munitions now.'

'Ah. He'll be spending long days at the factory then.'

'Yes. Mam says that's why he's so edgy. It's unlike him, though. I hope he's all right.'

'I'm sure he will be.' What a ridiculous thing to say, David thought. It was just one of those things one said automatically. 'He must have a lot on his mind,' he added. 'He'll be worried about Maud and the children. I'm sure he worries about you, too. And what with the air raids –'

'Yes. I suppose you're right. Anyway, let's talk of more cheerful things,' she said briskly.

David wished to God he could think of something cheerful. Anything!

'I'll have to rely on you for that, Lilian.' He gave her an

apologetic smile which she didn't return.

Instead, she reached out and touched his hand lightly.

'I'm sorry it was so bad, David, but you're right. We must be strong.'

It was there again, that sense of urgency in her voice. It sounded as if she really cared. Did she? Did he want her to care?

He couldn't answer that one. His heart wanted her to care, but his head – his head knew full well that he could be dead before the day was over.

'I'd better get a move on,' she said. 'I doubt if the bods from Air Ministry will appreciate being kept waiting. I'll have to drive very carefully too,' she added with a grin.

'Has the CO recovered?' he asked, smiling. Everyone on the camp had heard that Lilian almost put the CO in a ditch.

'I think so – I'm not facing a public flogging at dawn, so I assume so.'

And on that lighter note, they parted.

❧

∾ *Chapter Fourteen* ∾

JUNE 1941

Three days later, Lilian was being frog-marched down the road by Prue.

'The drinks are on me tonight,' Prue declared. 'Come on, Lil.'

'I'm walking as fast as I can!' Lilian gave her a sideways glance. 'What's got into you?'

'I have some news. I'll tell you when we get to the pub.'

'Not bad news?' Lilian was wary; she couldn't take much more bad news.

'Would the drinks be on me if it was bad news? I think not. I'd expect you to buy me a bottle of something. Patience, girl – all will be revealed.'

When they pushed open the door, they discovered the pub was empty. It was still early but, even so, it was highly unusual.

'I was beginning to think the end of the world had come,' John, the landlord greeted them. 'What will you have, ladies? The usual?'

John seemed to know what everyone's 'usual' was. He was a genial host, interested in everyone, and was forever giving free drinks to those in uniform. Lilian often wondered how he made a profit. This evening, Prue not only insisted on paying for their drinks, but even persuaded John to have a drink on her, which was unheard of.

'Go on then.' He had to give in. 'I've always been a softie for a pretty face.'

'And I've always been a softie for flattery, John,' Prue retorted.

'Is this a special occasion?' John asked.

'It certainly is.' Prue lifted her glass, chinked it against Lilian's first, then John's. 'You may drink a toast to the future Mrs Charles Wainwright.'

'Prue!' Lilian was just taking a sip; she almost choked.

'You're getting married?' John said in amazement.

'If I want to be Mrs Charles Wainwright,' Prue answered with a giggle, 'I think I'll have to, don't you?'

Lilian gave her friend a long hug and felt the sting of tears in her eyes. Dear Prue, her very best friend, was marrying the man who, in Lilian's eyes, was perfect for her. Oh, this was such good news! At last, they had some good news.

'I suppose you'll be having some posh do in the Cotswolds,' John put in. 'But if you want any sort of party here, just you say the word. We'll put on a good spread for you.'

'Oh, thank you, John – we may hold you to that.'

Prue was visibly moved by the kind gesture.

Minutes later, they carried their drinks to their favourite table in the corner and sat down.

'So,' Lilian said. 'Tell me all.'

'I asked Charlie to marry me, and he said yes.'

'You asked Charlie?'

'I did.' Prue sat back and grinned smugly. 'Why not? If I'd waited for Charlie to ask me, I'd have waited a lifetime. He was having one of his "I'm no longer a worthwhile human being" phases. They come and go.'

She looked sad but the moment quickly passed. 'Actually, when I asked him, he said no. However, I told him I was buying the dress and booking the church, and that if he didn't turn up, he'd have a jilted bride on his conscience for the rest of his days. He gave in fairly quickly.'

'I almost feel sorry for him,' Lilian teased. 'Prue, I'm so pleased for you. So very pleased. I've known all along that you were right for each other.'

'So have I really.' Prue was thoughtful. 'I suppose it was when he was wounded that it really hit home though. I kept wondering what my life would have been like if he'd been killed. I couldn't bear to think about it.'

Lilian knew exactly what she meant. She knew herself that if anything happened to David, she wouldn't cope. The thought should have shocked her, but it didn't. It wasn't the first time she had acknowledged the truth. She was in love with David; it was that simple.

The thought didn't make her happy, neither did it make her sad. It was a fact and there was nothing she could do about it. There was no point shouting her love from the rooftops, and there was no point sinking to the depths of despair because it had no future. All she could do was live with the knowledge that she was in love with David.

Briefly, she wondered what he would think if he knew. He wouldn't like it, of that she was certain. For one thing, there was no room for romance or any close attachments in his life – not until this war was over. For another, they came from different worlds. Every time she heard David speak she was reminded of that. If she'd had Prue's upbringing, then perhaps after the war... But she hadn't so it was a waste of time thinking about it. She and David had become friends, good friends she hoped, and she would have to be content with that...

'Are you listening, Lil?' Prue's impatient voice broke into her thoughts.

'Sorry? Yes. Yes, I was just thinking about –'

As if her thoughts had conjured him up, David walked into the pub. Lilian's heart clenched painfully at the sight of him. He was alone, and he came over to them.

'The same again?'

'This is on me, David.' Prue was on her feet and at the bar, leaving David looking very bemused.

'What's all that about?' he asked, sitting in the seat beside Lilian.

'Prue's celebrating. She'll explain all in a minute.' Lilian couldn't spoil Prue's moment of glory by telling him.

She looked around her – at Prue, at John pouring their drinks, at the pictures of hunting scenes on the wall – but her mind was full of David and how he looked. Most men looked smart in the RAF uniform and David was no exception, but how she would love to see him out of uniform, to know the war was over, and to sit with him simply because he wanted to be with her –

He'd lost weight since they had first met, she thought. He looked years older, too. Lines of weariness and strain were etched around his eyes. Blue-grey eyes, with tiny flecks of silver in them. He looked calm, and those eyes were smiling, but she knew the stress was taking its toll.

'Cheers, David!' Prue put drinks in front of them both and returned to the bar to fetch her own glass.

'Has Lilian told you my news?' she asked when she

joined them.

'No.' He looked to Lilian, then back at Prue. 'What exactly are we celebrating?'

'I'm getting married.' Every time Prue made the announcement, she looked happier, Lilian thought fondly.

'Congratulations!' Smiling, David leaned across the table and kissed her on the cheek. 'How wonderful! It's high time we had some good news. So – who's the lucky chap? When's the big day?'

Once Prue started talking about Charlie, there was no stopping her. David was given the man's life story – from the time Charlie was six years old and teaching Prue to ride, to his being wounded. Coming from Prue, though, it wasn't boring. Lilian had heard the stories a dozen times, but she still laughed at the way Prue told them.

'And do you have a date for the wedding?' David asked, when he could get a word in.

'Of course!' Prue grinned. 'I'd already booked the church when I asked Charlie to marry me.' She paused long enough to take a sip from her glass. 'I was telling Lilian before you came in – we're getting married in three weeks – the twenty-first.'

'Three weeks!' Lilian had no idea it was so close. She shouldn't have been surprised, she supposed. These days, with men being posted abroad and no one knowing what the future would bring, couples were getting married as quickly as possible. They didn't have time for endless planning.

'Yes – three weeks! Honestly, Lil, I knew you weren't listening to me.'

David and Lilian exchanged a small smile at her

words.

'It will be a very small affair,' Prue explained. 'Just close family. Charlie doesn't want any fuss, which I suppose is understandable. He's still a bit short in the self-confidence stakes.' Prue spoke as if she would soon sort that out! 'And I'm hoping you two will come – as a bit of moral support for me.'

Lilian stared at her. You two. Did Prue mean –?

'We'd be delighted,' David said immediately. 'Wouldn't we, Lilian?'

'Well – yes.'

Lilian didn't know quite what to make of that. How strange that Prue should ask her and David. It made it sound as if they were a couple, and she couldn't imagine David taking too kindly to that. Not that he seemed to have any qualms about it.

'If we can possibly get leave, we'll be there,' he assured Prue. 'Thank you. We'll be honoured.'

'Why us?' Lilian had to ask.

'Why you?' Prue looked at her in astonishment. 'I couldn't get married without my best friend in attendance!'

But Lilian had said 'why us?' not 'why me?'.

'Despite what Charlie says,' Prue went on, 'I want my friends to witness the happiest day of my life. In any case, Charlie will love you both, I know he will. He won't feel embarrassed and intimidated as he does with a lot of people at the moment.'

The pub started filling up and soon everyone knew Prue's good news. She was a popular character and soon the celebration was in full swing.

Seven of them walked back to camp together but, somehow, David and Lilian were apart from the rest.

Lilian walked with her hands in her pockets, savouring the moment. Years from now, she would remember this walk.

'I'm so pleased for Prue,' David remarked. 'She's always so generous – never fails to make people feel good. She deserves her happiness.'

'Yes, she does.' Lilian couldn't help adding, 'I thought you didn't approve of wartime romances.'

'It's not that I don't approve.' He sounded surprised, even a little hurt. 'I just know I couldn't get involved with anyone. I couldn't leave a wife to grieve – with Prue and Charlie, it's different. Charlie has been given an office job.'

'But he could be killed as easily as you could,' she pointed out. 'He could get hit by a bus tomorrow – or a bomb – and you could live long enough to celebrate your hundredth birthday.'

'True.' His voice was quiet. 'But so long as I'm flying planes that are laden with bombs over enemy territory, that's unlikely.'

Lilian shuddered at his words, and came right back to her earlier thoughts. If anything happened to him, she simply wouldn't cope. It sounded childish and melodramatic, but it was fact. She wouldn't deal with it.

'I hope we can make it to the wedding,' he added.

'So do I.' Lilian laughed suddenly. 'I've heard so much about Charlie, I keep forgetting I've never even met the poor chap.'

'Poor chap? He's marrying Prue! I'd say he was a very lucky chap.'

'Well, yes.' Lilian had to smile. 'But his life will never be the same again. I've never known anyone so bossy!'

'He sounds the type to revel in it.'

'Would you revel in it?' She was curious.

'Being bossed around by the woman I loved?' He looked at her and smiled. 'Probably.'

More than anything, Lilian wished she was the woman he loved. She wished she could slip her arm through his, rest her head against his shoulder, and tell him just how much she loved him. She couldn't. If she so much as hinted at her feelings for him, she wouldn't even have his friendship. She knew that. Her mother was often saying 'Half a loaf is better than no bread at all' and, in this instance, Lilian knew she was right. She would far rather have David's friendship, and keep her feelings to herself, than lose what little bit of contact they had...

∽ↂ∾

'Can you post letters to heaven, Mummy?' Rose asked.

Maud looked sharply at her daughter, but Rose's innocent face gazing back at her told her nothing of the child's thoughts.

She wasn't sure how to answer. It was Rose's birthday and they were on their way to the tea rooms for a birthday treat. She didn't want to spoil her day.

'Of course you can't!' John answered while his mother was still thinking about it.

'Oh!'

From that 'oh!' Maud couldn't tell if Rose was disappointed or not. Who knew what went through a five-year-old's mind?

'Did you want to send your dad a letter, sweetheart?' Maud asked quietly.

'Doesn't matter.' Rose shuffled her feet along the

pavement.

The children's attention was caught by a set of tin soldiers in the antique shop and Maud decided to let the subject drop. She wanted them to feel able to talk about their father, but she didn't want them dwelling on his absence – not today. A fifth birthday was supposed to be a happy event. It was difficult to feel happy though. Joe should have been with them. He should have been able to see his daughter on her birthday, and laugh at the way she had insisted on having ribbons in her hair before they left the farm... But Maud refused to spoil the children's day.

That morning, it hadn't known whether to rain or shine, but the sun had finally won the battle and it was pleasant walking through the village, looking in shop windows, or stopping to chat with friends. They'd met lots of people in the village, thanks to the popularity of Uncle Jack and Aunt Violet and, in a way, Maud would be sorry to leave. She had a job, too, helping out a few hours a week at the post office. The extra money was welcome, of course, but being able to talk to people and feel as if there was some purpose to her day was what Maud liked best

Aunt Violet had hinted many times that there was no need for Maud to return to Sunderland, but that was home. The children enjoyed life in the country, and so did she, but it wasn't where her roots were. As soon as the war was over, Maud would move back to the north-east.

'Here we are –' They'd reached the tea rooms and Maud pushed open the door.

She knew she was as biased as every other mother, but Maud was proud of her children. They were a joy to take out. Rose, five today, looked very angelic with her ribbons in her hair and John, six and three quarters as he told everyone, looked more grown up every day. He looked more like his father every day, too. Rose, on the other hand, resembled Lilian closer than anyone else.

Maud had to smile to herself at the thought. She only hoped it was confined to appearances. There was so much of Lilian that she loved, but the thought of bringing up a daughter with Lilian's temperament was a daunting one. But then again, Lilian had changed. It was ironic, Maud thought, but Joe's death had played a huge part in that. Lilian had swept through life in her own way, not realizing that this war would claim the lives of people she loved. During the last two weeks, Lilian had spent a couple of afternoons on the farm and, instead of trying Maud's patience, as she would have done a year ago, she seemed happy to relax with the children. Having spent years longing for Lilian to grow up and take life more seriously, Maud now hoped and prayed that the war didn't suffocate Lilian's sense of fun...

They heard the drone of planes flying overhead and Maud wondered if Lilian's David was flying. She always thought of him as that – Lilian's David. Maud had tried to get Lilian to talk about him, but her sister was unusually tight-lipped on the subject. But sometimes, words weren't necessary. Maud knew her sister well enough to see the truth.

Her question was answered a couple of minutes later. David strode along the street, looking inside. He had almost walked past when he recognised Maud and the children, and he immediately stopped and waved. He hesitated briefly, then retraced his steps to the door and came inside. The children were delighted to see him.

As was Maud.

'Will you join us?' she asked. 'We're celebrating Rose's birthday.'

'I'd love to. Thanks.' He pulled up a chair from a nearby table and sat down. 'How old are you, Rose?'

'Five!' She beamed at him. 'And I've got ribbons.' She shook her head from side to side, making her hair bounce.

'Very pretty they are too,' David said gallantly. 'Just like you.'

Maud had offered to treat David, but he ordered tea and more drinks for the children, as well as cakes, and insisted on treating them.

Rose was midway through a cake when she suddenly looked at David.

'Can you send letters to heaven?' she asked him.

Maud's spirits sank again at the question, but David was quick to answer.

'Only if you know a pilot,' he answered the child with a gentle smile. 'You have to post them in the sky, you see.'

Rose's smile illuminated her entire face. She was thrilled.

'If you write a letter, I'll post it when I'm flying,' David promised.

Rose was satisfied.

'Told you so!' she said to John.

The moment passed, and they chatted about all sorts of things.

'I feel terrible,' Maud confessed as they stepped outside. 'This was supposed to be my treat, not yours.'

'Then look upon it as a thank you for letting me share in the birthday party,' David answered with a smile.

'You can treat Rose to more ribbons for her hair. She looks adorable.'

'And she knows it!' Maud laughed as her daughter skipped on ahead, hand in hand with her brother.

'She reminds me of Lilian.'

There was a wistful catch in his voice which answered another of Maud's questions.

'I was thinking exactly the same thing earlier,' she told him with a smile. 'I was hoping it was only her looks. But I'm joking. For all her faults, we love her, don't we?'

'Of course. But she's seemed very quiet lately, hasn't she?'

'Yes, I know.' Maud looked at him, wondered if it was her place to speak, and then took a breath. 'You do know she's in love with you?'

He didn't reply. He didn't even alter his pace.

'It's none of my business, of course,' Maud said, feeling flustered. 'It's just that –'

'She's your only sister and you worry about her?' David finished for her and Maud nodded.

She wasn't sure what else she could say, and in the end said nothing. They walked on in silence with the children still a few yards ahead of them.

'These are uncertain times, Maud,' David said at last, breaking the silence.

'Yes.'

Maud left it at that, but her head was full of questions. It was as clear as day that Lilian was in love with David, and if she wasn't mistaken – and that wistful sound in his voice had spoken volumes – David was in love with her sister. They why, given the 'uncertain times', weren't they doing something about it?

Could it be, she wondered, that David thought himself above them? No! She dismissed the unkind thought. David wasn't like that. At least, she hoped he wasn't. Perhaps, if the circumstances were different, he would behave differently.

Her thoughts put a damper on her mood and she tried to dismiss them...

❧

~ *Chapter Fifteen* ~

JUNE 1941

'Look at this! Prue has even arranged the weather!'

'Would it dare rain on Prue's wedding day?' David laughed.

It was truly a perfect day, Lilian thought; the sun was warm, the sky was a deep blue, broken only by a few trails of wispy white cloud. As David drove them closer to Prue's home, the yellow Cotswold stone walls glared in the sunlight.

'Isn't this a lovely area,' David remarked.

'Isn't it just. No wonder Charlie loves it so much. According to Prue, he loves every tree and every blade of grass. I can understand that. It's beautiful.'

Lilian was so pleased they had been able to go – especially as she was to be Prue's bridesmaid, along with Prue's two young cousins. She had managed to get a day's leave. The squadron was being 'rested' – not before time, Lilian thought – and David should have gone home to London yesterday, but he'd stayed at the camp so he could drive Lilian to Chipping Campden. She was more grateful than she could say.

But even being with David couldn't quell her nerves. Prue was her best friend, and she loved her dearly, but she had never met Prue's family. She only knew that she and Prue came from very different backgrounds. It was all right for David; he would feel totally at home.

Lilian wouldn't.

'I hope Charlie's everything I believe him to be,' she said suddenly. 'I hope he's not a snob.'

'A snob?' David looked at her briefly and frowned. 'Prue wouldn't be marrying a snob!'

'No. No, of course she wouldn't.'

Lilian felt a little easier, but she was still nervous.

They were a couple of miles from Prue's home when David suddenly pulled into a field entrance, stopped the engine, and turned in his seat to look at her.

'What on earth's the matter, Lilian? You look terrified.'

'I am.' There was no point in lying to him. 'Ever since I've known Prue – and we met on our very first day as WAAF recruits when she arrived for training in her car – little things have always reminded me that we're very different. Her car for one thing. No one in my family has one – well, that's a lie actually. There is a rich relative who we have nothing to do with, and I'm sure he has a car, but no one has ever owned, or is ever likely to own a car. Then there's "Mummy" and "Daddy from Air Ministry" and the housekeeper –'

'Lilian! This is your friend you're talking about.'

'I know. I love her dearly, and I know she feels the same about me. What on earth will her family think of me though? And Charlie, come to that?'

'They'll love you just as much as Prue does.' From the way he looked at her, she might have been speaking in German.

'Will they?' Lilian was doubtful. 'I doubt if a girl from Sunderland whose father is a factory shop-floor manager is quite what Prue's mother would choose as bridesmaid at her daughter's wedding.' She gave him the ghost of a smile. 'It's all right for you, David. She'll be well impressed with the ex-Cambridge Pilot Officer Benson –'

Lilian was close to tears and couldn't say any more.

'Is that how you see me?' David asked curiously. 'Is that all I am? A man who studied at Cambridge who's risen to the rank of Pilot Officer?'

'No.'

'Well!' He let out his breath on a sigh. 'I would never have labelled you as a snob, Lilian.'

'I'm not a snob!'

'Of course you are. Presumably, if you suddenly inherited a fortune and got rid of your regional accent – your very attractive regional accent, I might add – you'd consider yourself superior in some way?'

'Of course not. That's different.'

'No, Lilian. It's exactly the same. It matters not a jot how much money your family has. Just as it doesn't matter whether your father is a king or a pauper. It's the person people should judge – not financial or social standing. And if people choose to judge other things, they're not worth bothering with.'

He started the engine but made no attempt to move.

'Believe me, Lilian, Prue's family are delightful. If they weren't, they wouldn't have a daughter like Prue. And if they weren't, she wouldn't love them.'

He drove off slowly, leaving Lilian to think about what he'd said.

She knew there was a lot of sense in his words, and she knew Prue's family would be gracious – unfortunately, that didn't stop her worrying. She was sure to make some glaring mistake. They would be sitting down to a meal after the service and Lilian had already had nightmares about that. She wouldn't have a clue what she was eating, or what knife she should be using...

'This is it!'

Lilian looked in horror at the large, square Cotswold stone house set back from the road and partially hidden by a huge oak tree. Prue lived here? No wonder the WAAF sleeping accommodation had been so hard for her to accept.

Given the choice, Lilian would have turned the car around and driven straight back to the camp. David was already bringing the car to a halt though.

Lilian was gazing at the imposing front door when it suddenly opened and Prue dashed out. Her friend was wearing the most hideous pair of trousers Lilian had ever seen, and her hair looked as if it hadn't been brushed for a week.

'I'm so pleased you could both be here.' Prue looked at David. 'You found us all right then?'

'Easily. Your directions were spot on.'

'David, I'll have to leave you with the parents, I'm afraid. We must see if this dress fits Lilian – heaven knows what we'll do if it doesn't. Come on, they're dying to meet you both.'

Lilian's legs shook as they went inside the house. The hall was vast, with a huge curving staircase leading off it.

'Through here.' Prue led them along the hall and pushed open a door at the end.

Rising to meet them was a man with a huge moustache, a small, dainty woman, a huge ginger cat, and two brown and white spaniels.

Lilian's hand was shaken vigorously.

'Delighted to meet you,' Prue's father said warmly.

'I've heard a lot about you, Lilian.'

'So thrilled you could make it, Lilian,' Prue's mother said, sounding equally warm and genuine.

David was welcomed in the same way and thankfully there was little need for Lilian to say anything. Once David was sharing a chair with the ginger cat and being handed a glass of sherry, she and Prue left them alone.

'Prue – this house is huge!' Lilian said as they walked up the staircase.

'I suppose it is. Think twice about accepting an invitation to stay for Christmas,' she warned with a laugh. 'There are warmer, less draughty barns around!'

For the first time, Lilian began to relax. It was Prue's day, no one else's, and it was silly to feel on edge.

'I wonder how Charlie's feeling,' she asked.

'He's probably regretting the day he met me,' Prue answered with a happy laugh. 'Still – he can't get out of it now.'

'I'm sure he doesn't want to.'

'So am I – really.' Prue pushed open a door and they stepped inside her bedroom. It was obviously Prue's room; Lilian could tell from the clutter that was scattered across the bed.

'It's nice to see how the other half live,' she murmured.

'Ha! It would be nice to live like this,' Prue retorted. 'If I could just smuggle my bed into the camp...' She pulled open a pair of doors and there, hanging up, was a frothy creation of silk and lace.

'Oh, Prue!'

It was gorgeous. It was the most feminine, romantic dress Lilian had ever seen.

'Nice, isn't it,' Prue said fondly.

She took it from the rail and spread it out on the bed, but not before Lilian had seen an almost identical dress in a pale shade of peach.

'Is that – I mean –'

'You don't like it?' Prue asked worriedly.

'I love it. Prue, it's beautiful. Far too lovely – I had no idea.'

'Let's see if it fits before we get too carried away,' Prue suggested, grinning. 'All the poor woman had to go on was my telling her you were more or less the same size as me, but about six inches taller. Oh, I do hope it fits!'

So did Lilian.

'She's coming to dress us in a couple of hours,' Prue went on, 'but I don't think she'll have time for any major alterations.'

Remarkably, and Lilian thought it must be a first, the dress was half an inch too long. It would drag along the floor and there was the danger Lilian would make a complete fool of herself by tripping over the hem, but apart from that, it was perfect. Lilian had spent so long in her WAAF uniform, she had forgotten how it felt to wear beautiful clothes. Not that she had ever worn anything quite as beautiful as this. With the dress emphasising her figure, Lilian felt every bit as beautiful as Lana Turner. Instead of feeling tall and awkward, she simply felt elegant and poised. How she wished her parents could see her now!

Prue took off those awful trousers and within minutes was transformed. Tears sprang to Lilian's eyes; she was speechless.

'I feel like Cinderella.' Laughing, Prue gazed at her reflection in the mirror. 'The vicar will begin his speech, and I'll look down to find myself wearing nothing but a pair of WAAF bloomers.'

'I've never seen anything like it.' Lilian's voice was little more than a whisper.

'It's the dress Mummy wore,' Prue explained, 'but with a few alterations. Quite a few, in fact. It is nice though, isn't it?'

'It's truly beautiful, Prue.'

'Your dress – and the two small ones – have been made to the same style. The colour's OK, isn't it, Lil? I don't suppose you would have chosen peach, but these days, it's so difficult to get –'

'It's the most wonderful thing I've ever worn, Prue.' And that was the truth.

They stopped admiring themselves when Prue's cousins, six-year-old Amelia and seven-year-old Katie, arrived with their mother, Sophie. The girls were a lively pair and it looked to Lilian as if poor Sophie had despaired long ago of keeping control over them. For all that, they were delightful and managed to look angelic in their dresses.

Then Miss Trowbridge, the dressmaker, arrived. She had a pin in her mouth when she walked through the door and, much to Lilian's relief, soon altered the hem on her dress. Lilian felt sure she would do something to embarrass all who knew her, but at least she wouldn't trip over her dress now.

Flowers came next; dark red roses for the bride and white roses for the bridesmaids. Lilian had no idea where they came from, or how much they cost, but every bloom was perfect. If this was Prue's idea of a 'small affair', Lilian hated to think what a lavish wedding would be like.

She didn't see David as she left the house, but she

assumed he was being well taken care of.

A car decorated with lengths of white ribbon arrived to take the three bridesmaids and Prue's mother to the church. Just as they were being driven towards the main road, a carriage drawn by two lively chestnut horses turned in.

'Prue refused to be married without the precious horses doing their bit,' her mother said with amusement. 'They do look smart though, don't they?'

'They do,' Lilian agreed. 'Are they Prue's horses?'

'The slighter smaller one is Prue's. The other is Charlie's.'

They were soon at the church and the four of them waited outside, their excitement – and Lilian's nerves – increasing as they heard the clip-clop of approaching horses.

Prue's mother had already checked to make sure that Charlie was safely inside the church. As if he would have dared to be anywhere else, Lilian thought with amusement.

The bride walked along the well-trodden stone path on her father's arm. In fact, she seemed to glide more than walk. It was most un-Prue-like, but so romantic. Prue looked as if she didn't have a care in the world. There was no trace of nerves and Lilian envied her. She looked cool, calm, elegant and serene.

Prue's mother fussed about with their dresses and flowers – not that anything needed fussing with – and then went into the church. The organ struck up and Lilian, with the two young girls in front of her, followed Prue and her father up the aisle.

The church looked beautiful. There were flowers everywhere, huge arrangements, and lengths of white ribbon had been fastened to the ends of the pews. Sunlight streaming through the stained glass windows gave the interior an added sparkle. Everything was so – stylish. Prue and her family had managed to make people forget there was a war on. There was no parachute silk at this wedding!

Lilian spotted David. He looked at Prue, then looked back to where Lilian was. His eyebrows rose a fraction, making her blush, and then some expression she couldn't read flitted across his face. He smiled at her, then looked away.

Lilian looked to where Charlie was waiting and she caught the depth of love in his eyes as he saw his bride. Lilian had to bite her lower lip to stop it trembling.

The sound of the organ faded away, leaving an awesome silence.

Prue and Charlie repeated their vows in clear, confident voices and soon it was all over. Prue was Mrs Charles Wainwright.

There was no doubting her happiness, or Charlie's, as they all stood in front of the church to have their photographs taken. Lilian hoped she looked happy on them. She was happy, but she was also nervous. They were now returning to Prue's parents' house where she had a meal to endure, the part of the day she had really been dreading. As it turned out, she needn't have worried. It was all fairly informal and Prue chattered for the duration. Charlie, every bit as lovely as Lilian had guessed, smiled indulgently at his new wife, only joining in the conversation when he could get a word in.

When the meal was over and the speeches made, everyone danced to the music provided by a group of four musicians, friends of Prue and Charlie's. Lilian thanked the Lord that she could dance!

'You look beautiful, Lilian,' David said as he claimed the first dance. 'Very beautiful.'

'Thank you.' She blushed at the compliment. 'What about Prue, though? Did you ever see a more lovely bride?'

'No,' he replied, smiling.

'Don't they make the perfect couple,' Lilian added, looking to where Prue was kneeling in front of Charlie. She wondered how Charlie must feel, watching everyone else dance while knowing his own dancing days were over. She doubted if the thought had even crossed his mind; he was more than content with life.

It was a lovely day and Lilian was sorry when it was over.

'You must come again, Lilian, when things are less hectic,' Prue's mother told her.

'Thank you. I'd like that very much.'

She and Prue went to change; Lilian into her WAAF uniform, and Prue into a new suit. She and Charlie were leaving shortly for a week in Bournemouth.

'What shall I do with the dress, Prue?'

'Do with it? How do you mean?'

'Where do you want me to put it?'

'Aren't you taking it with you?' Prue frowned. 'It's yours, Lil. Do as you please with it.'

'Mine?'

'Of course!' Prue shrieked with laughter. 'You idiot, Lil. You didn't think you were borrowing it for the day, did you?'

'Well – yes.'

'Of course not.' Prue hugged her, then held her at arm's length. 'It's your dress, Lil. It was made specially for you and no one else could ever look half as good in it. Dye it,' she added on a laugh, 'and wear it at your own wedding.'

Lilian ran a hand over the silk. Had she known Prue was giving her the dress, she wouldn't have worried half as much about it getting grubby.

'I might just do that. Thank you, Prue. Not just for the dress, but for asking me to be bridesmaid, for introducing me to your family, for inviting David, for being such a good friend, for –'

'For heaven's sake, Lil! Stop it – you'll have us both in tears. Thank you for being such a good friend. Now – help me out of this dress.'

Prue was soon wearing her new suit, in dark navy, and Lilian was once again in her uniform. Their goodbyes were quickly said and Lilian was again sitting beside David as he drove them back to the camp.

'How did you enjoy the day?' David asked her.

'It was wonderful. Didn't you think?'

'Yes. I did. And you really did look very beautiful, Lilian.'

'Thank you.' She didn't know what else to say. 'Prue has given me the dress. She suggested I dye it and use it when I get married.'

'And will you?'

'Dye it or get married?' she asked lightly.

'Either.' He slowed as they came up behind a tractor.

'I won't dye it. If I marry – oh, who knows?'

David overtook the tractor and they carried on their way. Less than a dozen miles further on, David did what he'd done that morning. He suddenly turned off the road and stopped the car.

'I was talking to Maud the other day,' he began

carefully. 'She was in the village – it was Rose's birthday and I joined them for tea.'

'She told me she'd seen you.' Lilian waited for more.

'She seems to think – perhaps I shouldn't say this, not to you, and certainly not to anyone else –'

'Get to the point, David!'

'Sorry.' He smiled, but Lilian could see that it took great effort. 'Maud thinks you're in love with me. Now –,' he was suddenly brisk '– I don't think we need to discuss the ins and outs of this, but –'

'She's right,' Lilian interrupted him softly. 'I am in love with you, David.'

She heard the breath catch in his throat, but apart from that there was no reaction to her statement.

'I realize nothing can come of it,' she went on, 'and I had no intention of mentioning it, but sometimes – well sometimes, I've wished you knew how I felt. When you're flying, I always wish you had gone knowing I love you. It's silly, I suppose, but...'

'It's not silly, Lilian.'

They lapsed into silence and Lilian would have given anything to know what was going through his mind. Finally, to her surprise, and disappointment, he started the car and drove off again. A deep frown was marring his features as he drove, making part of Lilian wish she had hotly denied Maud's claim. But mostly, she was glad he knew.

'Forget it, David,' she said softly. 'I can't turn my feelings on or off. I love you – fact. But I can live with that. It shouldn't affect our friendship.'

'No, of course not.' He didn't look convinced.

'I know how you feel about relationships,' she pressed on, 'and I realize we're from completely different backgrounds, but –'

'Damn it, Lilian!' He thumped the steering wheel, making her jump. 'Our backgrounds – different or otherwise – make no difference to anything. I do wish you'd stop talking such rubbish.'

He drove on, and Lilian decided to keep quiet. It seemed the more she said, the worse things became.

'Sorry,' he murmured, 'but really!'

Five minutes later, he stopped the car again. He turned in his seat, and looked at Lilian for a full minute before he spoke.

'The way I feel has nothing to do with our backgrounds or anything else.' He spoke with great patience. 'I simply feel – know – that it's dangerous to have feelings for anyone at a time like this. I saw how my mother struggled to bring me up alone. And now you have to watch your niece and nephew grow up without their father.'

'But you can't assume –'

'Can't you, Lilian? When all this is over, how many women like Maud are there going to be?'

'Well –'

'Too many,' he answered for her. 'I couldn't do that to you, Lilian. I couldn't do it to anyone. If things were different –' He sighed heavily. 'But they're not. I'm sorry, but I can't offer you anything.'

Lilian felt humble, and a little embarrassed.

'I don't expect anything, David.'

He nodded, somewhat abruptly, then started the car again.

It had been a perfect day, but now it was spoiled. What had possessed Maud to tell him? Come to that, how had Maud known? Lilian certainly hadn't told her. She hadn't told anyone.

They didn't exchange a single word all the way back to the camp.

David stopped the car, and leapt out to open her door and hand her the dress.

'Thank you,' she said, the words sounding stilted and awkward. 'For the lift and for coming with me. I – I appreciate it.'

'It was my pleasure,' he replied, sounding equally awkward.

She had taken two steps when he called her name. She turned round.

'Yes?'

He walked up to her.

'For what it's worth,' he said quietly, so quietly that she thought she might have imagined it, 'I love you too...'

∽∾∽

❦ *Chapter Sixteen* ❦

JULY 1941

'You're getting too good at this, Lilian!' Pete complained good-naturedly.

They were in the pub playing poker – Pete, Lilian, Prue and a couple of Pete's friends. Pete had been a pal of Ben's but they rarely had much to do with each other these days for some reason.

'I had a good teacher,' Lilian replied with a small shudder at the memory. 'Anyway, that's enough for me.'

'Me too. Let me get you a drink.'

They walked over to the bar, leaving Prue, Mark and Don at the card table.

'Prue looks happy,' Pete remarked as they waited to be served.

'Mrs Wainwright to you.' Lilian laughed. 'Has she told you all about Bournemouth?'

'Only half a dozen times.'

Prue had told everyone half a dozen times. Lilian was sure she'd been told exactly what they had for each meal. It had rained on three days out of the six and been dull and overcast for the other three. They'd met a lovely couple at the hotel – Mr and Mrs Fountain. Their bedroom – huge and beautifully furnished – had overlooked the sea. They'd held hands over dinner each evening. Prue had talked of nothing else.

'You look happy too,' Pete said, handing her a drink.

'Yes. I am.'

How could she be anything else? David loved her. Oh, she knew nothing would come of it – well not until the war was over. But then – just maybe. For now, though, she was content. She was loved by the most wonderful man in the world; it was enough. It was more than she had ever dreamed of.

Pete was enticed back to the card game, but Lilian stood at the bar with her drink. She was surrounded by people but happy with her own company.

It was still early when David came in. He walked straight over to her.

'Can I get you a drink?'

'No, thanks. I don't really want another.'

He looked at her almost empty glass.

'I've got the car outside,' he said. 'Would you like to drive out to the windmill?'

The windmill was little more than a ruin, but it was a lovely spot.

'Thanks. I'd like that.'

She emptied her glass and they set off.

When David had parked the car, they got out and walked, following the stream. Lilian slipped her arm through his and he made no protest. They had not spoken of their love again, but they would, Lilian thought. One day, when all this was over, they would speak of it once more. She could wait.

It was a warm evening; there was no breeze.

David took off his jacket for them to sit on and they watched the sun – a huge orange ball – sink below the horizon.

'It's hard to imagine the country's at war,' Lilian murmured. 'Listen –'

'I can't hear anything.' He frowned.

'Exactly! No planes, no bombs, no anti-aircraft fire, no sirens – nothing. Isn't it wonderful?'

'It's unusual,' he agreed dryly. 'But we are at war, Lilian.'

'Yes, I know.'

He lifted her hand and held it in his own.

'Was it worth anything?' he asked softly.

'Knowing you love me?' She smiled. 'Oh, yes. It means more to me than anything, David.' She ran her fingers across the back of his hand, admiring his strong wrists. 'I know how you feel about relationships right now – I think you're wrong, but I do understand how you feel.'

'You think I'm wrong? In what way?'

'I don't think you can decide not to have feelings – just because of the war. In fact, it's obvious you can't. I love you, you love me – we can't alter that. We can't pretend those feelings don't exist, simply because it's not convenient.'

'No,' he agreed, releasing her hand. 'But neither can life carry on as normal. We can't rush off, get married, and think of raising a family. We just can't do it, Lilian. At least, I won't do it.'

'I know.' She missed the warmth of his hand, and pulled on a blade of grass to twist it round her finger.

'Things won't always be like this, though,' he pointed out.

'I know that, too.'

He reached into his pocket, took something out and held it in his closed palm for a few moments.

'I want you to have this.' He opened his palm and Lilian saw a ring – one large ruby guarded by a cluster of diamonds. 'My grandfather gave it to my grandmother. It meant a lot to her – to them both – and it means a lot to me. I've always hoped that, one day, the woman I loved would wear it.'

'Oh, David.' The colour had drained from her face. 'I couldn't possibly take it. It's yours – it's valuable.' She knew that just from looking at it. 'And I don't need expensive jewellery. I only need to know you love me. I couldn't take it.'

'I'd like you to have it.' He put it in her hand and closed her fingers around it. 'I can't give you anything else, Lilian. Not now. Not yet. When the war's over, I'll put this ring on your finger. But if anything happens –'

'Don't!'

'If anything happens to me,' he continued firmly, 'then I'll have no need of it, will I? I want you to have it. You'll be able to sell it if nothing else.'

'I could never –' She sniffed, and groped in her pocket for a handkerchief. It was no use; hot tears spilled onto her cheeks. 'Sorry.'

'Don't cry, sweetheart.' David held her close. 'I wish I could give you the sun, the moon and the stars, my love. But I can't. Not yet.'

With her head buried in the warmth and safety of his chest, she uncurled her fingers and looked through a pool of tears at his ring.

'Have you had this with you all the time?' she asked.

'No. Of course not. I brought it back with me when I went home on leave – just after Prue's wedding. I brought it back because I wanted you to have it. It sounds silly, but so long as you have it, you'll know that I love you...'

She put the ring to her lips and then dropped it into her jacket pocket.

'I'll keep it safe until you can put it on my finger. Always remember though, that I don't need it. I love it, I'll treasure it always, but I don't need it. All I need is you.'

She lifted her hands, put one either side of his face, and wished she could have drowned in the love she saw in his eyes.

'Kiss me, David,' she whispered.

With a groan that came from deep in his throat, he held her face in his hands. His lips came down on hers with a hunger that matched her own. For all that, his kiss was all tenderness, all love…

Her fingers tangled in his hair, tugging on it, holding him close. She loved the taste of him.

'Make love to me, David…'

She unfastened the buttons on his shirt and slipped her hand inside. His heart was beating fast and strong, in time with her own.

'Lilian –'

'Ssh.' She put a finger to his lips to silence him. 'Make love to me, David – please.'

She covered his throat with kisses and slid her hands over his chest. She needed him, she needed to be closer to him than she had ever been to anyone. The future didn't concern her, nor the past. Only the here and now mattered…

❧

David woke early. He hadn't really slept, he had merely dozed fitfully. He supposed he should have been filled with regret, but he wasn't. Far from it.

He wished, more than anything, that Lilian was lying

beside him right now. He wished they were far from here, in a huge, soft bed, so he could make love to her all over again. He wanted to taste her sweetness again, to feel her soft skin beneath his hands, to hear her whispered words of love against his face, to give himself to her, to have her giving herself to him so freely, so lovingly...

Lying with his hands linked beneath his head, he relived every precious moment all over again – the way she had touched him, the way her soft hands had worshipped his body, that brief moment when he had hurt her – a bittersweet moment, a mixture of knowing he wouldn't hurt her for the world, and savouring the knowledge that he was the first man she had given herself to – the way she had laughed a little self-consciously, the way they had made love all over again, the way she had looked at him with the same sense of wonder he was feeling...

He hoped she didn't have any regrets. He didn't think so. Last night, when he had left her so reluctantly, she had lifted her smiling face to his.

'I love you, Pilot Officer David Benson.' Then, her face so serious, and so full of love for him, she had added softly, 'Now and always, my darling.'

He sprang out of bed. For the first time in a very long time, he felt glad to be alive. He had always believed in this war – he hated it, but he had always known they had no choice but to fight – but now he had a real purpose. Before, he had known they had to defeat the enemy to ensure freedom and a better life for the generations to come. Now, there was so much more to fight for. He would be fighting for Lilian, for the day when they would share that big, soft comfortable bed, for the day when he could put his ring on her finger, marry her, raise children, grow old with her...

Since the day war had been declared, it was the first time David could say he felt truly happy.

He was whistling cheerfully as he shaved. It would have been good to have had a quiet day ahead, with little more to do than think of Lilian. That was a forlorn hope, though. He was soon being briefed for the evening's bombing raid...

❧

Lilian hadn't slept either. She wondered if she could ever feel happier. It seemed impossible. And yet, on the day war was over, on the day she became David's wife, the day he made love to her again – perhaps she would be happier still.

She had put his ring on a chain around her neck and she kept fingering it, loving its feel beneath her fingers. She didn't need a token of his love. Last night, he had told her he loved a dozen times. She hadn't needed words either. The way he had made love to her – gentle and restrained when she wanted him to be, hungry and passionate when she needed him to be – had said more to her than words ever could.

She remembered the day she and Prue had cycled to the farm, when she'd asked Prue how a girl would know if she was in love. How absurd that seemed now. She had fallen in love with David, and she had known. No doubts, no questions – just a deep certainty that she would love him always. And that was just how it was meant to be. It wasn't a matter of right or wrong. What she felt for David could never be wrong. It just couldn't.

She was singing as she completed the daily vehicle inspection.

Even the sight of the planes roaring down the runway early that evening couldn't mar her happiness. It was a sight she was used to now.

She was busy for the rest of the day, driving here, there and everywhere it seemed. No matter what she did or who she spoke to though, her mind was full of David.

She lay awake, listening for the sound of the returning planes, but eventually fell asleep. She woke, in the early hours, dressed and paced around the camp in the near darkness. Only three planes had returned, and two of those were badly damaged.

She stood, waiting, at the edge of the runway listening for the sound of a plane.

The sound, when it finally came, was different. She watched the plane approaching the runway. It flew low then rose again. Lilian knew it was David's plane. The cockpit and the rear of the plane were badly damaged.

She stood there on the grass, her eyes never leaving the plane. It flew low again and bumped awkwardly onto the runway. A small fire was burning by the tail of the plane. She couldn't move. The plane was stationary, surrounded by vehicles and people, but she was frozen stock still. She felt light-headed, as if she would fall if she attempted to move.

The ambulance was nearby and she watched as two men climbed down from the plane. She saw the body lying on the stretcher.

And then she ran...

'Lilian!' It was Ben shouting her name. 'Lilian!'

She couldn't stop running, but he was quicker and

soon stopped her in her tracks, his hands painfully tight on her arms.

His flying clothes were covered in blood. His face was splattered with it, and his tears had made streaks in it. It seemed the more she stared at him and tried to speak, the more the tears rolled down his face.

'David is dead, Lilian.' The effort those four words took was immense. 'He said – he said "Tell Lilian – no regrets". I'm sorry, Lil.'

No regrets…

∽∾

❧ *Chapter Seventeen* ❧

SEPTEMBER 1941

Seven weeks later, Lilian was obeying orders and waiting to see the medical officer.

It would be a waste of time. She knew what was wrong with her, and it was nothing that a tonic, taking three pills a day or having a rest would cure. Her heart had been broken. The only man she could ever love had been snatched away from her and she no longer cared if she lived or died.

Prue, Maud – they all said time was a great healer. Lilian knew time wouldn't heal her broken heart. For seven weeks, all she had done was work. It didn't help, nothing helped, but there was nothing else to do. There was no one she wanted to see, no one she wanted to talk to, and nowhere she wanted to go.

Everyone had been kind – Maud, Prue, her friends, the staff. She appreciated their efforts, but she didn't want or need their kindness. She didn't want to eat or sleep, to be cheered up, to be listened to, to be consoled. All she wanted, all she needed was David. She had known for a long time that, without him, her life had no purpose. Now she had the proof of that. Her life was meaningless. The present was to be endured, and the future held nothing. God, she wished she had died with him...

At last she was called in to see the doctor. Lilian

answered her questions, suffered the humiliation of the examination, and waited without enthusiasm for the diagnosis.

'...added to which, you're pregnant.'

The doctor's words finally penetrated the numbness, causing a spark to flicker in Lilian's mind.

'Sorry?' Had she heard correctly?

'Mmm – I see you're not married. Well, there's no doubt, I'm afraid. You're pregnant.'

Lilian didn't wait to hear more. Later, she wasn't even sure if she had even answered the doctor. She had simply ran from that office.

And she kept on running, right out of the camp. The war, the WAAF – they could go hang themselves for all Lilian cared.

She half-walked and half-ran the three miles to the old windmill, and she was breathless as she followed the stream. When she reached the spot, the patch of grass that had once been warmed by the heat from their bodies, she sat down. This time, there was no jacket of David's to offer comfort. There was no hand to hold, no lips to kiss, no body to love...

And on top of everything else, she was pregnant.

'What the devil do I do now?' she whispered.

Pregnant. How could she go home and tell her parents she was having David's child. How the devil could she face –

David's child. The words went round and round her head. David's child. She was having David's child.

'Oh David! Forgive me.' She lifted her face to the sky he had loved so well. 'I thought you'd abandoned me, my love.'

David hadn't abandoned her; he had given her the

most precious gift of all. She hugged her warm feelings to herself. He'd given her new life, hope for the future. He had given her his child.

'Thank you, my darling,' she whispered.

It was ironic. The last thing, the very last thing David would have wanted was to leave her like this. Bad enough he should leave behind someone who loved him; so much worse that he should leave that woman to bring up his child alone.

Lilian smiled to herself. If he had to leave her, she wouldn't have things any other way. Except she would have had his wedding ring on her finger, she thought grimly. Not for herself, but for the sake of their child. She would take care of their child though; she would make sure he could hold his head high... He? For a moment, she had glimpsed that child in her mind's eye – a tiny replica of David. Boy or girl, no child would be more loved.

As an unmarried mother, life would be far from easy, she knew that. She could already imagine the disapproving whispers, and the averted heads when she went home. What she couldn't imagine was her father's reaction. She didn't try too hard, either.

No regrets, David had said.

'No regrets, my love,' Lilian whispered.

No regrets at all. Just gratitude for the precious hours they had spent together, for the love they had shared, and most of all, for the gift of a child...

∽◌∾

'You've brought shame on this house, Lilian!'

Her father's voice was like thunder. Her mother's

face was as white as the cloth on the table. Maud was looking at her feet and Lilian guessed her sister was quaking. Lilian refused to avert her gaze from her father's. She'd known what she would have to face and face it she would.

His anger didn't frighten her. She was too frustrated, too full of indignation. They simply couldn't understand what she and David had shared.

'How dare you come home to your mam and me in this state? We'll never hold up our heads in this town again.'

Lilian said nothing; there was nothing she could say. How could they understand how right this was for her?

Just when she might have appreciated the distraction of an air raid, Sunderland was quiet. She'd been relieved when Maud had said she'd come home with her, but Maud was no help in the face of their dad's fury.

'You let some man – God knows, you probably encouraged him –' her Dad's chest was rising and falling with fury. He paced the length of the kitchen and back. 'Perhaps it's our fault. We've always spoilt you. You've got away with murder in your time, Lilian, but you'll not get away with this.'

'Dad –'

'And there you stand –' he glared at her '– not an ounce of shame in your body. I could take my hand to you, my lady, for doing this to your mam. She's raised you and this is how you repay her. She won't be able to walk down her own street!'

Lilian could feel her own temper bubbling away inside her. She was standing there without shame. No one on earth, not even her father, would make her feel that what she and David had done was wrong.

'You give yourself to some man, as if you're a cheap –'

'That's enough!' Lilian cried. 'I won't stand here and take that. I gave myself to a man who was brave, decent, honest and good. To a man who loved me. To a man I loved. To a man who gave his life –' Her bottom lip quivered and she took a long, steadying breath. 'To a man,' she went on, 'who wanted to marry me as soon as this war is over. I gave myself to him – as you put it – the evening before he was killed. And you're right, Dad, I encouraged him.' Blind fury drove her on. 'I asked him to make love to me. I did that because I loved him, and because deep in my heart, I knew that one day I might have to face life without him.'

No one said a word. Lilian guessed her father was too furious for speech, and her mother and Maud were too shocked.

'And for your information,' she added scathingly, 'that man's name was David. Pilot Officer David Benson. And I don't care what anyone says; I'm having his child. Not only that,' she practically screamed at him, 'I'm proud to be having his child!'

'Proud? Proud to be bringing some bastard –'

'Clive!' Dorothy shrieked with horror.

'Yes, Dorothy. A bastard. That's all she's bringing to this family.'

'I will not –'

'Get out of my sight!' Dad's bellow cut Lilian off. 'Go to your room, and thank your lucky stars – and your mam – that I'm not throwing you out on the streets.

And that would be more than you deserve, young lady!'

'I won't –'

'Lilian – go to your room. Now!' Her mother's voice was more frustrated and worried than angry.

Lilian went, but she went with her head held high. She had known this would be difficult, but she had also known that David's love would see her through.

Minutes later, Maud joined her in their bedroom. Lilian was sitting by the window, with her elbows on the sill, staring out at the darkness. Maud sat by her side and put a comforting arm round Lilian's shoulders.

'Phew! That was even worse than I expected, Lil.'

'I won't feel ashamed, Maud,' Lilian said fiercely.

'I know.' Maud stood up, closed the curtains and switched on the light. 'Have you thought about putting it up for adoption? Heaven knows, you're not the only girl in this position.'

'Adoption?' Lilian couldn't believe it.

'Think about it. Adoption could be the best solution.'

'Over my dead body!'

'But you can't –'

'Save your breath, Maud. No one will take this baby from me. No one!'

'But what'll folk say?'

'They can say what they like. They can like it or lump it. They can go to hell for all I care.'

'Lil!' Maud shook her head in despair. 'You've always been too headstrong for your own good. You have no idea what it's going to be like. For the sake of the baby –'

'Not the baby, Maud. My baby. Mine and David's.'

'Don't be angry with me, Lil. I knew David – remember? And yes, he was everything you claim he was. I know he would have married you, and I know how much he would have hated to leave you in this – condition.'

'I'm not angry with you, Maud.' Lilian sighed. She was angry with the world, not with Maud.

'I've been thinking,' Maud said, choosing her words with care. 'I could adopt this child. I could say – well, we could say something. No one need ever know the truth.'

Lilian laughed softly.

'Maud, despite everything, I love you dearly. I really do. I know you mean well, and thank you, but the answer is no. Can no one understand – not even you?' She lay back on her bed, hands linked behind her head. 'When David was killed, I wanted to die too. I did. When I realized I was having his baby – I wasn't upset or angry or worried. I was happy. I was so very happy. David left a part of himself with me and nothing – apart from David coming back to me – could have made me happier. I'm happy to be having this child, Maud.'

'But you don't know –'

'I know exactly what it's going to be like,' Lilian said grimly. 'Half the folk I know won't acknowledge me. People will cross the road when they see me coming. I'll have no husband to support me. I'll have to work to keep myself and a child. My child will never know his father's love. Dad will probably never forgive me for bringing such shame to the family.'

'And you're prepared to put up with all that?'

'Yes.' Lilian would hate it, it infuriated her just to

think about it, but she would cope. 'I have no choice.'

'Will you at least think about –?'

'No.' Lilian sat up again. 'I won't, Maud. This child is mine. What David gave me, no one will take away. And now,' she added lightly, 'I'm getting into bed.'

They both climbed into their beds, but neither were sleepy.

'I know exactly how you feel, Lil,' Maud said softly. 'We're in the same boat, aren't we? Our men are gone – all we have is their children.'

'I suppose we are in the same boat.' Lilian hadn't thought of it like that.

Maud suddenly laughed.

'What's so funny?' Lilian asked, sliding down beneath the bedclothes.

'You! Fancy telling Dad you asked David to make love to you.' She spluttered with laughter and Lilian had to smile about it.

'Fancy him having the cheek to say I encouraged David!' She giggled. 'I suppose I did encourage him. And I'm so very glad I did.'

'Yes, but to tell Dad – I'm surprised he didn't take his belt to you!'

So was Lilian. She'd known how upset, disappointed and angry her parents would be. Over the years, there had been several girls – brazen hussies, as folk called them – in Lilian's shoes and they had all been treated as outcasts. Lilian herself had thought they were definitely not nice girls. How quick people were to condemn, she thought sadly.

'Thanks, Maud,' she said softly, 'for understanding. For not calling me a brazen hussy –'

'No – I think you're doing the right thing, Lil. I'm

really proud of you.'

Lilian couldn't sleep. Her heart ached constantly for David, and the more she told herself she must get some rest for the sake of the baby, the more she tossed and turned. Her one and only aim in life was to bring a healthy baby into the world. Without that purpose, she wouldn't have coped. But it wasn't easy. She had no appetite, but had to force herself to eat…

Her thoughts moved to David's mother as they so often did. Lilian wished they could have met – perhaps they would have done if things had been different. No doubt she would have wanted someone better for her son, but once she had seen how very much in love they were, perhaps she and Lilian would have been friends. The poor woman had no one now, except all those sisters, brothers, nephews and nieces David had spoken of. But Lilian guessed they would be of little consolation; the woman would miss her son dreadfully. It was all wrong for parents to outlive their children, it was against the laws of nature.

Lilian rolled onto her side and closed her eyes. Perhaps when their child was born, Lilian would write to David's mother and try to explain. She had a right to know she had a grandchild…

∾⌒∽

The next day, Lilian stayed in bed until she heard her father leave the house. She couldn't face him yet. When she went downstairs, she was relieved to find John and Rose demanding Mam's attention. The glances her mother threw in her direction told Lilian exactly how she felt about the situation.

Maud came downstairs, ate breakfast and then, much to Lilian's disappointment, took the children out, leaving Lilian alone with her mother. Her mother washed up, hurling plates into the sink, almost scrubbing the pattern from them, and banging them onto the draining board. Lilian picked up a tea towel and dried them.

'I'm sorry if you think I've let you down, Mam,' Lilian said quietly. That was all she could apologise for.

A plate was slammed down, making Lilian wince.

'I wish things could be different,' she went on. 'I wish more than I have ever wished anything that David had come home that day, and I wish I hadn't got pregnant until he'd married me –'

'Huh!' A cup hit the draining board with force. 'How do you know he would have married you? How do you know it wasn't just talk to get what he wanted?'

Lilian bit back the angry response that formed.

'Because I knew him,' she answered as calmly as she could. 'And because he gave me a ring, one that his grandfather had given to his grandmother – it meant a lot to them, and to David, and he wanted to put it on my finger as soon as the war was over.'

'What ring?' Her mother's tone was scathing.

Lilian fished inside her shirt for the chain and lifted out the ring for her to see. The diamonds sparkled in the light around the ruby.

'My!' Her mother was so impressed she forgot her anger for a moment. 'That should fetch a tidy penny.'

'I'll never sell it, Mam. I'll starve first.'

'You might have to starve!' And another cup hit the draining board. 'If there's an easy way to do something and a difficult one, you've always chosen the difficult one, Lilian. Your Dad – well!'

Lilian didn't need to be told how her father felt; that had been made plain enough.

'I don't know what the world's coming to!' her mother declared with a shake of her head. 'To think of a decent girl like you with some man we don't –'

'It's not like that!' Lilian cried suddenly. 'We've counted the planes take off and we've counted them land. Men haven't come back, Mam! You fell in love, Maud fell in love and I fell in love. It's all right for you – you've still got Dad. But Maud hasn't got Joe, and I haven't got David. Young men, the men girls of my age are falling in love with, are fighting. They're getting slaughtered every day. David knew he could be killed, and I knew it too. We knew we might only have a short time together, and we had to make the best of it.'

Tears were dangerously close and Lilian had to take a breath.

'I would do it all again, Mam, and nothing anyone can say will change my mind. I refuse, absolutely refuse, to feel bad about what David and I had. I'm sorry, but that's how I feel.'

Her mother said nothing, just shook her head.

'Prue and Charlie have bought a small house,' Lilian said quietly. 'Prue's offered me a home with them for as long as I want it. If you don't want me here –'

'Of course I want you here, Lilian!' And her mother burst into tears.

Lilian dropped her tea towel and put her arms round her.

'It'll be all right, Mam.'

'Will it, our Lilian? Will it?'

'Yes!'

Lilian only wished she could feel as confident about the future as she sounded...

ᗢ

~ *Chapter Eighteen* ~

APRIL 1942

At ten past four, on the morning of 10th April, 1942, Lilian's son entered the world, a healthy bundle weighing eight pounds and two ounces. He was perfect. Lilian counted his fingers and toes; they were perfect in each detail. She touched his soft skin and held his head in the crook of her elbow. She touched the fine silky hair, as dark as David's, and her heart swelled with love.

He was easy to hold, she realized with surprise. In the past, she'd marvelled at the way Maud had been able to dangle John off her hip while holding Rose at the same time, but it was easy. It felt as if her son had been designed to fit in her arms.

His lungs, she soon discovered, were strong and healthy. He screamed and screamed, and just when Lilian was starting to panic, he fell fast asleep. Lilian was exhausted, but she watched him sleep. Occasionally, his arms would fly into the air, and his little heart-shaped mouth kept twitching. He was the most beautiful baby Lilian had ever seen.

'Your dad would have been so proud of you,' she whispered, unable to resist stroking his soft cheek. 'And you would have been so proud of your Dad. You will be proud of him – I promise you that.'

The ward sister walked over to Lilian's bed and gazed down at him. Seeing nothing to fault for a change, she sat on the edge of Lilian's bed, pen and paper in hand.

'So – it's Miss Penrose, is it?'

Lilian hated the way she emphasised that Miss.

'It is.'

'Do we know the father's name?'

'Yes.' Confounded woman! 'David Benson.'

'And do we have a name for Baby?'

'David Joseph.'

'That'll be David Joseph Penrose?'

'Yes!'

With her form duly completed, the woman got to her feet and marched out of the room.

'Good riddance,' Lilian muttered, adding to her sleeping son, 'Honestly! "Do we have a name for Baby?" indeed.'

Lilian had decided on the day she discovered she was pregnant that, if she had a son, she would name him after his father and the uncle he would never know – two very special men who had given their lives for their country…

~~~

Young David was three months old when he had his first train ride. Lilian wondered if he could sense how nervous she was. She doubted it; he was too busy being bounced up and down on his Aunt Maud's knee.

'Thanks for coming with me, Maud,' Lilian said softly. 'I couldn't face it without some moral support.'

'Don't mention it. It'll be fine, Lil, try not to worry too much. You've managed to silence everyone in the street, Mam idolises little David, Dad's forgiven you –' She smiled. 'David's mam will be easy in comparison to that lot!'

Lilian wasn't so sure.

The last three months had been strange. Hard in some ways, but rewarding in others. At least Lilian had discovered who her true friends were. Her mother had come round before David was born and had spent long evenings knitting for him. Her father had taken longer but he'd soon fallen for David's sunny nature and was often seen kissing his grandson before he left for the factory.

Prue had fallen head over heels in love with young David. She'd sent flowers to the hospital and visited as soon as she could. Dear Prue – what a wonderful friend she'd turned out to be. Much to Lilian's amazement, Prue's mother had also sent flowers. With them had been a note: Do hope that you and your new baby will come and visit us. All best wishes for the future...

That note had reduced her to tears for the rest of the day. It was so kind, so thoughtful – Lilian had been overwhelmed. It had taken her straight back to the day of Prue's wedding when David had tried to convince her that Prue's parents would be lovely. How right he had been.

As for Maud, no one could have wished for a better sister. Without interfering, or making out that she knew best – which she undoubtedly did – she had helped Lilian no end with David. She was always ready to change him, dress him, sit and amuse him, or rock him back to sleep. Not only that, she was always ready to jump to Lilian's defence if anyone made any disparaging remark – and Lord knows, there had been plenty of those.

The street was divided. A few treated Lilian as they

always had, but many walked past her with their heads held high as if she were the scum of the earth. It hurt, but Lilian hid her feelings well.

And soon, she would hear what David's mother had to say when she discovered she had an illegitimate grandson. Lilian shivered at the thought. Mrs Benson was sure to be furiously angry. She would probably deny it, and refused to accept her grandson.

Lilian had no idea how the woman would react, she only knew she wouldn't rest until David's mother knew the truth. She had written at least a dozen letters, trying to explain the situation, and had torn each and every one into tiny shreds. It wasn't something you could say in a letter.

Lilian gazed at her son as he sat on Maud's knee, apparently watching the scenery rush past them. It would be hard for anyone to claim he wasn't David's son. The resemblance was far too strong. His hair, although thin and wispy now, was the same colour as David's, and his eyes were the same eyes...

'Do you remember when I joined the WAAF?' Lilian asked.

'Of course.' Maud nodded.

'Do you know what I wanted to get away from most?'

'Your wicked sister probably.'

'You're right.' Lilian had to smile. 'I never appreciated you, Maud. I always thought you were dull and boring, that you took life too seriously. I spent half my life wishing I had another sister, someone I could be great friends with.'

'I did the same,' Maud confessed.

'But now –' Lilian didn't know how to explain her feelings. 'Now, I couldn't wish for a better sister. It's not just the way you help me with David, or the way you've stood by me – although I appreciate that more than you'll ever know. It's just knowing I can always turn to you, and that you'll always be there for me.'

'Daft thing,' Maud scoffed, embarrassed.

'No.' Lilian was serious. 'That's all you can ever ask from a sister, isn't it?'

'I'll always be there for you,' Maud answered softly, 'just as I know you'll always be there for me – and there for my children.' She twisted her wedding ring round her finger. 'We'll make it, Lil. So long as we've got each other.'

Lilian nodded. There was no need for more; the rest was understood.

The train slowed to pull into the station and Lilian wondered if her legs would support her. She had David's mother's address, but she had no idea how to get there.

Surprisingly, it was easy. She asked a porter and discovered it was less than fifteen minutes away.

'I shall probably regret this to the end of my days,' she told Maud as they walked.

'No, you won't. You're right, Lil; the woman has a right to know. What she does is up to her, but you'll have done your bit.'

'Yes, but –'

'Yes, but nothing! She can like it or do the other thing. It's her choice.'

'That sounds like something I would have said.' Lilian laughed.

They found the house; an imposing sort of place. Lilian stood for a full minute staring at it, trying to visualise David living in it. She couldn't.

'I'll take little David for a walk,' Maud said, 'and we'll meet you outside in half an hour. Well, not outside. I'll meet you on the corner.' She pointed. 'OK?'

Lilian nodded. They'd already discussed this. Lilian would never turn up at David's mother's door with a baby in her arms.

'Half an hour?' She gave a wry smile. 'I doubt I'll even get past the front door.'

'Go on.' Maud nodded towards that front door. 'Go and get it over with.'

Lilian began walking away on legs that were shaking violently.

'Good luck!' Maud called after her.

She would need more than luck…

There was a bell push set in the stone and Lilian took a deep breath before pushing it. She heard it sound out, deep and strangely menacing, inside the house.

Within moments, the door opened and Lilian found herself face to face with a smartly-dressed, dark-haired woman. She was about to ask for Mrs Benson, but the woman visibly paled before her.

'Good heavens! You must be Lilian!'

'Well – yes. But how – I mean –' She'd spent hours rehearsing exactly what she was going to say, but she hadn't expected this and the words refused to come.

'David spoke of you,' Mrs Benson explained.

They looked at each other, and Lilian had no idea if she was welcome or not. She wondered what David had said about her that had made his mother recognise her on sight.

'What did he say?' She had to ask.

'Mmm?' Mrs Benson shook herself. 'Oh, I'm so sorry, my dear. Whatever must you think? Come in. Do come in. It's so very kind of you to call.'

Lilian was too surprised – and too self-conscious – to do anything but follow the woman inside. There would be time enough for Mrs Benson to show her the door later. For now, Lilian longed to see the house where David had grown up.

It was beautifully furnished with old and probably very valuable furniture. There was a lot of silver about, too, Lilian noticed. Rose bowls, candle holders, photograph frames. In the sitting-room, smiling at her from one of those frames, was David. Lilian felt the breath catch in her throat.

'May I?' she asked softly.

'Of course, my dear!'

Lilian picked up the framed photograph. It showed David graduating from Cambridge. Although it hadn't been taken many years ago, her David had been a far more mature, serious man. It was good to see him smiling such a carefree smile. She only wished she could see him smile again…

'I don't suppose you have many photographs of him,' Mrs Benson broke into her thoughts.

'Just one – it's of the whole squadron actually. It was taken a couple of weeks before –'

Mrs Benson nodded.

'I must find you some photographs. I have a lot. They might help.' She looked at Lilian's bare left hand. 'You don't wear David's ring?' She sounded surprised.

'You knew he'd given it to me?'

'Yes. I knew. I knew he loved you very much, Lilian.' She sat down and nodded at the chair opposite. 'He came home on leave – you and he had just been to a friend's wedding.'

Lilian nodded. She remembered it so well.

'I'm not saying David had been unhappy,' Mrs Benson went on, 'although I know this war – seeing his friends killed – affected him deeply, but I had never seen him as happy as he was then. He told me all about you. He was so optimistic about the future – he wanted to marry you, to spend the rest of his life with you.'

Lilian had had no idea he'd told his mother about her, let alone that he'd spoken of marriage.

'The ring meant a lot to him,' his mother went on. 'He so wanted you to wear it, Lilian.'

'He said he wanted to put it on my finger when the war ended,' Lilian said softly. 'Since the night he gave it to me, I've worn it on a chain around my neck.' She pulled the chain from her blouse to show the other woman.

'The thing is, Mrs Benson –' she hardly knew where to start '– the evening before David was killed –' This was even more difficult than she had expected. 'It wasn't David's fault. I encouraged him. I suppose I wanted whatever he could give me. I loved him so very much you see.'

Mrs Benson was frowning and Lilian knew the poor woman didn't have a clue what she was getting at. It was no wonder; she was making a dreadful job of it.

'The thing is –' She took a deep breath and blurted it out. 'Soon after David was killed, I discovered I was pregnant. I had a boy – he's three months old.'

'A child!'

Mrs Benson was on her feet. She strode over to the window and stared out, her back to Lilian. She said nothing, and Lilian didn't dare speak.

A clock somewhere in the room was loudly ticking away the minutes.

'Perhaps I'd better leave,' Lilian said, getting unsteadily to her feet.

'Oh, no! Please.' Mrs Benson turned round and Lilian saw the shimmer of tears in her eyes. 'Please – don't go. Tell me about him.'

'He's wonderful,' Lilian said, her voice softening as it always did when she spoke of their child. 'I named him David Joseph – David after his father, of course, and Joseph after my brother-in-law. Joe was killed too.'

'I have a grandson?' Her voice shook and Lilian suspected it was too much for her to take in. 'Could I see him sometime, Lilian?'

'Yes. Yes, of course.' There were no visible signs of anger; it was difficult to tell how she felt. 'My sister came with me today. I – David's with her at the moment. They've gone for a walk. We're meeting outside – well at the corner of the road – in half an hour.'

'He's here? In London? Oh, my!'

Another long silence followed. Lilian wanted to give her time to accept this startling news.

'And David didn't know?' she asked.

'No.' Lilian had already said she hadn't known she was pregnant until after David was killed – the poor woman was struggling to make sense of anything. 'When David died,' Lilian tried to explain, 'I wanted to die too. I worked, but all I was doing was making myself ill. In the end, they sent me to the medical officer – that was seven weeks later. It was only then that I knew I was pregnant.'

She sat down again.

'I don't know how you feel about this, Mrs Benson. I know it's a dreadful shock –'

'How on earth have you managed?' the other woman

asked suddenly. 'An unmarried mother? You poor thing – it must be very difficult.'

'It hasn't been easy,' Lilian acknowledged.

'I'm sure. I know how difficult it was for me, bringing up David alone – and at least I had his father's name and a wedding ring on my finger.' She looked again at Lilian's bare left hand. 'You should wear David's ring, my dear.'

Lilian didn't quite know how to respond to that, and they lapsed into silence. Strangely, it was an easy silence. Lilian was enjoying the feeling of being close to David, of being in the home he had known so well, and she suspected his mother was still trying to accept that she had a grandson.

When Lilian glanced up, she saw tears streaming down Mrs Benson's face. Yet, the woman was smiling.

'When David died – I thought that was it,' she said in a voice thick with emotion. 'To know that a part of him lives on – oh, I can't explain it.'

'You don't need to,' Lilian replied gently. 'I felt exactly the same. I thought David had abandoned me – not his fault, God knows, but that's how I felt. When I knew I was having his child, I finally saw some point to the future. He could have left me with nothing more precious.'

Mrs Benson nodded.

'You're a very brave girl, Lilian.'

'No. Not brave. Just grateful.'

Naturally enough, Mrs Benson was eager to see her grandson. They walked to the corner together and waited until Maud appeared with young David clasped safely in her arms.

Mrs Benson carried the child back to the house.

Apart from telling them he looked exactly as his father had at the same age, she said nothing. Lilian knew she was far too choked to speak.

Emotion claimed her several times that afternoon. When she had gathered herself though, Lilian realized she was a very strong, practical woman.

The four of them sat in the garden, enjoying the sunshine, as well as tea and sandwiches.

'You mustn't worry about the financial side of things,' she told Lilian quietly but firmly.

Lilian was horrified.

'Oh, no! You've got it all wrong. That's not why I came at all!'

'I know that, child.' Mrs Benson smiled kindly. 'I know why you came, and I thank you for it. But all the same – David would never forgive us if his child wasn't well provided for. I don't want to interfere, and I promise I won't, but we must work out some arrangement. Your life will be hard enough, Lilian, without having that to worry about too.'

'Life won't be hard,' Lilian said softly. 'I have precious memories of a very special man who loved me, I have his child, I have the support of my parents, your own friendship – I have some good friends, and –' she smiled across the grass at Maud '– I have a very special sister.'

They looked up as they heard the drone of planes.

'Must be RAF,' Mrs Benson said. 'There's been no warning.'

'Yes, they must be RAF,' Lilian agreed, a lump of emotion in her throat.

David wouldn't fly again, but she knew those pilots and their crews would do all they could to ensure his life hadn't been lost in vain.

One day, God willing, they would be at peace once more, and the world would remember men like David with gratitude – and with pride.

THE END

~∾~

THE WORLD AS IT WAS

Wartime England

World War II brought years of hardship and pain as rationing was introduced, cities were bombed and people were separated from their loved ones. But for many women these years also brought new work opportunities and independence. In August 1945 the Japanese surrendered, and the war was finally over. But for women like Lilian life would never be the same again.

KEY DATES

1939 1 September
Hitler invades Poland,
igniting WWII

1940 14 June
The Nazis occupy Paris

1941 7 December
Pearl Harbor attacked,
provoking the US into entering
the war

1944 6 June
D-day. The largest Allied
seaborne invasion ever

1945 8 May
World War II over in Europe

15 August
Japan's surrender ends
World War II

WOMEN'S WORLD

▼ In **1941**, the government cried out for help and British women responded in their thousands, working in munitions factories and the armed services. War was no longer just for men, and the role of women was set to change for ever. The 'little woman at home' would never be the same again.

WOMEN OF BRITAIN
COME INTO
THE FACTORIES

Although **MANY WOMEN** worked more efficiently than men, they were still treated as second-class workers, and their earnings were often less than half of those of the average man.

▶ **WOMEN** in the armed forces could join the WRNS (Women's Royal Naval Service), the WAAF (Women's Auxiliary Air Force), or the Auxiliary Territorial Service (ATS). Although training was hard and many of their tasks were dangerous, they were never put on active combat duty, and had good working conditions. They were fed on better rations than their families at home, and had free medical care.

Some **EVACUATED CHILDREN** went to houses that had already been organized for them. Others had to stand around in village halls, waiting to be chosen – rather like an auction sale. A black woman from East London remembered: *'We were the last to be picked. You couldn't blame them, they didn't have any coloured people there in those days... I think we stood there all morning.'*

▶ **1.5 MILLION CHILDREN** from towns and cities were evacuated to the safety of the countryside within two days. Railway platforms were filled with heart-breaking sights of children, tagged like parcels and carrying their favourite toys, with tearful mothers saying goodbye. Most children only stayed away for a year, as their mothers couldn't bear the separation.

▶ **THE WOMEN'S LAND ARMY** encouraged women to help cultivate much-needed extra crops. By 1941, 20,000 girls had volunteered – by the end of the war the number had risen to 80,000. Although some people thought farmwork was an easy option, Land Girls had one of the hardest jobs of all.

A typical working week was 50 hours and they only had seven days' paid holiday a year, compared with 28 days for women in the forces!

WOMEN'S LAND ARMY SONG:
*If you wanna go to heaven
    when you die
You must wear a green pullover
    and a tie,
You must wear a khaki bonnet
With WLA on it
If you wanna go to heaven
    when you die*

▶ **FOR MANY WOMEN,** the war brought a newfound freedom and independence. As one woman recalled,

'My generation had been taught to do as we were told. At work you did as your boss told you and went home to do what your husband told you. The war changed all that. It made me stand on my own two feet.'

▶ **FACTORY WOMEN** worked the same long shifts as men, but their work didn't stop when the whistle blew. They then had to find time for daily chores such as queueing for food rations, washing, cooking imaginative meals with limited foods, and generally running their homes and families.

WOMEN'S FACTORY WORK often involved handling ammunition and bombs, which could sometimes be dangerous. Although they wore protective clothing, the TNT in the shells often caused rashes and made their faces and hair go yellow.

◀ The **FEAR OF SPIES** was so great that the Ministry of Information ran a National Security campaign, warning people against speaking too freely. Along with the slogan 'Careless Talk Costs Lives' they invented characters such as Miss Leaky Mouth, Miss Teacup Whisper and Mr Pride in Prophecy to boost their campaign. The threat was taken so seriously that men and women in certain kinds of work were even discouraged from speaking about it to their marriage partners.

▲ **QUEUEING** for food and buses became a way of life for most women. Some described how they would often stop in a shopping district to speak to a friend, and suddenly find queues forming around them, with people asking 'What are we queueing for?'

SHOPPING was difficult for many women war workers. Family ration books could only be registered at one grocery shop, which meant that women had to shop during their lunch hours and/or on Saturday afternoons when shops were at their most crowded. Sometimes they even had to shop in the blackout!

▼ The **BRITISH PRIME MINISTER**, Winston Churchill, felt that morale in the forces would suffer if women carried firearms. Women felt angry that they could not defend their homes and took matters into their own hands, forming the Women's Defence Movement. By 1942, branches of the organization were teaching women how to handle rifles and grenades.

▶ **KING GEORGE VI** and his family were determined to share the hardship of their people. When the idea was suggested of evacuating the princesses to Canada, Queen Elizabeth refused, saying 'The children could not possibly leave without me... I would not go without the king.'

▼ During the **BLACKOUT**, every chink of light had to be removed to make it difficult for enemy bombers to find their targets. Thick curtains were used to cover the windows. When these ran out, women used black paint, brown paper and drawing pins instead. Although preparing for the blackout became a bore, ARP (Air Raids Precautions) wardens imposed strict fines on people who had light shining through their windows.

▶ Although the **ROYAL PRINCESSES** were very young at the outbreak of the war, Princess Elizabeth reached the age of conscription before the war's end, and served out the last few months as No.230873, Second Subaltern Elizabeth Windsor, in the ATS (Auxiliary Transport Service), where she soon became efficient at vehicle maintenance.

WATER was a problem after air-raids. When water pipes were bombed, queues stretched for miles. Until water carts were introduced, mothers and children would take buckets and basins – or anything else they had – to collect their water from leaky taps or burst water mains. One voluntary worker remembered using the contents of her father's hot-water bottle regularly: 'Tea first, socks last.'

The **ROYAL FAMILY** shared the country's fate. When Buckingham Palace was hit nine times during the Blitz , Queen Elizabeth (the Queen Mother) said 'I'm so glad we've been bombed. It makes me feel that I can look the East End in the face.'

ON 15 AUGUST 1945, Japan surrendered unconditionally, marking the end of the war. VJ (Victory over Japan) Day was declared on 15 August, amid great celebrations. The war was over.

WOMEN not only did men's jobs, but often did them better and faster. One woman working on the electric welding section of a ship-building firm produced 'thirty feet more than a man on similar work'. Even housebound women assembled parts of aeroplanes and guns from home.

▼ **VE (VICTORY IN EUROPE) DAY** was declared on 8 May 1945, and, although war was still being waged against Japan, England celebrated in style. The streets came alive as people sang, danced and let off fireworks. When night fell, all the lights were turned on to make the cities look as bright as possible. The years of darkness were over.

FASHION AND MAKE-UP

▼ **CLOTHES RATIONING** was introduced in 1941. From then on clothes could only be bought with coupons using a complicated 'points' system. By 1942 each woman had a yearly allowance of just 48 points – enough to buy a long-sleeved winter dress (11 points), a coat or suit (18), a dressing gown (8), one pair of shoes (5) and one pair of stockings (2). With what was left she could only buy 1 bra and 2 pairs of knickers a year!

UTILITY CLOTHES were introduced to make sure that there was enough clothing at affordable prices. These clothes were made from special cloth, and were cut to use the smallest amount of material, but because they were made by top designers, women still looked smart and stylish.

COSMETICS were hard to find - especially face powder, which was often just powdered, scented chalk. But inventive women found substitutes for everything else: olive oil and beeswax were used as moisturizers, burnt cork for mascara and soot for eyeshadow.

HOW TO PATCH ELBOWS AND TROUSERS
by Mrs. SEW-and-SEW

▲ **'MRS SEW-AND-SEW'** advertisements encouraged women to 'make do and mend' and every scrap of material was saved and used. Old shirts became baby clothes and knickers, flour sacks and sugar bags became cushion covers, and parachute silk was used to make curtains, underwear and wedding dresses.

◀ **LONG HAIR** was dangerous for women working in factories, so they wore headscarves knotted at the front to keep their hair out of the machines. Headscarves soon became more fashionable than hats for daily wear, and eventually came to be replaced by that ultimate 1940s fashion accessory, the turban.

◄ **CLOTHES** were commonly passed around between families and friends, to save money. Wedding dresses – made out of parachute silk or net curtains – were in particularly short supply. One wedding dress was worn by seven different women during the war.

SHAMPOOS were like gold dust, so women made their own versions using detergents and vinegar. Home-made perms were popular, as was peroxide, which women used to bleach their hair to make them look like American film stars.

▼ **LIPSTICK** was still on sale, as it was felt to be an important morale-booster for women, but many shop-bought versions were unpleasant to use. 'Our lipstick was like dry chalk to put on', one WAAF girl remembered.… 'It had a bitter taste and we waited for it to dry with our mouths open.' Many women used red liquorice sweets or boiled beetroot instead.

▶ **STOCKINGS** were a luxury that most women couldn't afford, so they went to great lengths to look as if they were wearing them. One popular method was to put gravy browning on their legs, then draw a 'seam' along them with an eyebrow pencil. One woman recalled, 'If it rained you were a right mess. The dogs used to come sniffing at your legs.'

◄ **WOMEN IN THE FORCES** had a definite pecking order in terms of uniforms. Naval uniforms were generally held to be the smartest, but the girls in the WAAF (Women's Auxiliary Air Force) thought their uniforms were the prettiest, and looked down on Army women. Army women in turn were sniffy about the uniforms of the girls in the Land Army.

WARTIME ROMANCES

For wartime women like Lilian, there were endless opportunities for love and romance, as young men and women were constantly thrown together in the line of duty. But with death an ever-present reality, 'living for the moment' became the order of the day. For some the course of true love ran smoothly, but many relationships ended once the blackout was over.

▼ **WARTIME ROMANCES** were commonplace, with many of them ending in marriage. The marriage rate for the last quarter of 1939 was the highest on record and one London jeweller sold more than ten times the usual number of wedding rings in the first weeks of September.

MENSTRUATION was surrounded by taboos. It was believed that butter would not set if churned by a menstruating woman, and women pilots were not allowed to fly planes when they had their periods on the grounds that they couldn't be trusted with the lives of passengers.

GIS were the last word in glamour and romance. One Land Army girl recalled her group being 'followed' by a circling helicopter. Within minutes, several GIs had parachuted out of it and asked them for dates.

◄ **DANCES** were popular places for meeting potential boyfriends – especially with the large numbers of newly arrived American, Australian and Canadian troops. At first, only single girls went, but gradually they were joined by young married women who felt lonely because their husbands were away.

RUMOURS warned that the incoming non-British troops would bring babies and venereal disease as well as nylon stockings, but women remembered the good times: 'So many nice lads... Norwegian, Polish, Canadian and of course the GIs...We recut our mothers' dance dresses, wore as much make-up as we could, and loved every minute.'

◄Many **GI ROMANCES** ended in marriage. At the end of the war, 80,000 British women left their families and homes and followed their American husbands to the USA – often against their parents' wishes.

CLOSE CONTACT between the sexes, combined with a sense of 'living for the moment' and general sexual ignorance, led to a rise in illegitimate births. By 1945, almost one baby in every three was born outside marriage. But attitudes to illegitimacy were still intolerant – many children were brought up by grandparents posing as parents and mothers pretending to be aunts.

►**SEXUAL IGNORANCE** was widespread during the war period. It was rumoured that girls could get pregnant if they got into the bathwater after their brothers or father, or if they sat on a man's knee.

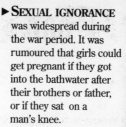

Although **BIRTH CONTROL CLINICS** had existed since the 1930s, members of the government found the subject of contraception 'distasteful'. But by 1943, they were reluctantly admitting that 'On social and medical grounds a shortage of any of the main types of rubber contraceptives was most undesirable'.

►**GONORRHEA** and syphilis became problem diseases in both military and civilian populations. By 1943 the incidence of VD was 139 per cent higher in the UK than at the beginning of the war. The government launched a propaganda campaign, with posters warning men about 'easy girls' and women about the danger of sterility.

The 'easy' girl-friend spreads Syphilis and Gonorrhœa, which unless properly treated may result in blindness, insanity, paralysis, premature death

◄ **WOMEN** in the armed forces were seen by many to have loose morals. Sex for unmarried women was even considered unpatriotic. *Woman* magazine told one of its readers that she was 'an enemy to her country, which does not want to be faced with the problem of supporting unwanted children'.

FOOD AND HEALTH

▶ **PEOPLE WERE ENCOURAGED** to experiment with foods they had never used before, such as nettles, dock leaves, horsemeat and even whale meat. Government posters of characters called 'Potato Pete' and 'Dr Carrot' extolled the virtues of weird and wonderful items such as potato cutlets, curried carrots, carrot jam, dandelion fritters – and even toffee carrots, instead of toffee apples.

ORANGES AND LEMONS disappeared altogether, and fresh fruits went on sale for extraordinary prices. A pound of grapes cost the equivalent of 10 days' wages for a British private soldier.

BANANAS disappeared early on. When children were given the odd one from GI stores, they didn't know how to eat them and often ate the skins instead of the flesh.

FOOD SUBSTITUTES were the order of the day. Coffee was made from ground dried acorns, salad dressings from soya flour, cakes were made to rise with household soda, and oatmeal was used for thickening sauces.

▶ The **'DIG FOR VICTORY'** campaign bombarded people with leaflets on how to grow their own food. By 1943 there were one and a half million allotments in England, and people grew vegetables everywhere: public parks, golf courses, railway embankments, the edge of football pitches ... even the moat of the Tower of London was given up to growing cabbages and potatoes.

◀ **THE GOVERNMENT** saw the role of house-wives as vital. Saving food, while also keeping families healthy, was now essential, and women were given advice on economical ways of cooking. Vegetables now had to be steamed, not boiled, to retain their goodness. One of the most popular government slogans was 'Food is a munition of war, don't waste it.'

◄ **FOR SOME CHILDREN**, the war brought improvements in diet. Under new government schemes every child was entitled to cod liver oil, extra milk supplies and cheap, or free, orange juice. Many poor children were better fed than they had been before the war.

Ironically, **RATIONING** and the wartime diet made people healthier. More vegetables and less fat reduced rates of heart disease and the banning of sugar meant that tooth decay improved.

▼ **A TYPICAL WEEK'S RATION** for an adult. Although little meat and few dairy products were allowed, vegetables were never rationed.

SUGAR was severely rationed in March 1941, and icing sugar was made illegal. Cakes were made with dried eggs and saccharine and decorated with mixtures of gelatine and sugar. Families who had children with birthdays close together would often use one birthday cake, divided down the middle with the appropriate number of candles on each side.

▶ **MANY PEOPLE** kept rabbits and chickens in their gardens. One East London woman remembered, 'A neighbour of ours kept rabbits and chickens. She used to go out to feed them with a tin bath on her head, right through the bombing. It sounds ridiculous now, but they were so important then.'

GI STORES stocked all sorts of goods that were rationed in Britain. At dances held in American bases, the girls were often showered with luxuries they couldn't afford, such as oranges and sugar. Some girls took the oranges home with them and took the peel from other people's plates to make marmalades.

▶ **CHILDREN** loved American GIs because they always had supplies of chocolate and chewing gum. 'Got any gum, chum?' became a national catchphrase.

295

ENTERTAINMENT AND LEISURE

✥

▼ **MANY PEOPLE** preferred to stay at home and listen to the radio, which offered comfort and reassurance in these difficult times. The nine o'clock news, in particular, became a daily ritual, and many programmes offered opportunities for people to send messages to their loved ones.

▶ **PAPER SHORTAGES** meant that few new books were printed, but reading was still popular. Many people took their books into the shelters during air-raid warnings. The long hours of waiting offered perfect opportunities for catching up on reading, and for families to read aloud to each other.

▼ **VERA LYNN** became the Forces' sweetheart, entertaining troops abroad and, on the radio, at home. One of her most popular songs was 'The White Cliffs of Dover' but she was best known for 'We'll Meet Again'. For those separated from their loved ones, the words said it all : 'We'll meet again… don't know where, don't know when, but I know we'll meet again some sunny day.'

▼ **THE ARRIVAL** of the GIs in Britain brought a welcome splash of glamour for British girls and dances at the American bases were always popular. The girls learnt all the new American dances such as the Jitterbug and the Jive, and the GIs joined in the Blackout Stomp – the latest British craze at the time.

◀ **CINEMAS** were closed when war broke out, for fear of air-raids, but by the end of 1939 they had nearly all re-opened and became the most popular entertainment of all. Famous wartime Blockbusters were *In Which We Serve* and *The Way Ahead*, but the undisputed hit film was *Gone with the Wind*.

MOST DANCE HALLS ran two bands, and they would often play 30 numbers and 30 encores in a single evening. Popular songs were Cole Porter's 'Don't Fence Me In' and pre-war favourites such as 'The Lambeth Walk'.

▼ **THE GERMAN SONG** 'Lilli Marlene', first heard by British troops in North Africa, became one of the biggest hits of the war.

TRANSPORT was difficult – petrol was rationed and bus journeys took a long time because of detours to avoid unexploded bombs, but some girls travelled miles for the sake of a dance.

ENTERTAINING at home was limited because food was rationed. Dinner guests at other people's houses were expected to take their own butter!

'MUSIC WHILE YOU WORK' schemes were introduced by the BBC radio to relieve the boredom of working long factory shifts. Later, singers often entertained workers in their lunch breaks, as well as civilians in Underground shelters.

▶ **YOUNG PEOPLE** loved to dance the nights away. Some dances were held at army quarters, but because of the shortage of venues new ones were found. Barns, fire stations, schools – and even opera houses – doubled up as dance-halls.

*L*OVE AND MARRIAGE

▶ **WARTIME WEDDINGS** were very makeshift affairs. Wedding dresses were made of net curtains or army-surplus parachute silk, rings were Utility – 9 carats instead of 22 – and cardboard and plaster wedding cakes were often used instead of the real thing.

Despite falling **BIRTH RATES** in the early war years, by 1945 births were up 17.9 per cent. Many women saw having a child as an antidote to loneliness and the breakdown of home life and the family. Others saw children as a way of keeping a man, as this popular song, sung at many Anglo-American clubs, suggests:

▼ *Oh give me something*
   to remember you by
   When you are far away from me
   Some little something
     little something
   When you are far across the seas

WEDDING PRESENTS were seen very differently in those days. For newly-weds about to set up home, the ideal gifts were now the ones that were the most practical: a packet of soap flakes, curtains (even though these were usually made from heavy blackout material) or a fuel-saving pressure cooker.

Delayed or **LOST MAIL** was a major cause of anxiety and depression for enlisted men and their loved ones, so the government tried to make sure that the post was as quick and reliable as possible. To save time, an official form was available on which men were allowed to tick boxes with options such as 'well', 'wounded but getting better' or 'will write soon'. S.W.A.L.K. ('sealed with a loving kiss') was often written on the back of the envelope.

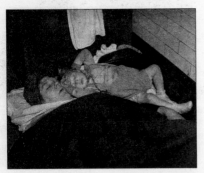

► Although it was acceptable for **FIGHTING MEN** to befriend women, they expected their wives at home to be totally faithful. Many of the British troops overseas were worried that their wives and sweethearts would fall prey to the charms of the GIs that came to England. Not only were their uniforms

more glamorous than those of the British soldiers, but they earnt more money. As one British soldier bitterly complained, 'British servicemen could not possibly entertain young women in the fashion an American could.'

MANY COUPLES were reunited at the end of the war to find that they were complete strangers. Some overcame their difficulties, but others were not so lucky. By 1945, the annual number of divorce petitions had risen from 10,000 (in 1938) to 24,000.

The **MOST DANGEROUS TIME** for a marriage, according to statistics, was the third year of separation. That is when most marriages were likely to break up.

RATIONING took its toll on young mothers. Pregnant women were advised to make cots out of old drawers, pad them with newspaper and line them with a nightdress.

▼ **MANY SOLDIERS** were away from home throughout the war. Others had a few days' leave at the most, and would often arrive home unannounced, to the surprise and delight of their families.

FATHERS who had left very young children behind often came back to find their children didn't know them. One war wife remembered her children saying: 'Mum, who's that man that keeps coming into our house and staying all night? We don't know him. Tell him to go away.'

▼ **HUSBANDS** and wives often knew little of each other's lives for long periods during the war. Although

women had taken on the demanding roles of running a job and a home, they were expected to keep quiet about their problems. It was considered 'unpatriotic' to write to men about anything that might upset them.

ℋOME

▼ **BATHROOMS** didn't exist in many wartime houses. A tin bath was  usually hung up on the back wall of the house and taken down when needed. Fuel for heating water was rationed, so families were encouraged to bath together to save energy. No more than 5 inches of water could be used, and many people painted a black line around the bath at this level so that they didn't overfill it.

STIRRUP PUMPS were a regular feature of wartime houses, and were kept at hand for putting out small fires from bombs. One person pumped up the water from the bucket, and another sprayed it on the fire.

ANDERSON SHELTERS (shell-like huts made from corrugated steel) were delivered to houses with gardens at the beginning of the war. The shelters were dug 3 feet into the ground and had to have at least 15 inches of earth covering the roof. They took up to six people, and offered protection from anything but a direct hit.

▼ **MORRISON SHELTERS** were introduced in 1941, and could be installed inside houses. Made of wire with reinforced frames, they offered vital protection as they always survived intact, even if the house was hit, and families could later be dug out, unharmed, from the rubble of their homes.

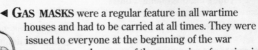

◄ **GAS MASKS** were a regular feature in all wartime houses and had to be carried at all times. They were issued to everyone at the beginning of the war because of the memories of gassing in the First World War, but were, in fact, never needed. Children had their own red and blue versions, known as 'Mickey Mouse' gas masks.